Economic Policies at
Cross-Purposes

ECONOMIC POLICIES AT CROSS-PURPOSES

The United States and
Developing Countries

Anne O. Krueger

The Brookings Institution
Washington, D.C.

Library of Congress Cataloging-in-Publication data:

Krueger, Anne O.
    Economic policies at cross-purposes : the United States and developing countries / Anne O. Krueger.
       p.   cm.
    Includes bibliographical references and index.
    ISBN 0-8157-5054-4 (cloth) — ISBN 0-8157-5053-6(paper)
    1. United States—Foreign economic relations—Developing countries. 2. Developing countries—Foreign economic relations—United States. 3. Economic assistance, American—Developing countries. I. Title.
HF1456.5D44K78   1993
337.730172'4—dc20
                                    92-35941
                                      CIP

9 8 7 6 5 4 3 2 1

The paper used in this publication meets the minimum requirements of the American National Standard for Information Sciences—
Permanence of paper for Printed Library Materials, ANSI Z39.48-1984.

Foreword

IN THE EARLY POSTWAR YEARS, U.S. economic policy toward developing countries consisted almost entirely of foreign aid. Over time developing countries have become increasingly differentiated. As that has happened, U.S. policies regarding international trade, capital flows, debt forgiveness, and the multilateral institutions have assumed growing importance. Unfortunately each set of policies has operated largely independently of the others. Indeed, in some instances, they have offset one another.

In this book, Anne Krueger analyzes the development of these American policies, showing how they have evolved at cross-purposes. She then illustrates her analysis by considering U.S. international economic policies for the Caribbean Basin Initiative and Korea. In each instance, domestic concerns—mostly over sugar and textiles in the case of the Caribbean, and over import competition and the trade balance in the case of Korea—have offset measures designed to support those countries' economic growth. Finally, the author uses these examples to illustrate the urgent need for greater consistency and coordination of American international economic policies.

Anne O. Krueger is Arts and Sciences Professor of Economics at Duke University and a nonresident senior fellow in the Economic Studies program at Brookings. Much of the research for this study was undertaken while she was at Brookings on leave from Duke. She is grateful to Henry J. Aaron and Charles L. Schultze of Brookings for their support of the project.

The author benefited greatly from the comments and suggestions of a number of people. They include David Finch, Stanley Fischer, Robert Z. Lawrence, Constantine Michalopoulos, and Ernest Stern, who read and made valuable comments on the entire manuscript; Rosalinda Quintanilla, who was very helpful in commenting on and suggesting additional sources for chapter 6; and James Fox, who was an invaluable resource in preparing chapter 7. Professor Chong-Hyun Nam, of Korea University, provided much of the background for the analysis of the impact of American trade policies on the Korean economy.

The author also wishes to thank the research assistants who helped to prepare the manuscript. Robert Slonim gathered statistics on developing countries' trade, globally and with the United States. Ömer Gokcekus undertook background work on the Generalized System of Preferences. Ozkan Zengin provided a useful paper on the Caribbean Basin Initiative. Pablo Barahona undertook the research on the costs of aid tying reported in chapter 4. Peter Dohlman assisted with background research on U.S. trade policies. Throughout much of the project, David Orsmond provided valuable research assistance, gathering data on the multilaterals and on trade, reading and commenting on the manuscript, and tracking down sources.

Gail McKinnis capably assisted with manuscript preparation throughout, with the help of Greg Sanders. Jay Smith edited the manuscript and Laura Kelly verified it for factual accuracy. Ted Laux prepared the index.

The views in this book are solely those of the author and should not be ascribed to the persons acknowledged above, or to the trustees, officers, or other staff members of the Brookings Institution.

BRUCE K. MAC LAURY
President

December 1992
Washington, D.C.

Contents

Tables

Economic Policies at
Cross-Purposes

1 ||| Introduction

WHEN THE REGIME OF Ferdinand Marcos was overthrown in the Philippines in 1986, the United States supported the newly elected government of Corazon Aquino. To that end, the U.S. Congress authorized $210 million of economic assistance to the Philippines in fiscal year 1987. At the same time, however, U.S. quotas on imported Philippine sugar were being reduced, causing the Philippines to lose $89 million, equal to 42 percent of the U.S. aid allocated.[1] In addition, Philippine exports of textiles and apparel to the United States were restricted under the Multifiber Arrangement even as the United States was urging the Philippines to remove protectionist trade barriers to stimulate export growth.[2]

This vignette is typical of U.S. international economic policy vis-à-vis a number of developing countries: the United States extends foreign aid and official lending to enhance economic performance but offsets many, if not all, of the aid's potential benefits with other policies.

While there are obvious reasons for this state of affairs, U.S. international economic policy toward developing countries is undoubtedly in disarray. For many developing countries, the bewildering conflict among U.S. policy instruments leads to antagonism, or at least suspicion. A more coherent set of U.S. international economic policies toward the developing countries could greatly increase the benefits of trade, aid, and other policies without any increase in government expenditures.

The need to reassess U.S. policy is heightened by the fact that developing countries are becoming increasingly important in the international economy. In some cases, such as in East Asia, this newfound importance is a result of rapid economic growth; in others, it derives from both economic and political considerations, as in Latin America and the Middle East.

Table 1-1.   **The Role of Developing Countries in U.S. Trade, 1989**

Commodity group	U.S. exports to developing countries		U.S. imports from developing countries	
	Billions of dollars	Percent of all U.S. exports	Billions of dollars	Percent of all U.S. imports
Food	15.69	36.7	14.06	49.7
Raw materials	5.48	33.1	2.51	23.3
Ores and other minerals	1.96	28.0	1.84	32.9
Fuels	3.36	33.7	40.97	73.0
Nonferrous metals	1.29	25.6	2.34	21.2
Total primary products[a]	27.77	34.1	61.71	55.2
Iron and steel	1.58	42.8	2.31	20.2
Chemicals	13.56	35.7	3.25	14.9
Other semimanufactures	6.17	34.5	11.53	31.8
Machinery and transport equipment	51.88	31.2	49.80	23.6
Power generating machinery	2.71	27.3	.83	12.9
Other nonelectrical machinery	12.09	37.0	4.39	13.6
Office and telecommunication equipment	15.98	33.7	27.91	44.2
Electrical machinery and apparatus	6.08	41.3	8.09	44.6
Automotive products	5.76	18.6	6.66	8.46
Other transport equipment	9.26	30.3	1.92	16.1
Textiles	1.61	36.8	2.67	41.5
Clothing	1.46	66.1	19.91	76.5
Other consumer goods	7.80	23.8	23.37	43.2
Total manufactures[a]	84.06	31.7	112.84	30.7
Total trade[a]	117.47	32.3	178.09	36.1

Source: GATT, *International Trade, 89–90*, vol. 2 (GATT, 1990), table A6; percentages calculated by author.
a. Totals include some items not included in any commodity category.

Table 1-1 gives data on the role of developing countries in U.S. exports and imports in 1989, a fairly representative year. Overall, developing countries import about one-third of U.S. exports and are the source of about the same proportion of U.S. imports. However, they are considerably more important for individual commodities: 73 percent of U.S. fuel imports—predominantly petroleum—originate in developing countries, and developing countries account for more than 40 percent of U.S. exports of iron and steel and of electrical machinery and apparatus.

When developing countries experience severe economic difficulties, as they did in the early 1980s, demand for U.S. exports is reduced. In the early 1980s U.S. exports to Latin America fell by about a third in response to the debt crisis, and that drop is argued to have greatly increased the severity of the U.S. recession in 1982–83.[3]

In addition to its economic and geographical interests in developing countries, the United States also has a broader stake. Recognizing the poverty in many developing countries, many U.S. citizens believe that the United States, as a rich country, bears a responsibility to assist in economic development on humanitarian grounds. Moreover, most analysts believe that successful economic development is a necessary, if not sufficient, condition for the stable and peaceful evolution of the world economy.

In the past two years, another reason for concern has emerged. The countries of Eastern Europe and the Commonwealth of Independent States (CIS) have won independence and begun difficult transitions to democracy and a market economy. Their rapid and, to the extent possible, painless transition to democracy and reasonable standards of living is greatly in the interest of the United States. In the debates over how best to smooth the transition, questions surrounding the efficacy of foreign aid and debt forgiveness, the role of the multilateral institutions, and the desirability of relaxing restrictions on imports from those countries have arisen. The formulation of a more coherent U.S. policy is urgent on that score alone.

The purpose of this study is to examine the major instruments of U.S. international economic policy toward developing countries, including U.S. policies on foreign aid, the multilateral institutions, trade, and debt. Analysis of the impact of these policies and recognition of the extent to which they are at cross-purposes will, it is hoped, provide impetus for their improvement.

The organization of the work is as follows. Chapter 2 provides a brief overview of the evolution of U.S. international economic policy toward the developing countries after World War II. Although the purpose of this volume is not to analyze *why* U.S. policies are what they are,[4] or to provide a history of these policies, an understanding of the evolution of policy helps set the stage for what follows. In a sense, U.S. policy toward the developing countries was formulated at a time when they were relatively homogeneous and without much clout in the international economy. While economic policies toward developed countries were formed along functional lines, policy toward developing countries was based largely on foreign aid. As developing countries have evolved, becoming much more important and much less homogeneous, U.S. policy toward them does not appear to have been systematically reassessed.

Chapter 3 provides a summary of current understanding of the development process, focusing on policies of developing countries that are conducive to economic growth and on how the international economy affects growth prospects. Readers familiar with current thought on economic development and the policy reforms of the 1980s may wish to proceed directly to the subsequent three chapters, each of which deals with one of three major areas of U.S. policy toward the developing countries—foreign aid; the multilateral institutions, especially in regard to their role during the debt crisis; and international trade. Each of these policy domains has a sizable technical content that must be addressed if the relationship to economic development is to be understood.

Foreign aid, for example, consists of concessional assistance in support of development projects and programs in developing countries. The U.S. foreign aid program has been undertaken for a variety of motives, as the variety of categories of assistance attests. Any assessment of the effectiveness of foreign aid must take these diverse motives into consideration. Chapter 4 addresses these issues.

In addition to its bilateral aid program, the United States has also been the largest shareholder in the International Monetary Fund and the World Bank and a major shareholder in the regional development banks. As a result, U.S. policies affecting the behavior and performance of the multilateral institutions have also had a significant impact on developing countries. During the 1980s, when many developing countries encountered major economic difficulties and were unable to service their debts without international support, the United States actively formulated policy responses, influenced the activities of the multilateral institutions, and used a variety of policies to promote debt rescheduling and forgiveness. The impact of U.S. policies on the multilateral institutions, including their responses to the debt crisis, is the subject of chapter 5.

U.S. policies toward imports from developing countries affect their access to markets and the response of their exporters to changes in incentives. One of the critical considerations in assessing the net impact of U.S. policies toward developing countries is the relationship between foreign aid and official lending on the one hand, and trade on the other. U.S. trade policies affecting developing countries are the subject of chapter 6.

When a number of different agencies, with differing constituencies and objectives, are responsible for the formulation and execution of policy in a number of different areas, conflict among the effects of these policies is probably inevitable. Although some of those conflicts are discussed in the chapters dealing with aid, the multilaterals, and trade, this discussion remains somewhat abstract. Chapters 7 and 8, therefore, complement that material by examining the interaction of U.S. policies in two particular situations: the Caribbean and the Republic of Korea.

Chapter 7 provides an account of the Caribbean Basin Initiative (CBI), inaugurated by President Ronald Reagan in 1983. The CBI was a response to the economic difficulties of the Caribbean countries; improvement in their economic performance was deemed vital to U.S. interests. At the Reagan administration's request, Congress authorized and appropriated additional foreign aid for the CBI countries. However, trade, aid, and debt policies have often been at cross-purposes with the overall Caribbean initiative. These conflicts provide one concrete example of the incoherence of U.S. international economic policies.

Chapter 8 analyzes U.S. policy toward Korea in similar terms. Korea's enormous economic success is in part attributable to U.S. foreign aid extended in previous years. Korea is thus important to the United States as an example of what foreign aid, combined with appropriate economic policies in the recipient country, can achieve. Korea's continued economic growth is in the U.S. interest both because it is essential to the stability of Korean democracy and because Korea has become a "showcase" of successful U.S. foreign aid policy. Nevertheless, recent international economic relations with Korea, handled through the U.S. Trade Representative (USTR) and the Treasury Department, have been acrimonious. The United States has restricted some Korean imports and has strongly pressured Korea to liberalize its import policies and to appreciate the nominal exchange rate of its currency. The United States has advocated some of these policies even when they were clearly detrimental to Korean economic growth.

A final chapter, chapter 9, then summarizes the argument and calls for greater coherence among U.S. international economic policies toward developing countries. Such coherence would require the United States to define a clearer set of policy objectives and to realize the costs of the current conflict among policy instruments. If this volume contributes to greater awareness of those costs, it will have achieved its objectives.

2 ||| The United States and the Developing Countries

THE END OF WORLD WAR II ushered in one of those rare moments in world history when an idealistic but feasible vision of the future world order guided policymaking. Although the United States emerged victorious and dominant politically as well as economically, U.S. policy was guided more by a vision of what the world system should be than by short-term calculations of U.S. interest. The United States rallied support for an open, multilateral trading system, multilateral economic institutions, and foreign aid on a grand scale. Never before in history had the victors provided so much aid to the vanquished and recognized their interest in rebuilding the war-torn economies of allies and enemies alike. And rarely had a major power voluntarily promoted economic organizations that limited its own scope for unilateral action in favor of a world system.

Even before the end of the war, there had been considerable planning for the postwar economic order. That planning culminated in three international organizations, the International Bank for Reconstruction and Development (IBRD), the International Monetary Fund (IMF), and the General Agreement on Tariffs and Trade (GATT).[1] In the design of the world economic system, attention centered almost entirely on the concerns of the industrialized countries.[2]

Despite all the planning, the degree of economic dislocation in the immediate postwar period was much greater than had been anticipated. As economic recoveries in Europe and Japan floundered, U.S. policymakers understandably focused on the problems of reconstruction in those regions.[3] By 1947–48 the severe economic problems of those countries were seen as a major threat to the desired postwar order. The fledgling IBRD and IMF clearly lacked the resources to undertake a task as massive as the reconstruction of postwar Europe and Japan. The only country capable of doing so—the United States—extended vast quantities of resources under the Marshall Plan to the countries whose economies had been greatly damaged, if not destroyed, by the war.[4]

In the early 1950s, U.S. attention continued to focus primarily on the economies of Europe and East Asia. Nonetheless, the prosperity of the world economy contributed greatly to a favorable environment for the developing countries. The United States provided strong support for an open, multilateral trading system starting with the period of postwar reconstruction and continuing into the 1970s. Under U.S. leadership, the liberalization of international trade was far reaching.[5] The rapid growth of the European and Japanese economies was further stimulated by trade liberalization, as was the strong expansion of world trade. That expansion itself contributed significantly to the growth prospects of developing countries. Opportunities for trade with the industrialized countries create greater growth potential for developing countries than does reliance on their own internal markets.[6]

Once the European and Japanese recoveries gained momentum in the mid-1950s, U.S. attention gradually turned to the newly independent countries of Asia and Africa and to the economic aspirations of their leaders. Some of the idealism that governed postwar U.S. foreign policy also motivated support for colonial independence movements.[7] One by one, newly independent governments replaced colonial rule in "underdeveloped" (as they were then called) countries. Although some developing countries—Turkey, Thailand, and most of Latin America—had already become politically independent,[8] the postwar emergence of newly independent countries provided a "minimum critical mass" and enabled a sense of commonality among citizens of developing countries.

In those early years, developing countries had remarkably similar economic structures, with low living standards, low savings rates, high illiteracy rates, relatively short life expectancies, large fractions of population and GNP in agriculture, and dependence on primary product exports to earn foreign exchange for imports of goods not produced domestically. Most leaders in developing countries recognized their common situation and believed strongly that rapid economic development was politically, as well as economically, in the national interest. Articulate and charismatic leaders, especially in the Indian subcontinent, focused squarely on the aspirations for economic development and higher living standards in developing countries.

In the U.S. government, foreign aid came to be regarded as the major economic policy instrument for the developing countries. The success of the Marshall Plan made it natural that foreign aid would be seen as the major tool with which to encourage the growth of developing countries. Policymakers gave little thought to the differences between the war-devastated European countries, with their highly skilled labor forces and industrial histories, and the developing countries, where the task was one of creating new earnings streams, not of reviving earlier ones. In addition, economic thought about the development process centered on the proposition that workers in developing countries did not have enough capital to permit productive employment. Given low savings rates, a "transfer of resources" to developing countries in the form of aid was expected to increase capital per head and hence permit more rapid growth.[9] Also contributing to the emphasis on aid was the belief that the developing countries were so small that individually they had little effect on the major industrialized countries. Moreover, with their specialization in minerals and tropical agriculture and their low income levels, their economies seemed so "different" from those of the developed countries that they were thought to warrant special treatment within the international economic system.

The U.S. foreign aid program did not spring full-blown; instead, it evolved in response to experience. In addition to the Marshall Plan (which included aid to Turkey, like the Point Four program before it), the United States established early, large-scale aid programs to Korea and Taiwan because of strategic interests in the Far East. Until the early 1960s, U.S. aid was administered by the Mutual Security Agency. As the name implies, national security concerns in Turkey, Korea, Taiwan, and other "sensitive" countries were paramount during that period. Only in the early 1960s was the agency's name changed to the U.S. Agency for International Development.

Although many other industrialized countries organized foreign aid programs, the economic reality of the 1950s and 1960s was that the United States was so large and so rich relative to other industrialized countries that U.S. foreign aid was dominant.

Political support for foreign aid came from two distinct sources. For some, humanitarian considerations were the driving force. Those individuals supported foreign aid either because they felt that it was morally right to help the poor or because they believed that failure to develop satisfactorily would lead to conflict between rich and poor nations in the longer run. However, U.S. foreign policy increasingly focused on "containment" of the Soviet Union. As a national consensus began to support that view, it was widely believed that rapid economic growth in the developing countries would prevent the emergence of pro-communist governments there. Foreign aid was regarded as the policy instrument most conducive to rapid growth and thus received much support for national security reasons. From the mid-1950s until the 1990s, political support for U.S. foreign aid came from this coalition of two groups with extremely different motives. The disarray in foreign aid has resulted in part from the often divergent objectives of its supporters.

During these early years, the economies of developing countries were peripheral to the international economy, and U.S. policy toward them was perceived to center largely on its foreign aid program. The exports of developing countries were primarily raw materials, mostly exempt from import duties in the United States. Developing countries were failing to diversify and expand nontraditional exports because of their attempts to undertake "import substitution" and reduce their imports. The balance-of-payments difficulties that resulted restricted their potential as a market for U.S. exports. Hence, from a U.S. perspective, policies that centered on interactions between the economies of developing countries and the U.S. economy were hardly necessary; the aim of policy was to foster their growth.

This is not to say that U.S. policies did not affect developing countries—they did. Because the United States was so economically dominant, its stockpiling of raw materials and maintenance of sugar quotas had major effects on individual countries. But for the most part, such policies were undertaken unilaterally by the United States with little regard to their impact on developing countries. Most important of all, as noted, U.S. sponsorship of multilateral trade liberalization and the rapid growth of the international economy that ensued provided major benefits to developing countries.

During the 1950s and 1960s U.S. international economic policy thus became bifurcated. Issues such as exchange rates, trade, and private capital flows were important in relations with other industrialized countries. Foreign aid and official lending—both bilateral and multilateral—were the focus of economic relations with developing countries.

During the 1960s U.S. foreign aid was so large relative to that of other industrialized countries and the multilateral institutions that the United States largely determined international foreign aid policy. As rapid growth in Europe and Japan continued, however, their bilateral foreign aid programs increased more rapidly than that of the United States. At the same time, the shares of European countries and Japan in the multilateral institutions increased. As the U.S. predominance diminished, the multilateral institutions assumed greater responsibility as formulators of development policy, and U.S. participation in the multilaterals became increasingly important. While bilateral foreign aid was the responsibility of the U.S. Agency for International Development, the Treasury Department played the lead role in determining U.S. policy toward the multilaterals.

Despite occasional policy contradictions, the United States bilaterally and multilaterally[10] supported what was perceived to be in the best interest of developing countries themselves.[11] Their roles in the world economy were not large enough to generate trade and investment frictions. The less developed countries[12] adopted highly restrictive trade and payments regimes, and many were not members of GATT. Even for those that were, Article 18 of GATT provided an exemption from the obligation to maintain an open trading regime.[13] It was generally understood that developing countries should receive the benefits of reciprocal tariff reductions among industrialized countries under GATT without themselves having to make comparable tariff cuts.[14] U.S. trade with developing countries was small, the United States was dominant economically, and trade was not perceived to be of central importance. The United States exported less than 5 percent of GNP in the 1950s and 1960s, and of that only about 38 percent went to developing countries.[15]

While this perception of the irrelevance of developing countries in trade policy was largely appropriate in the 1950s, the world economy was already gradually changing. Some aid recipients, most notably Korea and Taiwan, built upon the rapid growth of the world economy and adopted economic policies that would permit their rapid trajectory into the class of "newly industrializing countries" (NICs).

Table 2-1 provides data on trade expansion that vividly demonstrates the changing structure of the international economy. World trade grew exceptionally fast between 1950 and 1970.[16] The United States accounted for almost one-fifth of world exports in the 1950s and early 1960s, while industrialized countries as a group increased their share of world trade markedly. Between 1950 and 1970, the export earnings of developing countries grew, though much more slowly than overall world trade. As a result, their share of world trade fell

Table 2-1. **Growth and Shares in World Trade, Selected Years, 1950–90**

Area	1950	1960	1970	1980	1990
	Value of exports (billions of U.S. dollars)				
World	57	114	283	1,910	3,310
Industrialized countries	36	84	220	1,254	2,458
United States	10	21	43	225	394
Other	26	63	177	1,029	2,064
Developing countries	21	30	61	656	852
Oil-exporting countries	4	7	17	301	168
Oil-importing countries	17	23	44	356	684
Africa	3	6	11	93	74
Asia	6	7	17	164	452
Western hemisphere	6	7	16	103	128
	Share of world exports (percent)				
Industrialized countries	63	74	78	66	74
United States	17	18	15	12	12
Other	46	55	62	54	62
Developing countries	37	26	22	34	26
Africa	5	5	4	5	2
Asia	11	6	6	9	14
Western hemisphere	11	6	6	5	4

Sources: International Monetary Fund, *International Financial Statistics Yearbook, 1980*, pp. 62–65, and *1991*, pp. 120–23.

from 37 to 22 percent, largely reflecting their policies of import substitution.

After 1970 several factors changed. First, the Asian developing countries' share of world exports dramatically increased, as Korea, Taiwan, Hong Kong, and Singapore emerged as major traders. Second, as oil's importance and price increased during the 1970s, the exports of oil-exporting developing countries increased rapidly, and the industrialized countries' share of world trade fell. Finally, the relative position of western hemisphere and African developing countries declined: countries in both regions experienced much slower rates of export growth than the world economy as a whole.

By 1990, therefore, the relative importance of different groups of trading nations was quite different than it had been even twenty years earlier. East Asia emerged as a major trading power; Africa and Latin America were less important than before. For its part, the United States accounted for about one-eighth of world exports in 1990, far less than the one-fifth share it held some three decades earlier.

With healthy growth of the international economy in the 1960s, even those developing countries that did not take full advantage of rapidly expanding world markets were able to benefit and increase their investment rates. Many achieved growth rates of real per capita income and improvements in health and educational standards unprecedented in their histories. Even India, whose per capita income grew by a disappointing 1.5 percent annual average, was experiencing growth at a rate more than three times that of the preceding century.[17]

U.S. awareness of the developing countries as something other than poor and economically unimportant aid recipients probably dates first to 1973–74, when the oil-exporting countries of OPEC restricted oil supplies and increased the price of oil dramatically. The global recession of 1974–75 was widely attributed to the oil price increase. Because a variety of developing countries participated in OPEC, they suddenly appeared very important to the U.S. economy, and their potential impact could no longer be ignored.[18]

At the same time, the shares of East Asian NICs in U.S. markets for textiles, clothing, footwear, electronic appliances, and other labor-intensive goods were rising dramatically. The very success of the East Asian NICs made them important trading nations; inevitably, protectionists in the United States and other developed countries raised questions about the NICs' own import regimes, as their penetration of markets for labor-intensive manufactured goods increased.[19]

Many U.S. observers asked why aid should continue for developing economies given the success of Korea and Taiwan, failing to recognize that they were the exception rather than the rule. Living standards in most developing countries were still abysmally low in comparison with those in industrialized countries; citizens in developing countries therefore regarded their economies as entitled to preferential treatment. However, businessmen in industrialized countries confronted with competition from East Asian imports began to regard the East Asian NICs and developing countries in general more as competitors than as countries deserving of aid.

Awareness that the goods competing with U.S. manufactures came from places such as Korea, Taiwan, Brazil, and Hong Kong placed trade issues clearly on the negotiating agenda with the NICs. But when trade issues arose, the United States relied on mechanisms established for dealing with other industrialized countries. Inevitably, the same processes and trading rules in effect for developed countries were applied to the NICs and other developing countries.

As if the emergence of trade rivals and the oil price increase did not require enough adjustment, another set of difficult issues arose in the early 1980s. Planners of the postwar international economic order had assumed that private international capital markets would not provide for the capital needs of the very poor developing countries, and they established the World Bank (earlier the IBRD—see chapter 5) as a multilateral lending institution. The expectation that most long-term international capital flows would be official was correct in the 1940s. By the late 1950s Europe's recovery had progressed enough to allow European countries to rely once again on private capital flows.

By the 1960s success at exporting permitted many developing countries to begin borrowing in the private international capital market. Private international bankers learned that those countries could be highly creditworthy borrowers, as foreign loans elevated domestic investment beyond levels possible with domestic savings and yielded rates of return high enough to finance the debt. When the first oil price increase took place in 1973–74, many oil-importing countries found their trade and current account balances sharply in deficit. They were confronted with the unpleasant choice of greatly restricting domestic investment to correct their current account deficits or of borrowing abroad to sustain investment levels. Many of the more advanced developing countries, including the Philippines, Thailand, Korea, Turkey, and many Latin American and North African countries, borrowed to finance those current account deficits. In some cases, this borrowing financed investments in activities yielding high rates of return; in others, however, foreign lending merely permitted the government to maintain consumption and investment levels in activities without adequate returns. During the late 1970s worldwide inflation allowed borrowing to continue without a commensurate increase in debt-service ratios, because most lending was at fixed nominal rates of interest. When in 1980 inflation persisted while worldwide recession began, lenders shifted to floating rates. The exports of developing countries fell sharply, and they borrowed again to finance their current account deficits. Outstanding indebtedness thus rose sharply at the same time as debt-service costs increased and worldwide inflation fell.

The recession that began in 1980 was deeper and more prolonged than earlier downturns, and for some countries initial levels of indebtedness were significantly higher than they had been in 1973–74. When, in addition, world nominal (and real, since there was no increase in the prices of international traded goods) interest rates rose, many of the apparently more successful and advanced developing countries were unable to service their debt. The consequence was the "debt crisis" that ensued starting late in the summer of 1982.

The debt crisis posed a number of issues for debtor countries and for U.S. international economic policy. For developing countries, the critical questions centered on the causes of their heavy debt burdens; the linkages between their falling growth rates, their indebtedness, and the state of the world economy; and the best means to resume growth and restore creditworthiness. For the United States, the debt crisis raised foreign policy concerns regarding Mexico and other countries deemed important; anxiety about the fragility of democratic movements in Latin America and elsewhere; and questions about the stability of the international financial system.[20] Because the multilateral institutions played a key role in the resolution of the debt crisis, U.S. policy toward those institutions, which sought to ensure an orderly stream of debt repayment, was also critical.

In many instances more was at stake than indebtedness and its servicing. Previous complacency about "sustained growth" in developing countries was shattered by the realization that the impressive growth rates of earlier years had in part been achieved in ways that mortgaged future living standards.

The severity of the economic difficulties of the 1980s for many developing countries has not visibly affected U.S. attitudes and policies toward them. On the contrary, the contradictions in U.S. policy have increased. Some U.S. officials have directly and indirectly (through the multilaterals) advocated policy reforms in many developing countries to encourage rapid export growth as a means of correcting policy distortions, resuming economic growth, and restoring creditworthiness. At the same time, other officials have actively sought to restrain the export promotion policies adopted by some developing countries.[21]

Foreign policy concerns in particular countries and regions have further complicated U.S. economic relations with developing countries. In the case of Egypt, the Camp David peace accords negotiated by President Jimmy Carter in 1977 committed the United States to a massive program of foreign assistance. Mexico has long assumed importance for the United States because of its size, proximity, and oil reserves and now assumes even more thanks to the proposed free-trade agreement. The Caribbean is perceived to be important because of its proximity, and Korea has historically been regarded as a strategic ally. Bilateral relations with these specific countries have complicated U.S. relations with the developing world as a whole.

By the early 1990s, almost all the instruments of U.S. international economic policy affected developing countries in significant ways. U.S. policies on trade, capital flows, debt, and foreign aid all occupy important positions in bilateral relations. Even as the issue agenda has broadened, the scope of action for U.S. officials has narrowed, for the increased importance of developing countries has intensified domestic political pressures in the United States on certain economic issues.

Different segments of the U.S. administration and Congress formulate specific aspects of U.S. policy, which are subject to conflicting pressures. Policy has become increasingly fragmented as the number of economic and political issues affecting U.S. relations with developing countries has increased. On occasion, divergent U.S. policies may even cancel each other out! In relations with other industrialized countries, the United States does not confront certain issues, such as debt, official lending, and foreign aid, that complicate the policy agenda with developing countries.

However, many U.S. policies—the Caribbean Basin Initiative, the Baker and Brady debt plans, support of the World Bank, IMF, and regional development banks, the Enterprise for the Americas Initiative, and foreign aid—deliberately and publicly seek to assist developing countries. When these policies and others offset in part each other's potential benefits, the damage to U.S. relations with the countries in question can be sizable.

The very success of many developing countries has increased their importance to the United States. Table 2-1 offers some data indicating the great importance of developing countries in U.S. trade in 1989. Developing countries account for more than one-third of all U.S. exports and imports and even greater shares of many individual manufactured exports. Yet those data ignore other important linkages: immigration, drugs, flows of students, and, perhaps most important of all, foreign policy concerns.

U.S. policy toward the developing countries has evolved in piecemeal fashion over several decades. Given the disaster many developing countries experienced in the 1980s, the increased differentiation among them, and the crucial transitions of former Soviet and East European countries, U.S. policy toward developing countries deserves a comprehensive reassessment. Such an undertaking is ambitious, as it must include a range of policies covering trade, commodity markets, debt, foreign aid, foreign investment, the multilateral institutions, and the role of the private sector. Each policy has been crafted subject to particular political and economic pressures, often without major regard to its interaction with other policies.

The original idealism that prompted U.S. support of foreign aid, the multilateral institutions, and the development efforts of poor countries still influences foreign policy. The costs and benefits of the gradual retreat to more parochial interests in the formulation of U.S. policy ought to be weighed against the potential costs and benefits of a more coherent set of policies. As the political and economic importance of developing countries increases, U.S. policies motivated by short-term particular interests may have sizable negative consequences in the long run. Scrutiny of the benefits and costs of these policies in the short run may inform judgments as to the wisdom of their continuation.

3 ‖ Trade, Aid, and the International Economy: Development in the Postwar Era

REGARDLESS OF THE MANY MOTIVES behind them, U.S. policies toward the developing countries have been grounded in a strong national consensus that the development of these countries was in the U.S. interest.[1] Certainly, the rationale for bilateral foreign aid programs and for support of multilateral lending institutions has been that they would promote development. Although the U.S. foreign aid program after World War II was driven by a combination of humanitarian, foreign policy, and national security concerns, all its advocates agreed that it would enhance the development prospects of the recipient countries, and that development was a desirable policy objective.[2]

Just as U.S. foreign aid and trade policies have evolved in response to the realities and prevailing ideas of the time, so too have the development strategies of developing countries. In more than forty years of postwar experience in more than one hundred countries, policymakers have learned a great deal about the development process. This chapter sketches the evolution of development thought in the postwar years, discussing also how it influenced policy in developing countries and in the United States. The evolution of these policies and of the developing economies themselves reflects the lessons of experience, which are also detailed. Much early thought and policy turned out to have consequences quite different from those anticipated, and many policies designed to facilitate rapid development were, in fact, bottlenecks to development.

The 1980s presented new problems for the developing countries, and this chapter discusses the imperative of policy reform and the implications for U.S. international economic policies. Throughout,

18

the focus is on the determinants of economic development and the ways in which U.S. international economic policies and the world economy can affect the growth prospects and potential of developing countries.

Development Thought in the Early Years

Development thought has evolved in response to both experience and ongoing economic research. My purpose is not to provide a full history of development thought, but to focus on those aspects of "early" development thought that informed development and aid policy and set the stage for current reforms in many developing countries. To that end, a description of development thought from the early 1950s to at least the late 1960s will suffice.[3]

To almost any world traveler in the 1950s, the differences between developed and developing countries, or underdeveloped countries, as they were then called, were obvious. The most important difference, of course, was the vast disparity in living standards, but many other social indicators also divided the two worlds. In developing countries, life expectancies were significantly shorter, infant mortality rates much higher, and educational attainments much lower than in developed countries. In developing countries, larger shares of the population and labor force engaged in agriculture, drawing a sharp contrast with the extensive industrial and urban activities of developed countries. Unlike their wealthier counterparts, developing countries specialized in primary commodity exports and depended on imports for many manufactured goods.

In the developing countries themselves, memories of colonial rule, a sense of dependency (based in part on the structure of trade) and vulnerability vis-à-vis the developed countries, and the desire for higher living standards combined to prompt most political leaders and the modernizing elites to attach great importance to achieving "industrialization" and rapid economic growth. Their implicit belief was that industrialization was the key to development, and that governments should undertake measures to achieve it.

The views of political and intellectual leaders in developing countries were shared in large part by economists who became interested in the development process. Robert Bates described the line of thought well: "Like all nations in the developing world, the nations of Africa seek rapid development. Their people demand larger incomes and higher standards of living. Common sense, the evidence of history, and economic doctrine all communicate a single message: that these objectives can best be secured by shifting from economies based on the production of agricultural commodities to economies based on industry and manufacturing."[4]

To be sure, economists such as Gottfried Haberler and Harry Johnson noted very early that the challenge was one of increasing productivity in all lines of economic activity, and that the shift from agriculture to industry was more the outcome of successful development than the primary cause.[5] Yet they were at that time in a minority. Even today, few observers would quarrel with the basic proposition that living standards generally rise as the share of nonagricultural sectors in economic activity increases. But in the 1950s and early 1960s, that proposition was taken to mean that incremental resources should go to industry and that agricultural development could largely be neglected.

With this basic bias toward industrialization, the next step was to analyze how it might come about. Several important ideas dominated a consensus among academics and policymakers about industrialization in developing countries. Most believed that: (a) markets failed in developing countries, and price incentives produced little response, especially in agriculture; (b) government should play an activist role in leading industrialization; (c) poor countries remained poor because of a vicious circle with low savings rates, scarce capital, and low output and incomes; and (d) a strong suspicion of the international market was appropriate.

Each of these ideas directly influenced economic policymaking in important ways. The experience of the Great Depression and Keynesian ideas about the role of government encouraged distrust of the market mechanism.[6] It seemed self-evident that, had markets not failed, developing countries would have achieved the growth rates and living standards of the developed countries. Additionally, peasants were assumed not to respond to incentives, so governments could expect little "supply response" in agriculture.[7] Concerns about lack of entrepreneurship, poorly functioning labor and capital markets, and monopolistic pricing were common.

Economic theory also provided a valid case for "infant industry" protection under certain circumstances. When a country would in the long run become competitive in a new industry already established elsewhere, theory showed that investors, despite the promise of long-run profitability, might not start the industry because profits might be dissipated in spillover effects that they would not recapture. Those wishing to industrialize thus appealed often to the infant industry argument to support their contention that markets would not generate industrialization for latecomers to the process.[8]

The intellectual climate was also receptive to an activist government role in the development process. The apparent success of the Soviet Union in achieving rapid industrialization under central planning seemed to suggest that governments could effectively undertake responsibility for establishing and managing industrial enterprises. Paul Rosenstein-Rodan argued that "the whole industry to be created is to be treated and planned like one huge firm or trust."[9] Jan Tinbergen, in the 1980s, summarized the conclusion that was even more widely held in the 1940s and 1950s: "As an outcome of many discussions and on the basis of experience. . . . Many European economists and politicians have concluded that the type of ownership of the means of production is much less important for an enterprise's efficiency than the quality of its management. . . . So efficiency considerations need not be a stumbling block if public enterprise is chosen as a means for furthering a country's development."[10]

Thus suspicion of market mechanisms was combined, implicitly or explicitly, with a belief that governments could undertake economic activities and achieve an outcome that maximized social welfare and avoided market failures. Most observers did not even contemplate that the state might undertake an economic activity using more of all factors of production than efficiency considerations warranted.

Another pillar of early development thought was the belief that a shortage of capital was the key explanation of "underdevelopment." Accelerating the rate of capital accumulation, therefore, would presumably enable rapid economic growth.[11] To be sure, all observers recognized that development would require educating the population, improving health and social services, and strengthening economic institutions. But it was widely believed that achieving desirable social outcomes in education and health care would be straightforward if resources were only available.

Finally, suspicion of international markets had multiple origins. First, there was the colonial heritage of most developing countries and the strong nationalist sentiment that accompanied independence movements. Second, the experience of the Great Depression in the 1930s, when global trade and finance collapsed, was important. Third, there was a strong "elasticity pessimism" about the prospects of primary commodity exports. Many analysts noted that the demand for primary commodities was price inelastic and believed that if developing countries attempted to remain specialized and rely on primary exports for growth, the prices of those commodities would decline so much that growth might in fact prove immiserizing.[12] This concern, in turn, led to the belief that growth would have to originate in the production of industrial goods that replaced imports—a strategy then called "import substitution," or inward-oriented development.

Development Policies in the Early Years

Informed by this early thought, almost all developing countries adopted fairly similar economic policies. Most encouraged domestic (import substitution) manufacturing investment, suppressed agricultural prices, expanded existing and started new public enterprises, attempted to stimulate savings and investment through taxation and credit allocation, and regulated private economic activity. These policies relied extensively on government intervention, private sector controls, direct assumption of economic functions, and insulation of the domestic economy from the world economy.

Measures to encourage new domestic industries included both public sector investment and private sector incentives. Incentives were usually in the form of subsidized investment credits; tax incentives to produce new industrial goods; preferential access to foreign exchange for investment and intermediate goods and raw materials; and high levels of import protection, if not outright prohibition of imports of goods that could be domestically produced. In addition, policymakers were extremely reluctant to alter the nominal exchange rates of their currencies, even when highly overvalued, because they feared raising the prices of imported capital and intermediate goods for import-substitution industries.[13]

Protectionist and exchange rate policies were extremely important in channeling new resources to the import-substitution industries. In the first decade after these policies were adopted—the 1950s in India, Pakistan, and much of Latin America, and the 1960s in much of Africa—industrial production grew quickly in many countries. The most rapidly growing part of the economy was import-substitution industry, which had been profitable to investors (including the government) behind high walls of protection. Protection allowed their prices and costs to far exceed international prices and created little incentive for efficiency. Over time, as these industries increased their share of industrial and total output, the negative consequences of import substitution became more and more evident.

Agricultural commodity prices to producers were suppressed through a variety of mechanisms. In some countries, agricultural exports were explicitly taxed. More often, state enterprises were given monopoly control over the marketing of traditional agricultural exports. These monopolies sold in world markets at prices that exceeded the prices they paid to farmers by considerably more than their costs of collecting and exporting the commodities.[14] The net effect was strong discrimination against agriculture and a general neglect of agricultural development.[15]

In most developing countries, public enterprises multiplied and assumed a variety of functions, including manufacturing, mining, tourism, banking, insurance, transportation, and communications. In many developing countries, public enterprises accounted for more than half, and in some cases even three-quarters, of investment and value added in manufacturing and mining activities.

In the belief that stimulating savings and investment was important and the responsibility of the public sector, governments increased tax rates, hoping to increase public savings. They also provided cheap credit to new industrial investors. For this purpose, low ceilings limited the interest rates commercial banks could charge, and government-owned financial enterprises supplied credit for industrial investment projects. Because interest rates were suppressed and often lagged below the rate of inflation, especially when it accelerated, the demand for credit greatly exceeded the supply. This scarcity enabled governments either to direct the credit allocation of private banks among industries or to provide credit directly to private and public firms that undertook new ventures the government favored in the drive for industrialization.

Finally, suspicious of markets, developing countries instituted a variety of controls over private economic activity. In many countries, labor markets were closely regulated. Minimum wages were often set at levels significantly above those prevailing throughout much of the economy, taxes were imposed to cover social insurance, and employers were required to provide housing, education, training, and a host of other measures that substantially raised the costs of employing labor. In addition to the credit controls already discussed, there were

Table 3-1. **Per Capita Income Levels and Growth Rates, Groups of Countries, 1950, 1965–89[a]**

Group	GDP per capita (1980 U.S. dollars)			Growth rate of GDP per capita (average annual rate)		
	1950	1973	1989	1965–73	1973–80	1980–89
Asia	487	1,214	2,812	n.a.	n.a.	n.a.
East Asia	n.a.	n.a.	n.a.	5.1	4.7	6.7
South Asia	n.a.	n.a.	n.a.	1.2	1.7	3.2
Latin America	1,729	2,969	3,164	3.7	2.6	−0.6
Sub-Saharan Africa	348	558	513	3.2	0.1	−2.2
EMENA[b]	940	2,017	3,164	5.5	2.1	0.8
Developing countries[c]	839	1,599	2,796	3.7	3.0	2.3
OECD countries[c]	3,298	7,396	10,104	3.1	2.6	2.5

Sources: World Bank, *World Development Report, 1990* (Oxford University Press, 1990), p. 16, and *1991*, p. 14.
n.a. Not available.
a. Numbers are simple averages for the countries for which data are available.
b. EMENA is Europe, the Middle East, and North Africa.
c. Growth rates for all OECD countries and for all developing countries for the 1965–73 and 1973–80 periods are interpolated.

often price controls over particular ranges of commodities or even over all items. Among scores of other controls, which varied from country to country, were investment licensing (in India firms could not legally produce *more* than the capacity indicated on their license), shipping permits, quality regulations, and so on.

Development Experience up to the 1980s

In hindsight, the quarter-century starting about 1948 appears to be a period of great success in development. When in the 1970s the World Bank commissioned David Morawetz to analyze the previous twenty-five years, he noted that actual growth rates in developing countries had greatly exceeded the expectations of the 1950s, though with great variation among countries.[16] Table 3-1 gives data on per capita income levels and growth rates for various groups of countries. Most countries registered impressive gains, especially until 1973.[17]

Savings rates also rose in almost all developing countries, often achieving levels that had been considered unfeasible. Moreover, indicators of the quality of life, such as health, educational attainment, and nutritional status, all began to show signs of improvement. Even from the perspective of the early 1990s, successful efforts to increase life expectancies, raise literacy rates, and reduce infant mortality significantly in almost all developing countries are among the greatest achievements.[18]

Policies and Outcomes

Although some economists were initially skeptical about the efficacy of market-distorting policies, the fact that countries such as Brazil and Turkey—both of which had heavily interventionist policies and highly restrictive trade regimes—were growing at historically unprecedented rates of 6 and 7 percent muted their criticism. In response to questions about the effectiveness of inward-oriented, interventionist policies, their defenders could point to relatively rapid growth rates as evidence that they were not imposing high costs.

However, even in the rapidly growing import-substitution countries, growth was not entirely smooth. By the 1970s a number of countries that relied on heavy governmental involvement and import substitution began to experience slower growth, and even stagnation. Simultaneously, the East Asian NICs, which had earlier abandoned import substitution in favor of growth-oriented policies and greater integration with the world economy, were growing very rapidly. Even among other developing countries, those that appeared to be most insulated from the world economy appeared to have lower growth rates.[19]

As indicated, governments were initially willing to provide newly established domestic industries with protection against imports. These industries produced substitutes for imports but usually depended on the import of raw materials, intermediate goods, and spare parts to maintain production levels. Import demand therefore grew rapidly, as established factories imported to maintain production, and new firms imported capital goods to accelerate investment. Meanwhile, export growth was sluggish, because of overvalued exchange rates and the allocation of resources for import substitution. Policymakers did not immediately realize that the scarcity of foreign exchange was effectively limiting investment.[20] As import licensing became more restrictive, the inefficiency costs of trade regimes multiplied, and delays in receiving shipments of spare parts and material inputs constrained production in many new import-substitution enterprises. Incentives to evade the import regime mounted, and the authorities had to impose export controls to capture foreign exchange earnings (which were higher in the unofficial market).

Another difficulty was that after an initial phase during which industrial production rose rapidly, import substitution became increasingly costly and capital-intensive. While the early import-substitution industries were often reasonably labor-intensive and produced goods with fairly large domestic markets, growth could continue only if new import-substitution industries were developed.[21] These new enterprises were often more capital-intensive and uneconomic on the small scale that matched the domestic demand in developing countries. As a result, the incremental output generated by new investments diminished. In many developing countries, growth rates remained stubbornly constant, or even declined, despite rising savings and investment rates.

Growing fiscal deficits accompanied investments in new import-substitution industries. Either because of political pressures to maintain growth, or simply because of the momentum of existing policies, fiscal deficits (after aid and other capital flows) tended to increase as a percentage of GNP. As they did so, inflation rates, which were in any event higher than those in developed countries, tended to accelerate. As a result, over the years, the average rate of inflation in most developing countries rose. When political pressure against inflation mounted, development expenditures were often cut, with adverse consequences for growth.

Over time, the government bureaucracies that administered development programs and private sector controls grew increasingly cumbersome. In part, they expanded because the economies themselves had been growing and becoming more complex. Government agencies also grew in attempts to stem the evasion of increasingly restrictive control mechanisms, a very difficult task because evasion was so profitable, for both businessmen and bureaucrats.[22]

While administrative difficulties continued to plague countries that relied on import substitution and government controls, the East Asian NICs altered their development strategy to rely on export-oriented growth. Although specific policies varied significantly among the NICs, each adopted a fairly realistic exchange rate policy and provided uniform export incentives almost as great as those for import-substitution industries. They improved the quality of their infrastructure, allocated resources to education, and began removing controls on labor, financial, and other markets.

The success of these policy reformers was spectacular in Korea, Taiwan, Singapore, and Hong Kong. They achieved sustained real growth rates of 8 to 9 percent and even higher. Among the most important lessons, their experience demonstrated that it was possible to achieve rapid growth through integration with the international econ-

omy, and that growth more rapid than that achieved by import-substituting countries such as Turkey and Brazil was possible.

However, as long as growth remained at reasonably high rates, most
countries maintained import-substitution policies and relied on government to direct much of the economy. When, in the 1970s, the price
of oil increased, many of those countries failed to adjust their domestic economic policies. Even some oil-importing countries did not re-
align the domestic price of oil and oil products, despite the much larger
import bill.[23] Their inaction was possible largely because they were
able to borrow in the private market to cover their excess of foreign-
exchange expenditures, although domestic inflation rates shot up
markedly after 1973.

During the 1970s developing countries borrowed more heavily than
ever before, and more credit was from private lenders, especially commercial banks. While some encountered debt-service difficulties one
or more times during the 1970s, most managed to continue growing,
even if more slowly than before (table 3-1), because of two phenomena. On the one hand, many started with very little outstanding debt.
On the other, most borrowing was at fixed nominal interest rates when,
during the late 1970s, worldwide inflation accelerated. As a result,
between 1976 and 1980, the real value of the developing countries'
outstanding debt increased much more slowly than it otherwise would
have.[24] Meanwhile, interest charges were 7 to 9 percent annually, while
the U.S. dollar prices (in which most debt was denominated) of internationally traded goods were increasing at an average annual rate of
10 percent or more. Thus debt-service ratios were not increasing.

Lessons of the 1960s and 1970s

Although few developing countries dramatically altered their basic
policy framework in the 1960s and 1970s, general understanding of
the development process improved considerably. Agricultural development thought began to change after T. W. Schultz demonstrated
that farmers were calculating, rational maximizers. Simultaneously, as
growth failed to accelerate as much as anticipated when investment
rates increased, analysts began to emphasize other factors that were
important development inputs.

They particularly stressed the significance of investments in people,
especially in health and education.[25] Experience in many countries,

notably India, demonstrated the infeasibility of rapid development through industrialization without attention to agriculture.[26] Workers at the International Rice Research Institute in the Philippines developed high-yielding strains of rice, and researchers in Mexico developed high-yielding wheat. Although these discoveries of the Green Revolution significantly increased the output of major foodgrains, they required far more supporting inputs of water, pesticides, and fertilizer to be effective. In addition, seed itself had to be adapted to widely varying climatic conditions. These challenges, in turn, increased the role of agricultural research and extension.

Many other important lessons emerged from field experience, as numerous developing countries sought to organize irrigation facilities, schools, family planning clinics, and a host of other programs.[27] By the late 1960s the idea that a shortage of physical capital was the key impediment to development had long been discredited. While it remains true that sustained rapid development is not possible with a low rate of investment, many other factors were recognized as determinants of the rate of economic growth, including investment in human capital and the role of incentives in a variety of microeconomic settings. The belief that individuals in developing countries were unresponsive to incentives waned.

By the end of the 1970s it was also widely recognized that a shortage of foreign exchange had significantly retarded growth, and that the outward-oriented trade strategies of the East Asian NICs had numerous advantages. Their success was so impressive that many in developed countries, including the United States, began to perceive them as important competitors in international trade, rather than as aid recipients.

Most important of all, however, policymakers and academics began to recognize that the overall policy framework was a crucial determinant of success in development. No longer did they believe that additional resources would inevitably imply more rapid growth; economic efficiency, achieved through appropriate market incentives, was also important.

A key lesson of these decades is that developing countries cannot rely on their own internal markets and import substitution for sustainable growth. For rapid and successful growth, they must rely on the international market and comparative advantage. Only by doing so can they take advantage of relatively abundant unskilled labor,

Table 3-2. **Growth Rates and Policy Orientation of Developing Countries, 1975–89**
Average annual rate of GDP growth

Developing country group	1975–82	1983–89
Strongly outward-oriented	8.4	7.7
Moderately outward-oriented	4.6	4.1
Moderately inward-oriented	4.0	2.7
Strongly inward-oriented	2.3	2.2

Source: IMF, *World Economic Outlook* (October 1990), p. 69.

economize on scarce capital, and avoid high levels of protection to domestic industry.

In that context, the healthy growth of the international economy and access to the markets of industrialized countries are crucial to the growth prospects of developing countries. Those (including Turkey and Chile) that have adopted outward-oriented policies have experienced rapid export growth. If markets in developed countries are more protected, or if the growth of world trade slows, the growth potential of countries that provide appropriate incentives for exports will be commensurately restrained. Of course, countries that continue a strategy of import substitution will also experience slower growth when the world economy is stagnant.

Thus the policies of developing countries themselves and the state of the world economy affect their growth prospects. When global trade is sluggish, all developing countries grow more slowly, although inward-oriented countries grow even more slowly than outward-oriented ones. When worldwide growth is rapid, all developing countries benefit, but once again, those with policies more conducive to growth excel.

These lessons began to gain recognition at the beginning of the 1980s, and the experience of that decade has reinforced them. Table 3-2 gives data on the growth rates of developing countries, grouped by their policy stance, for the periods 1975–82 and 1983–89. All countries experienced slower growth in the second period, but the strongly inward-oriented countries grew more slowly in both periods.

Developments in the 1960s and 1970s

In part because growth continued, and in part because the lessons of the 1950s and 1960s were only beginning to be learned, U.S. aid officials and the multilateral organizations continued supporting developing countries whose policy regimes had remained unaltered since the 1950s. In the 1960s the U.S. bilateral aid program shifted away from financing infrastructure, industrial, and other projects in favor of comprehensive development programs. By and large, however, this program support operated in the context of the prevailing policy framework.[28] Though aid officials cautioned against excessive protection, import licensing, negative real interest rates, price controls, and other policies, their warnings had little long-term effect and were heeded only when a balance-of-payments crisis erupted.

In the event of such a crisis, the international community—bilateral donors and the multilateral institutions—became involved with policy, usually under the leadership of the IMF. "Consortia" of donors would then meet and pledge support to a country undertaking an IMF stabilization program.

In each country, some combination of unacceptably high inflation and balance-of-payments disequilibrium prompted the government to approach the international community for assistance. Usually, the conditions of international support were adjustment of the nominal exchange rate, a ceiling on government borrowing, and a limit on credit creation. Once taken, these measures tended to reduce inflationary pressures and improve the balance of payments as flight capital was repatriated[29] and as exports responded to the more favorable exchange rate. In addition, a recession often accompanied or followed the stabilization program, both because import shortages extended to intermediate goods and raw materials, slowing industrial production, and because reduced government expenditures and credit creation slowed economic activity.

Some countries were unable to maintain their unrealistic policies as early as the late 1970s. Other countries, however, managed to maintain their policy regimes until 1982–83. Like the oil crisis of 1973–74, the 1979 oil price increase preceded a worldwide recession. Unlike 1973–74, however, in 1979 the industrialized countries did not resort to expansionary policies to attempt to counter the recession. As a consequence, the recession was prolonged and severe, and the world prices of many traded commodities declined. As the balance of payments of developing countries deteriorated, their borrowing increased. While foreign aid was much less important for middle-income countries, aid programs continued to provide resources for poorer countries, as they had in earlier years.

The Experience of the 1980s

The 1980s provided a harsher environment for countries pursuing economic development than earlier decades. On the one hand, the real growth rate of the world economy slowed abruptly in the first half of the decade. At the same time, worldwide inflation abruptly decreased, while real interest rates soared. The combination presented a great challenge for leaders in developing countries. Officials in developed countries concerned with the fortunes of developing countries also faced new policy challenges as they sought to support their growth and manage the debt problem.

The Debt Crisis and Its Consequences

In mid-1982, the government of Mexico announced that it could no longer service its debt. The announcement was startling, especially because large oil fields had been found in Mexico in the late 1970s and the country, as a major oil exporter, had recently been deemed very creditworthy.

The Mexican announcement prompted the commercial banks to reassess their willingness to extend additional credit to developing countries. As a result, the banks suddenly stopped lending to almost all of them. At the same time, as the world prices of many developing country exports were declining, nominal interest rates remained very high, and debt levels mounted sharply. The abrupt drop in bank lending alone would have required serious macroeconomic adjustments in most borrowing countries even if debt had not been outstanding, commodity prices had not fallen, and real interest rates had not risen. However, given the debt, the recession, and low commodity prices, country after country had difficulties servicing the debt and appealed to the IMF, the World Bank, and bilateral donors for assistance. The outward-oriented countries of East Asia managed to avoid debt-service crises and to make adjustments without external support, but for most other developing countries, the situation was much more serious.

As country after country announced its inability to continue servicing the debt, growth rates fell still further. In Mexico, for example, sharp expenditure cuts and other responses to the crisis contributed to a dramatic change in real GDP growth, from a rate of 7.9 percent in 1981 to −5.3 percent in 1983.[30] For middle-income developing countries that import oil, real per capita income fell 0.2 percent annually from 1980 to 1985; the same indicator had increased an average of 3.3 percent each year from 1973 to 1980.[31]

Most analysts initially attributed declining growth rates to the debt crisis and the worldwide recession. However, when in 1983 and 1984 nominal interest rates started to fall and the worldwide recovery began, some countries continued to stagnate while others resumed rapid growth. Growth rates in the East Asian NICs fell by much less than those in other countries after 1979 and accelerated sharply after 1983 (table 3-2). Turkey's economic growth also began to accelerate as its policy reforms stimulated economic activity. Other countries, however—especially in sub-Saharan Africa and Latin America—continued to experience declines in per capita incomes.

As the 1980s progressed, the lessons of the 1970s were, if anything, accentuated: it became increasingly evident that differences in economic policies contributed significantly to differences in economic growth rates. In the 1980s the impact of policies on economic performance was far more widely recognized than in the 1950s and 1960s, when the world economy was highly conducive to growth and import substitution was in its initial stages. Korea's debt as a percentage of GNP, for example, was not very different from that of many Latin American countries in 1982–83. But Korea's debt as a percentage of exports was much lower because of its outward orientation. In another example, growth in Chile sharply accelerated in the late 1980s after major policy reforms, despite one of the largest debt burdens in Latin America and a severe drop in the price of Chile's most important commodity export, copper, during the early 1980s.

In that decade it also became evident that successful policy reform is a very difficult process, for both political and economic reasons. Reform requires a large shift in incentives, and to achieve results people must believe the changes will last. However, a number of factors conspire to raise doubts about the sustainability of policy reform, especially in its early stages.

Invariably, governments must remove controls that have benefited many citizens. Public expenditure cuts negatively affect those who receive incomes or transfers from the government. Tax revenue increases are difficult for obvious reasons. Dismantling a highly restrictive trade regime reduces the profitability of many import-substitution activities and challenges producers to become more efficient. Removing food subsidies, pricing public services realistically, and other necessary reforms all provoke understandable opposition.

In addition to these difficulties, the inevitable costs of policy reform are borne early in the process, while the benefits are not visible until later. Even those who stand to gain much in the longer run may perceive their prospects as uncertain, if not diminished. Political opposition to reforms is therefore strong, raising doubts as to whether they can be sustained. In the face of staunch opposition, the response can be slower, and as a consequence, uncertainty increases. Evidence suggests that four or five years may pass before the benefits of policy reforms are widely evident.[32]

Implications for U.S. Policy toward Developing Countries

As understanding of the development process has improved with experience, analysts have reached several conclusions that are extremely important for U.S. policy. Among the lessons, the domestic economic policies of many developing countries are incompatible with sustained economic growth, and the range of activities that the international community can productively finance and that will significantly contribute to long-term development is quite limited. Furthermore, policy reform is a difficult task that industrialized countries and the multilateral institutions can facilitate with appropriate support. Finally, with appropriate policies, developing countries will grow more rapidly when the international economy is strong and world markets are open to their exports.

When policies are inappropriate, the effectiveness of many forms of assistance (which can be productive under appropriate policies) is greatly reduced. It makes little sense, for example, to attempt to encourage agricultural development by financing subsidies for the use of fertilizers, pesticides, and other agricultural inputs when government policies severely depress output prices. Certainly, it does not enhance development prospects to offer "balance-of-payments support" by lending to countries with highly protectionist trade regimes and an unrealistic exchange rate. Since these policies will ultimately have to be altered, lending only permits counterproductive policies to persist longer than they would otherwise. Moreover, when reform occurs, the borrowing country will face larger debt-service obligations than it would have in the absence of lending.

Thus when policies appear inimical to growth, overall lending in support of development programs is unlikely to achieve developmental objectives. However, supporting programs that invest in people and lay the foundation for greater factor productivity after policy reform can increase development potential, if not short-run growth rates.

Although general support is unwarranted when policies are inappropriate, assistance selectively targeted to support reforms can smooth the transition and make success come more rapidly. When the immediate impetus to reform is imbalance in a country's external accounts, assistance can also facilitate adjustment, especially if imports have severely fallen before the initiation of reform. If, as in Turkey in 1980, a lack of oil imports has virtually shut down the transport system, while factories have been unable to obtain raw materials, intermediate goods, and spare parts for months, assistance in the form of foreign exchange can significantly accelerate the recovery of production levels.[33]

Perhaps even more significant for foreign assistance in the 1990s, a number of heavily indebted countries have very low domestic savings rates after years of slow growth. In these circumstances, even after reforms, the rate of investment would remain very low if savings were the only source of investment funds. The implementation of reforms and very high real interest rates in liberalized financial markets strongly suggest that additional resources can be productively employed. But, by definition, heavily indebted countries with low savings rates are not creditworthy and have little access to private international capital markets. In these circumstances, additional resources from official sources in support of reform can generate very high returns.[34]

Strong international trade expansion in an open, multilateral trading system provides the environment most conducive to the growth of the developing countries and the success of policy reform. For this reason, foreign aid and official lending cannot be viewed as alternatives to trade; they are complements. Trade opportunities can be as important as foreign aid in fostering the rapid growth of developing countries. Because of the crucial importance of the world economy to developing countries, the United States can no longer regard foreign aid and support of the multilateral institutions as policies for developing countries, treating trade and other international economic policies as entirely separate.

Harry G. Johnson pointed out the analytical relationship between trade and aid as early as the mid-1960s: "Foreign aid serves two functions in the development process. First, it provides real resources additional to what can be extracted from the domestic economy, increasing the total available for investment; second, since resources are foreign, it averts the real income losses to the country involved in transforming domestic into foreign resources."[35] Those additional resources can be used as readily in support of export expansion (and the development of infrastructure necessary for exporting) as in the production of import substitutes. Insofar as policies are appropriate, capital inflows (official or private) can permit a higher level of investment consistent with any economy's structure. For countries still at very early stages of development, the technical assistance component of foreign aid can also be very important.

Finally, sustained economic growth in the developed countries itself contributes significantly to the growth prospects of developing countries, as long as it is accompanied by open markets. Thus policies on trade, aid, debt, and the multilaterals must each be assessed to obtain an overview of U.S. policy toward developing countries. Many of the shortcomings in the current U.S. position arise because of conflicts between these policy instruments.

4 ||| U.S. Foreign Aid

AS THE CHIEF POLICY LINKAGE between developing and developed countries for many years, foreign aid successfully facilitated an increase in investment rates in many small developing countries, financing as much as 50 percent or more of investment.[1] The United States was the world's major provider of this aid in the decades after World War II. In recent years, the view of foreign aid has become far less simplistic. Transformations in the understanding of the development process and in the developing world itself have irrevocably altered the perceived role of foreign aid. Appropriate policies and access to international markets are now regarded as paramount; no longer is a "transfer of resources" and high rate of investment alone deemed adequate to ensure rapid economic growth.[2]

These changes have affected the operation of U.S. foreign assistance programs. Even for supporters of aid, its mission is no longer as clear as it was; as political support for foreign aid has weakened,[3] these supporters have increasingly accepted special provisos governing the allocation and administration of aid to win the support of doubters. These provisos have arguably reduced aid's effectiveness. Expectations as to what could be accomplished with given amounts of aid have been excessively optimistic. For these and other reasons, "aid fatigue" has emerged in the United States.[4] Confronted with the low per capita incomes and widespread poverty that remain in numerous countries, many aid supporters have come to question its effectiveness.

Moreover, aid no longer dominates bilateral relations between the United States and developing countries. As some developing countries have achieved rapid growth, economic issues such as trade, investment, and foreign debt and political issues such as authoritarianism, national security, and the environment have assumed increased importance relative to foreign aid. Most of these matters are handled by government agencies other than the U.S. Agency for International Development, giving rise to questions about the coherence of U.S. policies toward developing countries.

In addition, the role of the United States as an aid donor has declined in both absolute and relative terms. The United States contributed just over 20 percent of total bilateral assistance in the late 1980s (table 4-5). European countries and Japan have increased their foreign aid programs as their real incomes have risen. The multilateral lending institutions—the World Bank, IMF, and regional development banks— have also increased in relative and absolute importance. The United States remains a major participant in the multilateral organizations, but it is by no means dominant, holding just less than a 20 percent share in both the IMF and the World Bank.[5] Nonetheless, most Americans perceive that U.S. foreign aid programs continue to lie at the heart of relations with developing countries. The same holds internationally: many issues of international economic policy are handled through the OECD, whose membership largely excludes developing countries. The Development Assistance Committee of the OECD is the major forum where donor countries coordinate their aid efforts.[6]

One of the difficulties of discussing foreign aid is the large number of technical concepts and terms. As the variety of foreign aid instruments has increased, so too has the number of terms. An appendix to this chapter provides an introduction to concessional assistance, official development assistance, and other frequently encountered but technical aid terms. This chapter moves from an overview of the evolution of U.S. foreign aid to an evaluation of its effectiveness and a summary of its current state.

The Evolution of U.S. Foreign Aid

Only after the postwar recovery of Europe and Japan seemed self-sustaining did U.S. attention turn to the problems of economic development. Since the Marshall Plan, U.S. foreign aid has declined in real terms. Measured in 1988 dollars, foreign aid averaged $35 billion annually during the Marshall Plan years, held steady at about U.S. $22 billion annually until the mid-1970s, and then fell to an average of about $15 billion annually after 1976, though with sizable annual fluctuations.[7]

As a percentage of U.S. GNP, foreign aid fell even more sharply.

Foreign aid constituted 3 percent of GNP in 1949 but fell thereafter to about 1 percent of GNP in the 1950s. By the late 1980s, it represented only 0.27 percent of U.S. GNP.[8]

The formal organization directing the U.S. foreign aid program has changed several times. It began as the Economic Cooperation Administration in 1949–53 and then became the Mutual Security Agency. In 1961 it assumed its present title, the U.S. Agency for International Development (USAID). As the names imply, the United States first directed aid toward the industrialized, war-devastated countries. Not until the early 1960s were the reconstruction needs of Europe met, and the foreign aid program then began to focus on the support of economic development.[9]

U.S. foreign aid has been administered largely through "AID missions," teams of USAID personnel located in recipient countries. The presence of fairly large AID staffs on location has been a hallmark of the U.S. aid program, distinguishing it from that of the World Bank and other bilateral and multilateral agencies.[10] This distinctive characteristic should be recalled when considering the "comparative advantage" of U.S. aid and that of other aid donors.

U.S. foreign aid has affected almost all aspects of its recipients' economies, financing roads, railroads, bridges, telephone networks, electrical generating capacity, ports, irrigation dams, and feeder wells. In addition, U.S. technicians have provided technical assistance as well as physical capital.[11] U.S. aid has supported the development of local agricultural research and extension institutions and assisted in the improvement of educational and public health systems, among other accomplishments. In many U.S. projects, the local learning that resulted enhanced local capabilities for additional projects.

The presence of AID missions also enabled AID economists to participate in discussions of economic policy in the recipient country. In some instances, local AID employees later assumed major responsibilities in their governments, especially in the Korean case.[12] In many instances, this "policy dialogue" helped increase the recipient country's ability to formulate improved economic policy,[13] as AID officials introduced project appraisal guidelines, highway design standards, and central banking techniques.

The late 1950s and 1960s represented the heyday of U.S. foreign aid. Political leaders in most developing countries regarded foreign aid as crucially important. Aid constituted a significant fraction of available investment resources and was perceived, by both donors and recipients, as a key element in hopes for rapid development. During those years, the United States was the dominant donor country. Although some other industrialized countries had begun to formulate aid programs, their efforts paled beside that of the United States. U.S. foreign aid missions, therefore, played crucial roles in the discussion of economic development policies in a number of developing countries, and AID mission directors often enjoyed higher standing than U.S. ambassadors in recipient countries. The U.S. foreign aid program was then in its formative stages. In some instances, such as in Korea and Taiwan, the exigencies of the situation prompted program assistance, a form of generalized support, but the primary emphasis was on project support, whose foreign exchange component was financed.[14] In most recipient countries, foreign aid began with a strong project orientation.

U.S. aid was so important that AID officials regularly participated in discussions of domestic economic policy: without aid, governments simply could not undertake desired development programs. The extent of their interaction raised problems for both U.S. officials and foreign politicians. Sensitive domestic economic issues became subject to discussion and negotiation with a powerful foreign government. In countries with recent colonial histories, this matter was especially touchy. Meanwhile, Congress held U.S. officials accountable not only for aid expenditures but for almost all the policies of recipient country governments.

As early as the 1960s, some of the tensions and conflicts that eventually led to aid fatigue were beginning to surface. In countries where the leadership was pursuing economically disastrous policies, AID officials often tried unsuccessfully to influence policy.[15] Eventually AID officials recognized that project aid did not provide a vehicle for discussions of overall economic policies with the central government, while additional project support made little sense until the government improved the overall framework of economic incentives.

As a result, "program aid" in support of overall development plans became a larger component of the aid effort. President John F. Kennedy's Latin American "Alliance for Progress" initiative exemplified this trend, as it encouraged each eligible Latin American country to formulate a development plan that the United States would then support.[16]

Even in its heyday, total official development assistance seldom accounted for more than 2 to 3 percent of GNP in recipient countries.

Despite its modest scale, foreign aid was surrounded by unreasonable expectations of rapid economic advances. Because aid officials were held accountable for all expenditures in recipient countries,[17] as excesses of economic policies became evident and growth rates failed to increase as much as expected, concerns with the U.S. foreign aid program increased.

By the late 1960s U.S. foreign aid appropriation bills were encountering considerable opposition. For a variety of reasons, including the hostility of many developing countries to the United States, the difficulties with economic policy already discussed, and the slow rate of progress compared with the Marshall Plan's success, aid fatigue was increasing. President Richard Nixon appointed the Peterson Commission (table 4-8) to evaluate U.S. foreign aid programs and recommend changes.

The Peterson Commission advocated several major reforms that were accepted and implemented. It noted the reduced relative importance of the United States as a donor, as the rapidly growing European countries had already begun expanding their aid programs, and multilateral assistance to low-income countries had increased with the establishment of the International Development Association (IDA).[18] In response it recommended that the economic assistance component of the U.S. aid program focus on project lending. Consistent with this thrust, it also recommended that the United States support the lead of the IMF and World Bank in evaluating the overall policy framework of each developing country. USAID thus reduced its staff capacity for analysis of overall economic frameworks, relying instead on the IMF and World Bank and shifting its emphasis back to project aid and technical assistance. Increasingly, USAID personnel were specialists in health, education, population, nutrition, agriculture, and other sectoral and subsectoral fields.

Focus on overall economic policies was left largely to the multilateral institutions. The World Bank's activities, which had already been increasing, began a major expansion in the early 1970s with the acceptance of the Peterson Commission report. Most professional observers still believed growth rates were satisfactory, and there were few fundamental challenges to the prevailing policy regimes.

In the 1970s additional questions about aid and its effects were raised. In particular, analysts pointed out that in many countries the poor had not been the chief beneficiaries of growth. While in hindsight the policies that encouraged import substitution and government controls appear largely responsible for this phenomenon (to the extent that it was real), Congress responded by mandating that foreign aid concentrate on meeting "basic human needs." U.S. foreign aid was thus to emphasize projects that directly assisted the poor.

Despite the obvious appeal of this emphasis to those supporting aid out of humanitarian motives, economists realized that this mandate would deter assistance for some highly worthwhile projects that might, indirectly, permit even greater increases in the poor's well-being. Expansion of port facilities, for example, might permit the development of new, labor-intensive export industries that would provide employment for many poor people, who would work more productively and earn higher real wages than before. The basic human needs approach, however, discouraged such infrastructure investments in favor of rural projects that would "directly" improve the well-being of rural people where they resided. The approach encouraged projects that would directly finance rural employment programs, the provision of safe drinking water, improvements in public health facilities, and agricultural extension services. While some such activities are clearly economic investments, the focus on basic human needs at times diverted resources from investments that would, indirectly, have yielded even larger benefits for poor people.

One can convincingly argue that many projects designed to increase the well-being of the poor are very worthwhile investments. Moreover, in light of the many development programs of the 1960s that neglected these investments, the change in emphasis had economic merit. The new approach, however, also constrained what could be done with foreign aid and probably shifted the focus of aid programs more than would have been desirable even in the interest of increasing the earning power and well-being of the poor.

When, in the aftermath of the early 1980s debt crisis, worldwide attention centered on the overall economic policy framework of developing countries, USAID was unable to play an effective role, having lost its capacities for macroeconomic analysis. Debt policy was primarily the responsibility of the Treasury Department. USAID dealt almost exclusively with low-income countries, mainly in the form of project assistance. In contrast to its overriding importance to recipient governments in the 1950s and 1960s, U.S. aid was only one of several sources of assistance in the late 1980s, and other donors and the multilateral institutions were often far more important. By the early 1990s USAID was continuing to provide significant project aid for low-income countries, but its presence was far less visible than before, as more and more economic policy toward developing countries was formulated and executed by the U.S. Trade Representative, the Treasury Department, the Agriculture Department, and other agencies.

The Policy Dialogue

As noted, during the 1950s and 1960s USAID economists recognized that economic policies in some countries were detrimental to growth, and they naturally engaged local officials in policy dialogue. In some instances, policy discussions dealt with project lending, when concerns over agricultural pricing, credit subsidies, fertilizer distribution, or import access arose in particular sectors.

At the economy-wide level, however, the policy dialogue was more important, often involving the AID mission director and top staff. These discussions were ongoing, as U.S. policy was to support the overall development efforts (usually embodied in a development plan) of the country concerned. In some countries, a consortium of aid donors held formal meetings in which senior local officials presented expenditure and revenue plans and anticipated financing and balance-of-payments shortfalls. The donors then pledged aid in support of the plans, if they were deemed appropriate.[19]

Especially when U.S. aid was predominant, the United States was a major participant in the consortia.[20] When there were serious concerns about the wisdom of current or planned economic policies, consortia could postpone meetings or fail to act, thereby exerting considerable pressure on recipient governments to change their policies. Because of the importance of U.S. assistance, the policy stances of U.S. aid officials were especially influential.

In most countries, U.S. officials used their influence to push policies in the appropriate directions, toward less restrictive import and exchange practices, more export incentives, more realistic interest rates, smaller fiscal deficits, and so on.[21] In many instances, political opposition to these measures was strong, and even when government leaders altered their policies by considerably less than suggested, they often responded more out of a need for aid than out of any conviction that the new policies were appropriate.

Certain political constraints limited the effectiveness of all policy dialogues. These constraints originated both in the United States and

Table 4-1. **Geographic Distribution of U.S. Foreign Economic Assistance, Selected Time Periods, 1946–90**[a]
Billions of U.S. dollars, with percent of total assistance in parentheses

Region	1946–48	1949–52	1953–61	1962–86	1987–90
Africa	b	b	1.1	14.3	4.4
			(4.6)	(9.7)	(11.2)
East Asia	2.0	3.0	7.6	17.8	2.0
	(16.0)	(12.4)	(31.5)	(12.1)	(5.1)
Europe	8.6	13.6	4.5	2.4	b
	(68.8)	(69.9)	(18.6)	(4.7)	
Latin America	b	b	1.5	18.4	6.3
			(6.2)	(12.5)	(16.1)
Near East and South Asia	0.6	1.3	7.6	50.8	12.6
	(4.8)	(7.0)	(31.5)	(34.7)	(32.3)
Total	12.5	18.6	24.1	146.3	39.0

Source: USAID, *U.S. Overseas Loans and Grants and Assistance from International Organizations: Obligations and Loan Authorizations, July 1, 1945–September 30, 1990* (Washington, 1990), various pages.
a. Area figures do not add to the total because of the omissions of Oceania and of expenditures—primarily for the multilateral institutions—that cannot be allocated by region.
b. Less than $500 million.

in recipient countries, making it especially difficult to judge the "accuracy" of policy advice and the extent to which U.S. influence improved economic performance. Nonetheless, policy dialogues undoubtedly contributed to an understanding of economic policy in many developing countries.

Volume and Destination of Aid Flows

Table 4-1 presents data on the volume of U.S. aid flows and their importance to various geographic regions since 1946. All data are in current prices, which understate the magnitude of foreign aid in the early postwar years relative to later periods.[22] USAID breaks the entire period since 1946 into five subperiods: the "Postwar Relief" period, from 1946 to 1948; the Marshall Plan period, from 1949 to 1952; the Mutual Security Act period, from 1953 to 1961; and the Foreign Assistance Act period, from 1962 to the present, subdivided again to the 1962–86 and 1987–89 subperiods.

As noted, the bulk of U.S. aid in the immediate postwar period went to Europe and East Asia essentially as a reconstruction program. Although aid flows to the Near East and South Asia increased somewhat in the Marshall Plan years, Europe and East Asia received more than 80 percent of all U.S. foreign assistance. Bilateral aid from the United States to individual recipients accounted for more than five-sixths of the world's total aid at that time.

The period from 1953 to 1961 was mixed, in that Europe, Japan, Taiwan, and Korea all continued to receive aid, but aid to Europe and Japan fell sharply as their growth accelerated, while aid to Korea and Taiwan rose significantly. African, Latin American, and other developing countries also began to increase their shares of the U.S. foreign aid budget.

By the 1960s, U.S. support for reconstruction in Europe was ending. Total aid to Europe from 1953 to 1961 was only $4.5 billion, compared with $13.6 billion in the preceding four years. As its name change in 1961 indicated, the U.S. foreign aid program began to focus squarely on developing countries. By the mid-1960s, East Asia's share of U.S. aid had fallen dramatically, as that region's major aid recipients, Korea and Taiwan, achieved such rapid growth that they no longer warranted aid. Assistance to Africa and Latin America has increased steadily in relative importance, although Africa still received less than one-eighth of all bilateral U.S. assistance in the most recent period. The Near East and South Asia have received about one-third of all bilateral U.S. aid since 1953, although the amounts received by individual countries changed markedly.

Table 4-2 summarizes U.S. economic assistance to the developing countries that received the most aid. Each developing country that received more than $500 million from the United States between 1953 and 1961 or more than $1 billion between 1962 and 1986 is listed separately.

In the 1950s the largest developing country recipients of U.S. aid in absolute dollar terms were India, Korea, Pakistan, Turkey, Vietnam, and Yugoslavia. In per capita terms, of course, aid to India and Pakistan was far smaller. On a per capita basis, the largest aid recipients were Costa Rica, Israel, Taiwan, and Turkey.

The 1962–86 period covers several eras in U.S. foreign policy, and foreign aid flows reflected the different emphases of each era. Vietnam was a large recipient in the early part of the period. Egypt and Israel received the most aid during the entire 1962–86 period, especially in the latter part. Israel had also received a sizable amount of assistance in the 1950s, when Egypt's receipts were much smaller (even in 1970 aid to Egypt per capita was less than $1). After the Camp David peace accords in 1977, however, each country's economic (and military) as-

Table 4-2. **Major Recipients of U.S. Aid, 1953–61, 1962–86, and 1987–1990**[a]

Country	U.S. aid received (millions of dollars)			Percent of total U.S.aid, 1962–86	Aid per capita, 1970 (1970 dollars)
	1953–61	1962–86	1987–90		
Bangladesh	0	2,835	605	1.9	n.a.
Brazil	314	2,232	14	1.5	1.0
Chile	171	1,067	10	0.7	6.3
Colombia	107	1,419	54	1.0	5.6
Costa Rica	52	1,049	519	0.7	4.6
Dominican Republic	2	1,229	203	0.8	8.1
Egypt	302	12,986	3,950	8.9	0.0
El Salvador	11	1,758	1,331	1.2	2.9
India	2,408	8,995	606	6.1	0.8
Indonesia	221	3,084	313	2.1	1.6
Iran	548	196	0	b	2.1
Israel	507	12,083	4,795	8.3	28.9
Jordan	276	1,401	196	1.0	6.1
Korea	2,579	2,857	0	2.0	6.4
Morocco	290	1,182	362	0.8	4.3
Pakistan	1,419	5,358	1,527	3.7	2.1
Peru	101	1,118	292	0.8	1.0
Philippines	286	2,112	1,177	1.4	1.7
Portugal	28	1,022	186	0.7	c
Spain	914	183	8	b	0.0
Sudan	54	1,314	238	0.9	n.a.
Taiwan	979	311	0	b	c
Thailand	264	769	123	b	1.0
Turkey	1,093	2,992	211	2.0	2.5
Vietnam	1,548	6,014	0	4.1	22.8
Yugoslavia	1,038	536	0	b	c
Total economic aid	24,053	146,321	39,041	...	...

Sources: First four columns: USAID, *U.S. Overseas Loans and Grants and Assistance*; last column: U.S. Department of Commerce, *Historical Statistics of the United States: Colonial Times to 1970*, pt. 2 (Washington, 1975), pp. 872–75 (for aid data); and IMF, *International Financial Statistics Yearbook, 1988* (Washington, 1988), various pages (for population data).

n.a. Not available.

a. The countries included are all those with more than $500 million aid in the 1953–61 period or more than $1.0 billion in the 1962–86 period. Totals include countries that received less than those amounts in the respective periods.

b. Less than $0.5 million in aid.

c. There were net payments to the United States.

Table 4-3. **U.S. Foreign Economic Aid, by Major Programs, 1977–88**[a]
Billions of 1989 U.S. dollars

Year	Assistance				Economic Support Fund	Total
	Development	Food	Other	Multilateral		
1977	2.2	2.3	0.5	2.3	3.3	10.6
1978	2.9	2.2	0.4	2.4	3.9	11.8
1979	2.6	2.1	0.6	3.1	3.2	11.6
1980	2.4	2.2	0.9	2.6	3.3	11.4
1981	2.3	2.1	0.8	1.7	3.0	9.9
1982	2.3	1.7	0.7	1.9	3.5	10.1
1983	2.4	1.7	0.6	2.1	3.6	10.4
1984	2.5	1.8	0.6	2.0	3.7	10.6
1985	2.8	2.3	0.7	2.2	6.0	14.0
1986	2.6	1.8	0.6	1.6	5.4	12.0
1987	2.4	1.6	0.7	1.6	4.2	10.5
1988	2.5	1.5	0.6	1.5	3.6	9.6

Source: *Presentation of the Task Force on Foreign Assistance to the House Foreign Affairs Committee* (Hamilton Report), 101st Cong. 1 sess. (February 1989), p. 8.
a. Military assistance, which is included in the foreign aid appropriation totals, is not included in this table. Military aid averaged about $6 billion annually in the 1980s.

sistance rose sharply. Egypt and Israel continue to be the largest recipients of U.S. foreign aid, receiving together approximately $4 billion annually in recent years.[23]

In the 1980s increased emphasis on Central American and Caribbean countries is clear from the data in table 4-2. Costa Rica, the Dominican Republic, and El Salvador all became major recipients, despite their relatively small populations.[24] Foreign assistance to most other Latin American countries diminished during that decade, as growth had raised their income levels above those of most aid recipients.

Categories of U.S. Assistance

U.S. foreign aid is divided into several categories. Table 4-3 breaks U.S. programs into five categories for the period 1977–89. "Development assistance" is the category closest to the popular notion of foreign aid designed to help developing countries raise living standards. Total development assistance, which is spread over many countries, has fluctuated between $2.2 and $2.9 billion annually (in 1989 dollars) since the late 1970s. Food aid consists of shipments of grain and other commodities (primarily fats and oils) that are sold to developing countries, usually on soft terms. Food aid was a very important part of the U.S. program in the 1950s and 1960s. By the late 1970s food aid programs had diminished considerably in both absolute and relative importance.[25] Other economic assistance, as the name implies, covers projects in agriculture, transportation, infrastructure, and other fields, as well as program support.

Multilateral assistance effectively serves to increase the capital of the various multilateral institutions, discussed further in chapter 5. The Economic Support Fund (ESF) channels payments to countries in which the United States has a special national security interest; it has long been an important part of the U.S. aid program. The United States has often allocated ESF funds to countries without bright development prospects, justifying the support with security reasons. Given its purposes, ESF surprised few observers when it sometimes failed to foster more rapid economic growth in recipient countries.

Although military aid can contribute to (or detract from) a country's development, it does not receive further consideration here. In some obvious instances, such as Korea, when the recipient government would have undertaken very high military expenditures in any event, U.S. military aid clearly freed resources for economic development. In other cases, however, military aid simply financed greater military expenditures than would otherwise have been possible.

Total U.S. foreign assistance for economic development since 1977 has fluctuated at about $10 billion annually (in 1989 prices) over the past decade and a half. Of that amount, approximately one-quarter has gone to the multilateral institutions, with the rest allocated to bilateral programs. While there are no objective criteria for determining the "right" amount of aid, U.S. foreign aid constitutes a smaller percentage of GDP than that of any other major industrialized country, despite the fact that the United States has a higher per capita income and greater foreign policy concerns than most of them.

Repayment of Aid

Almost all U.S. foreign aid has initially been in the form of loans.[26] The terms have been concessional, varying with the type of assistance. For much of U.S. food aid, for example, countries paid in local (nonconvertible) currency, which was then deposited in a local account for

U.S. use. The United States then drew on these soft currency deposits to pay local embassy expenses, finance Fulbright scholars, lend in support of economic development, and cover other local costs incurred by the U.S. government. The United States has extended other loans at moderate or low interest rates, with very long repayment periods.[27]

Although the United States has extended bilateral foreign aid in the form of loans, in many instances it has forgiven debt. The U.S. government forgave Egypt's debt after the Persian Gulf War and has forgiven about half of Poland's debt since its transition from Communist rule. In these and similar instances, forgiveness has been politically motivated.

In addition, however, the U.S. government has forgiven the official debt of very low-income countries. In the summer of 1991, for example, the United States declared sub-Saharan African countries with IMF programs in place eligible for the write-off of loans.[28] Earlier write-off programs had covered $350 million and future write-offs were anticipated.[29]

U.S. Aid in Relation to That of Other Donors

In the early years of foreign aid, as noted, the wealth and economic size of the United States insured its position as the major aid donor. In 1960 the United States provided 85 percent of all bilateral aid, or 55 percent of total development assistance in that year. By 1970 the U.S. share of bilateral aid was 45 percent, and by 1989 it had fallen to 16 percent.[30] The trend for recent years is visible in table 4-4.

U.S. foreign economic assistance during the 1980s was virtually constant in nominal terms, while OECD assistance as a whole increased by 70 percent. In part, the declining U.S. share reflects U.S. success under the Marshall Plan in enabling the rapid growth of other OECD countries, which as a result have been able to increase their aid contributions significantly. In part, however, the declining U.S. share, especially in the 1980s, reflects the failure of U.S. foreign aid to keep pace with inflation, much less to grow.

Table 4-5 completes the picture with data on total resource flows to developing countries from the United States and from all OECD countries. As late as 1965 U.S. foreign aid accounted for 51 percent of all long-term capital flows to developing countries. By 1975 total

Table 4-4. **Relative Importance of U.S. Official Development Assistance (ODA), Selected Years, 1960–89**
Billions of U.S. dollars unless otherwise specified

Year	U.S. ODA	OECD ODA	U.S. share of OECD ODA (percent)
1960	2.7	4.6	58.6
1965	4.0	6.5	61.5
1970	3.2	7.0	45.7
1975	4.2	13.9	30.2
1980	7.1	27.3	26.0
1985	9.4	29.4	32.0
1989	7.7	46.7	16.4

Sources: World Bank, *World Development Report, 1980* (pp. 140–41), for 1960 figures; *1990* (pp. 214–15), for 1965–85; and *1991* (p. 240), for 1989.

aid had increased in value but decreased as a percentage of capital flows, as developing countries relied more on the private international capital market, borrowing from private banks and encouraging direct foreign investment. From 1975 to 1985, total capital flows to developing countries increased by less than one-eighth in nominal terms. In real terms they fell as private capital flows to developing countries were sharply reduced in the aftermath of the debt crisis and the worldwide recession of the early 1980s. Although total development assistance rose to $29.5 billion in 1985 (out of total capital flows of $45 billion) from the 1975 level of $13.6 billion, the drop in private flows largely offset that increase.

Thus by the late 1980s the U.S. share of total official development assistance (ODA) had fallen sharply. In Tunisia and Turkey, for example, U.S. ODA was 11.1 and 11.6 percent of the total they received. Outside of Central America and the Caribbean, the U.S. share of total ODA exceeded 33 percent only in Ecuador (34 percent), Egypt (68 percent), Israel (97.8 percent), Liberia (49.5 percent), Peru (34.9 percent), the Philippines (38.4 percent), Portugal (61.2 percent), and Uruguay (40.7 percent). While total ODA as a percentage of all long-term capital flows to developing countries had increased, it was relatively small as a percentage of the resources expended upon development in those countries. For example, in 1986 total ODA represented 0.3, 0.9, 4.7, and 13.7 percent of government expenditures in Brazil, India, Pakistan, and Sri Lanka respectively.[31] In 1989 ODA amounted to an average of 2.2 percent of GNP among low-income countries and 0.6 percent among middle-income countries.[32]

Table 4-5. **Flow of Financial Resources to Developing Countries, Selected Years, 1965–87**
Billions of current U.S. dollars

Type of resource	United States				All OECD			
	1965	1975	1985	1987	1965	1975	1985	1987
Official development assistance	3.4	4.0	9.4	8.9	5.9	13.6	29.5	41.4
Bilateral aid	3.3	2.9	8.2	7.0	5.5	9.8	21.9	29.9
Multilateral aid	0.1	1.1	1.2	1.9	0.4	3.8	7.5	11.6
Other official flows	0.1	0.9	0.2	−1.8	0.3	3.0	3.4	2.0
Voluntary agency grants	n.a.	0.8	1.5	1.6	n.a.	1.3	2.9	3.5
Private flows								
Direct investment	1.3	7.2	1.0	8.0	2.5	10.5	6.5	20.9
Bilateral portfolio investment	0.4	2.4	−10.6	−4.4	0.7	5.2	−4.5	−2.4
Multilateral portfolio investment	0.2	1.9	0.3	0.3	0.2	2.5	6.6	2.7
Private export credits	0.0	0.3	0.1	0.4	0.8	4.1	0.8	−2.4
Total flows	5.3	17.5	1.8	13.4	10.3	40.4	45.2	65.7

Sources: Organization for Economic Cooperation and Development (OECD), *Development Cooperation*, vol. 1974 (pp. 232–33), for 1965 figures; vol. 1977 (pp. 187–88), for 1975 figures; vol. 1989 (pp. 279–80), for 1985–87 figures.
n.a. Not available.

Although aid began as the major form of development finance and the United States began as its major source, over time the importance of aid diminished greatly, and the relative importance of the United States dropped even more markedly. While the U.S. program remains large in absolute terms, in few countries is U.S. aid sizable enough to provide a sharp impetus to economic growth itself.

As table 4-5 indicates, much non-U.S. ODA is administered through bilateral programs. The multilateral organizations, however, have increased their role in ODA both absolutely and relatively. In many countries, the World Bank, the IMF, and the relevant regional development bank[33] disburse more resources than any bilateral donor, including the United States. Yet as one of the largest contributors to the multilateral organizations, the United States exerts significant influence over their activities. The Treasury Department is the arm of the U.S. government with responsibility for the multilateral organizations, while USAID maintains control of the bilateral U.S. aid program.

The Effectiveness of Foreign Aid

A major source of frustration for analysts of foreign aid has been the difficulty of assessing its effects. On the one hand, supporters of aid point to triumphs in certain countries, including phenomenal economic growth, health and nutrition improvements, crop yield increases, and other visibly successful projects. On the other hand, opponents of aid point to countries such as India, Sudan, and Tanzania, where poverty remains an intractable problem.

Some critics of aid assert that successful individual projects do not prove that aid contributed significantly to overall success. They claim that aid's side-effects—draining highly skilled people from potentially more productive activities, increasing reliance on foreign savings, and expanding the role of government—may have offset or more than offset its benefits at the project level.[34]

Obtaining an irrefutable assessment of aid's effectiveness would require standardized techniques for ascertaining what would have happened without foreign aid. Specifying counterfactual projections in that way is clearly infeasible, so no analysis can be definitive. In any event, most observers concur that aid has been highly successful in fostering economic development in some instances and moderately successful in many others. They also recognize that no program as complex and constrained as foreign aid is going to appear completely successful when evaluated after the fact. Indeed, any aid program that seems without mistakes in retrospect may arguably have been too conservative!

Over the years donors have learned a great deal, making aid gradually more effective. Yet for a number of reasons, aid has achieved less than it might have in support of development goals. The objective of this segment is not to assess the precise score of U.S. foreign aid programs but to summarize the main conclusions of studies of aid effectiveness in light of the problems they pose for U.S. foreign policy.[35]

Aid's Successes and Failures

The four developing countries that received the most U.S. aid in the 1950s were Brazil, Korea, Taiwan, and Turkey. In all but Brazil, U.S. national security objectives were a major consideration: in Korea, the United States offered significant assistance before and after the Korean war; in Taiwan, the security concern was the Peoples' Republic of China; and in Turkey, the Soviet Union shared the border of a NATO ally whose stability was assumed to depend on successful economic development. Not surprisingly, military support was an important component of overall U.S. assistance in each case.

In all four countries, foreign assistance was an important component of total resources during the 1950s. The most extreme case was Korea, where aid receipts peaked at more than 10 percent of GNP between 1955 and 1957, and where aid financed more than three-quarters of imports and almost all investment.[36] In Taiwan, U.S. foreign assistance was also important, accounting for 30 to 40 percent of domestic investment and 6 to 8 percent of GNP between 1951 and 1962.[37] In Turkey, U.S. aid accounted for a smaller percentage of GNP—from 2 to 4 percent—but over a much longer time period, from the mid-1950s until the early 1970s. In Brazil, U.S. aid peaked at almost 3 percent of GNP in the 1960s.

Interestingly, Brazil, Taiwan, and Turkey experienced growth rates significantly above average during the 1950s and 1960s, and Korea's growth accelerated sharply in the 1960s. In Korea and Taiwan, once rapid growth began, real growth rates surpassed those that had been considered feasible, averaging almost 10 percent annually. Moreover, these countries sustained similar growth rates in the 1970s and 1980s, long after U.S. aid had been phased out. By contrast, Brazil and Turkey did not manage to sustain rapid growth. Brazil's growth continued at real annual rates of 6 to 8 percent until the 1980s, while Turkey's growth halted in the mid-1970s and did not resume until the government undertook major economic policy reforms in the early 1980s.

Without a doubt U.S. aid significantly contributed to rapid and sustained growth in Korea and Taiwan. Project aid helped construct vital infrastructure services, increase access to education, improve health services, and develop agricultural research and extension services.[38] USAID officials in Korea and Turkey were involved in bringing about the policy reforms that enabled rapid rates of growth. These policy dialogues were important both because U.S. officials were analyzing economic policies and their effects,[39] and because foreign economists who subsequently became key policymakers worked in USAID missions and interacted with U.S. colleagues.

Aid was also important in Turkey and Brazil, especially on the project side, and certainly contributed to their relatively high growth rates in early years. Until the 1980s, however, the overall policy framework in those countries, with extensive government intervention and an inward-oriented trade strategy, was not compatible with long-run sustained growth. As a result, U.S. aid did not provide the lasting boost that it did in Korea and Taiwan. When Turkey did reform its economic policies in the early 1980s, many observers gave early USAID projects credit for facilitating the export boom that followed.[40] For example, many of the Turkish entrepreneurs who successfully obtained construction contracts throughout the Middle East had gained their initial experience with USAID projects in the 1950s and 1960s. Likewise, previous development of roads and ports, financed in part by aid, permitted economic activity to expand more rapidly than it otherwise could. Many Turkish officials instrumental in the reforms had received their technical training abroad, financed in part by USAID.

Of course, aid has not consistently improved the growth or development of its recipients. In contrast to the four early success stories are many sub-Saharan countries, whose living standards have declined over the past two decades, despite aid receipts relatively large in terms of GNP. For many years Tanzania was perhaps most visible as an aid recipient. With its charismatic leaders adopting a "third way" toward development, Tanzania became a focal point for many donors, yet failed to achieve satisfactory growth.[41]

Evaluating the impact of aid is very difficult in macroeconomic terms, where the overall policy framework of a developing country is far more important than its aid receipts in the long run. On the microeconomic side, however, the impact of individual projects is more easily assessed.[42] In the mid-1980s OECD donors appointed an expert group on aid evaluation to compile a report on the success of aid projects, evaluated in terms of their impact on development and living standards. The group primarily analyzed capital investment projects, because evaluation techniques for technical assistance projects are far less satisfactory. Their conclusions, which resembled those of similar World Bank and European Community studies, were summarized in the Annual Report of the OECD's Development Assistance Committee (DAC):

In round figures, most attempts to come up with some sort of scoresheet based on a review of existing evaluation findings, hedged . . . with all the qualifications that an exercise of such crudity requires, seem to arrive at numbers roughly as follows. . . . Approximately one-third of aid-financed projects can be judged highly successful, in the sense that they fully achieved or even surpassed their stated objectives. Another third can be judged satisfactory, in the sense that the results were reasonably close to the objectives as originally conceived. . . . The remainder have been in various degrees and for various reasons disappointing. Within this last third, which is the area where one finds the horror stories on which assertions of the failure of aid are based, some projects had problems that proved remediable; some produced a benefit that hardly justified the original investment, but still constituted some sort of positive return; and some, perhaps 19 percent, had to be regarded as a total loss.[43]

Around the world, evidence suggests that project aid used to finance public investments in education, health, and nutrition generates high returns in the great majority of cases.[44] In countries where projects helped adapt agricultural research and extension for local conditions, increases in yields and rural living standards have been sustained.[45]

Project aid used to supplant markets, for example by subsidizing rural credit or financing industrial development at negative real interest rates, has been far less effective. Aid has also been far less effective where governmental controls (such as an overvalued exchange rate) distort market signals and skew resource allocation. For example, some countries implicitly tax export crops and protect food crops through an overvalued exchange rate, creating incentives for farmers to shift from export to food crops, even though the former may have a higher "social" rate of return.[46] In these countries, aid projects that increase the supply of agricultural inputs or develop research and extension have a far lower rate of return than in countries where producers confront incentives that appropriately reflect the trade-offs of international trade. Project aid has also been hampered by many donors' unwillingness to finance the maintenance and local currency expenditures of their projects. Many donors continue to finance new projects even when maintaining existing ones might be more beneficial. Their failure to cover local costs has also encouraged projects that use a large share of imported goods.

In the early postwar years, foreign aid was a new undertaking, and in several countries it proved a stunning success. In many others, of course, failures were numerous. From this mixed record, the development community has learned many lessons. Some have already been incorporated into aid programs, which may enjoy a higher success rate in the future thanks to the reforms.

Constraints on Aid Effectiveness

Two implicit assumptions have characterized the discussion thus far, neither of which is correct: that the promotion of economic development is the only objective of the U.S. aid program and its recipients, and that aid officials are free to allocate aid as they desire in pursuit of that goal. By contrast, U.S. aid officials have sought to achieve multiple objectives and have often encountered significant obstacles. The effectiveness of aid programs, therefore, must be judged in light of their objectives and constraints.

Regarding objectives, neither the donor nor the recipient of foreign aid has economic development as its sole policy objective. In the United States, political considerations influence the foreign aid program in many ways. The most obvious may be the massive aid programs to Egypt and Israel, offered at the time of the Camp David peace accords in 1977. Supporters of Greece have insisted for years that Turkey (with a population of 55 million and a 1989 per capita income of $1,390) receive no more than $10 in U.S. aid for every $7 received by Greece (with a population of 10 million and a 1989 per capita income of $5,350). Security considerations during the Cold War resulted in high levels of U.S. support to Taiwan, Korea, Sudan, and Central America.

Project aid tends to face fewer political constraints than other less narrowly defined forms of assistance.[47] In countries with economic policies clearly inimical to development, political considerations may prevent aid officials from insisting on policy changes as a precondition for aid. The most extreme and well-known case appears to have been Egypt after the Camp David peace accords,[48] but the problem intrudes to a certain degree in any discussion of domestic economic policies with foreign governments.

The fundamental issue in this regard is that of "leverage," or "conditionality." How much leverage can donors exercise over the behavior of recipients in return for official aid? When and to what extent should assistance be conditional on policy performance by recipient countries? The questions are complex and have no easy answer.[49]

In some instances the case for conditionality is fairly clear-cut. The IMF, for example, should hardly decide to support a stabilization program that seems unlikely to achieve its objectives.[50] Nor should the World Bank pledge support for policy reform in structural adjustment programs unless the agenda of policy reforms shows promise of success.

To the extent that the United States stresses security and political issues in an aid allocation, however, aid officials are unlikely to be able to withhold foreign assistance when domestic policies do not seem to maximize development. In some instances, the U.S. government has been so eager to support new regimes that aid officials have had almost no room to question development plans.[51]

The issue becomes even more complex when the political objectives of recipients are multiple. National leaders may at times decide (correctly or otherwise) that they must undertake policies inconsistent with development to remain in office. To maintain support they often subsidize urban food consumption, place projects in uneconomic regional locations, increase military expenditures, and construct large and highly visible showpiece projects, such as athletic stadiums, places of worship, modern airports, and even advanced hospitals when the majority of the population has no access to medical care. All governments have noneconomic objectives on behalf of which they expend resources that could otherwise go to development. Military expenditures, such as those incurred by Pakistan and India, are the largest, but not the only, such objective.[52]

When deciding whether to condition their assistance, donors must delicately weigh the potential economic benefits of certain policy reforms against their political costs to the government in power. The task is by no means easy.

Another class of political constraints originates not abroad but in donor countries such as the United States: the administrative and legal requirements of foreign aid authorization and appropriation bills. As support for U.S. foreign aid has eroded over time, legislators have placed an increasing number of restrictions on foreign aid appropriation bills, attempting to rally political support with a convenient policy tool.

One such restriction is "tied aid," which requires that foreign aid funds be spent on goods and services from the donor country. Such provisions reduce the value of aid to its recipients but garner support from segments of the domestic business community that look forward to additional contracts with recipient countries.

In 1976 an estimated 82 percent of bilateral U.S. aid was tied, com-

Table 4-6. **Estimated Cost of Tied Aid in India and Korea, 1960–72**
Percentage loss per dollar of aid

Year	India	Korea	Year	India	Korea
1960	n.a.	13	1967	9	0
1961	n.a.	11	1968	13	6
1962	n.a.	11	1969	19	1
1963	n.a.	6	1970	17	n.a.
1964	15	5	1971	12	n.a.
1965	16	6	1972	15	n.a.
1966	14	3			

Source: Pablo F. Barahona, "The Excess Cost of Tying Non-Project Aid: Some Empirical Evidence," Duke University, Department of Economics, 1989, pp. 16–19.
n.a. Not available.

pared with a 66 percent average among all OECD donors. By 1985–86, when these donors had all cooperated to relax tying, 57 percent of U.S. aid was tied, slightly more than the 54 percent average for all OECD donors.[53]

The amount that tying reduces the value of aid varies with a number of factors, including the international competitiveness of producers in the donor country, the range of product lines in which a donor country's producers are competitive,[54] the number of producers of any given item in the donor country,[55] and the foreign exchange constraints of the recipient country. Recipients that earn enough foreign exchange on their own to contribute "free" foreign exchange to aid projects that depend on high-cost foreign producers presumably attain greater value for their aid resources. By contrast, tied aid more adversely affected countries such as Pakistan and India, which maintained overvalued exchange rates and thus had few foreign exchange reserves for project financing.

With so many factors in play, the cost of tied aid is difficult to estimate. In the late 1960s a dollar of tied aid was estimated to be worth an average of 15 to 20 percent less than a dollar of untied aid.[56] A more recent study, using unit value data for individual commodity imports in different countries, estimated the costs of tied aid between 1960 and 1970 in Korea and between 1964 and 1972 in India. For Korea, exports grew rapidly and import restrictions were removed during these years. For India, a shortage of foreign exchange dominated the period, although the government did devaluate the currency in 1966 and temporarily ease import restrictions thereafter. The results appear in table 4-6.

The estimated reduction in aid value for each country was similar during years of foreign exchange shortage. In 1960 the estimated cost to Korea was about 13 percent of aid, while in 1964 India's cost was about 15 percent. As Korea liberalized its economy during the 1960s, the cost of tied aid fell substantially; by 1970 no additional cost was evident. For India, the cost of tied aid did decline immediately after the devaluation but appears to have increased again once the effects of the post-devaluation import liberalization faded. These estimates of tied aid's costs do not include the administrative costs to the recipient of insuring that aid is spent in the "correct" country.[57]

Tied aid imposes costs primarily on the recipient country, since the initial dollar amounts of aid lose some value. The donor country, however, does incur the administrative cost of ensuring that recipient countries comply with tied aid provisions. The United States and other donors also incur some indirect costs when their officials simultaneously advocate the liberalization of foreign exchange markets *and* the establishment of administrative mechanisms to tie aid flows. Indeed, in Indonesia in the late 1960s, the Indonesian rupiah was convertible, while the U.S. dollar sold at a discount in the black market, because dollar aid receipts were tied!

One particularly difficult issue that arises in connection with tied aid is the use of export credits. Most countries, including the United States, have an agency, usually called an export-import bank, that provides credit to finance export transactions. These credits, usually available at somewhat subsidized rates, are designed to enhance the competitiveness of the nation's exporters vis-à-vis those in other countries. Export credits have often been used to induce governments in developing countries to undertake projects that are not always fully or even partially consistent with development. To prevent gross resource misallocation from the competitive use of export credits, the OECD has begun to regulate the minimum terms that may be offered by its members' export-import banks to developing countries.[58]

Although the use of export credits as a means of export promotion may be deplorable on grounds of economic efficiency, a separate discussion of them would not be warranted in a discussion of aid. However, by the 1970s, some developed countries were resorting to "mixed credits" as a means of export promotion. These mixed credits were a combination of aid and export credits targeted for particular projects. This practice obviously invited abuse, as donors could readily divert foreign aid to projects where national exporters could sell their products. Until 1983 the United States largely eschewed the use of mixed credits[59] and vigorously supported restrictions on their use within the OECD. However, as other countries continued these practices, Congress passed the Trade and Development Enhancement Act of 1983, which authorized the Export-Import Bank and USAID jointly to provide tied aid credits. The aid component of these credits falls under Economic Support Fund assistance. To date, the United States has used very little of its foreign aid in the form of mixed credits, wielding the authority to do so essentially as a bargaining tool to dissuade other countries from competing with tied aid.

In addition to tying aid, Congress has constrained the ability of aid officials to administer aid in a number of other ways. Some restrictions are consistent with foreign policy objectives or commitments, such as U.S. aid to Israel and Egypt. In these cases, Congress mandates assistance not only by countries, but also by assistance categories. For example, in the 1988 foreign aid bill Israel received precisely $1.8 billion in military aid and $1.2 billion in economic aid.[60]

Congress also divides all aid expenditures into various categories during the processes of authorization and appropriation. The $14.3 billion appropriation for fiscal year 1989, for example, included $1.5 billion for the various development banks, including the IDA, the Special Facility for sub-Saharan Africa, and a catch-all, "International Organizations and Programs." Development assistance totaled $6.3 billion, which was divided into 29 separate categories, including agricultural aid ($493 million), international disaster aid ($25 million), the Economic Support Fund ($3.2 billion), the Peace Corps ($153.5 million), migration and refugee aid ($361 million), international narcotics control ($101 million), and the Foreign Service Retirement and Disability Fund ($40 million). The smallest single allocation within the bilateral aid program was $8.6 million for science and technology assistance. The largest was for the Economic Support Fund (ESF), which provides resources to friendly governments. In many cases, ESF support goes to countries whose overall economic prospects appear dim, and whose political stability and friendship toward the United States therefore seem in jeopardy. Even so, U.S. aid officials tend to welcome ESF funds because they carry fewer restrictions than other forms of aid. The 1989 bill also authorized $5.7 billion in military assistance, broken down into five categories. Finally, the bill contained funding for five additional programs not counted toward the total figure of

Table 4-7. **Legislative Constraints on U.S. Foreign Aid, Selected Years, 1948–89**

Year	Appropriated[a]		Pages (number)	Earmarking (percent of total assistance)	General provisions (number)
	Billions of current U.S. dollars	Billions of constant U.S. dollars			
1948	6.0	21.1	5	3.0	6
1956	3.8	11.5	3	3.5	5
1961	3.9	11.7	5	1.0	11
1967	2.3	6.5	9	0.5	23
1973	5.8	12.7	13	6.5	16
1978	9.1	13.0	12	33.0	25
1981	10.0	10.4	11	41.0	25
1989	14.6	12.8	72	52.0	100

Sources: Foreign Aid Appropriations Act, 1949 (P.L. 80-793); Mutual Security Appropriations Act of 1957 (P.L. 84-853); Foreign Assistance and Related Agencies Appropriations Act of 1962 (P.L. 87-329), 1968 (P.L. 90-137), 1974 (P.L. 93-240), 1979 (P.L. 95-481), 1982 (P.L. 97-121); and Foreign Operations, Export Financing, and Related Programs Appropriations Act, 1991 (P.L. 101-167).

a. Constant dollar estimates are the nominal dollar values deflated by the U.S. producer price index for finished goods, 1982 = 100. Price data are from *Economic Report of the President, February 1991*, table B-63.

$14.3 billion, including the Export-Import Bank and the Overseas Private Investment Corporation (OPIC).[61]

As if earmarking aid into twenty-nine categories were not enough, Congress has imposed many restrictions (maximum and minimum) on expenditures for individual countries and programs. The 1989 appropriation, for example, earmarked $2 million for the Solidarity movement in Poland and also required that the administration spend between $10 million and $35 million on aid to the Republic of Ireland and Northern Ireland. For the Philippines, the bill appropriated $124 million from ESF and $40 million in development aid, in addition to military aid. It designated another $5 million for a program to provide artificial limbs for civilians wounded in conflicts in countries such as El Salvador, Mozambique, and Vietnam.[62]

Such restrictions have proliferated over time. Table 4-7 provides an indication of the increasing complexity and restrictiveness of foreign aid legislation in the postwar era. The data are for selected years and are taken from appropriations, rather than authorizations, for purposes of comparison. Bills from reasonably indicative years were chosen, although in recent years Congress has crafted aid legislation in the form of continuing resolutions, not acts, with increasing frequency. Passage of the 1989 appropriation in 1988 marked the first new act since 1981.

Though crude, these indicators illustrate the increasing complexity

Table 4-8.   **U.S. Commissions on Foreign Aid**

Instigator	Date	Commission name	Chairman
Dwight D. Eisenhower	1958–59	President's Committee to Study the United States Military Assistance Program	William Draper
John F. Kennedy	1962–63	Committee to Strengthen the Security of the Free World	Lucius Clay
Richard M. Nixon	1969–70	Presidential Task Force on International Development	Peter Peterson
Ronald Reagan	1983	Commission on Security and Economic Assistance	Frank Carlucci
House of Representatives	1988	Task Force of the House Foreign Affairs Committee	Lee Hamilton

Sources: David Wallace, "Commissions on Foreign Aid: An Evolution of Thought," in John Wilhelm and Gerry Feinstein, eds., *U.S. Foreign Assistance: Investment or Folly?* (Praeger, 1984), pp. 18–23; and Larry Nowels and Ellen Collier, "Foreign Policy Budget: Priorities for the 102nd Congress," Congressional Research Service, May 22, 1991, p. 13.

of aid legislation. Not only did Congress earmark an increasing percentage of total assistance for particular purposes, but it drafted an increasing number of general provisions that had much the same effect. One general provision, for example, "effectively forced the Pentagon to finance a program to rid the Portuguese Azores Islands of a Japanese beetle infestation," while another prohibited any aid to Panama as long as Manuel Noriega remained president of that country.[63]

Congress also imposed a large number of reporting requirements on the agencies that administer U.S. aid. Administrators had to report to Congress on a variety of issues, such as the environmental impact of economic assistance, ensure that aid is tied, guarantee small businesses an opportunity to bid on aid projects, and so on. By the late 1980s simply fulfilling these requirements occupied an estimated 140 workyears annually![64]

Efforts to Improve Aid Effectiveness

Because foreign aid is such a complex instrument, the U.S. government has sponsored repeated examinations of its foreign aid program. Table 4-8 lists all the U.S. commissions, assembled almost every five years, except for the 1970s. Separate international commissions also assessed the assistance programs of all industrialized countries in the late 1960s and again in the early 1980s.[65]

Two commissions are particularly worthy of note. The first is the Peterson Commission, which recommended that the United States reduce its bilateral aid and rely on the multilateral institutions for analysis of recipients' overall economic policies, restricting the U.S. program to project assistance. The government generally followed this recommendation, greatly diminishing USAID's capacity to undertake macroeconomic analysis. The second group is a congressional task force chaired by Representative Lee Hamilton, which in 1988–89 analyzed the aid program and recommended a variety of changes. One of its principal objectives was to simplify the restrictions surrounding the operation of aid greatly. The task force found that "Scattered through the Foreign Assistance Act are 33 objectives. . . . Foreign aid legislation contains 288 individual reporting requirements. . . . Earmarks have increased to unprecedented levels. . . . Congress receives over 700 notifications of project changes each year. . . . In addition, there are numerous directives, restrictions, conditions, and prohibitions in the foreign aid legislation. . . . The result is an aid program that is driven by process rather than by content and substance."[66]

Although the task force appeared almost unanimous in its recommendations, a bill that would have greatly reduced legislative constraints on foreign aid passed the House of Representatives but failed in the Senate,[67] primarily because numerous senators wanted to preserve special provisions in earlier bills that favored their constituencies.

The frequent appointment of these commissions reflects the fundamental unease with which politicians view the aid program. Politics generates popular demand for foreign aid, largely from citizens concerned with humanitarian issues in poor countries. Passage of aid bills, however, has involved a "Christmas tree" approach, as legislators decorate appropriations with politically useful caveats, exemptions, mandates, and requirements.

Aid at Cross-Purposes with Other U.S. Policies

Although policy conflicts occur at all levels, the most visible has been the apparent inconsistency between policy dialogues with developing countries and actual U.S. trade policies. In many instances, USAID officials have taken strong positions on recipients' policies, urging more open trade regimes, greater reliance on free markets, and less government intervention in the economy even as other U.S. policies undercut the message. In Bangladesh, for example, U.S. authorities actively urged the government to promote manufactured exports of labor-intensive goods. Policies changed as a result, and some clothing exports soared in response. Soon after the boom, U.S. trade officials confronted Bangladeshi authorities eager to negotiate quotas that would restrict apparel exports to the United States! Such restrictions have been in place since 1986.[68]

Other policy conflicts were smaller and less visible. The fact that some U.S. aid was tied so that it had to be spent in the United States contradicted the principles of open trade espoused by U.S. officials. Often accompanying U.S. food aid were restrictions on the agricultural exports of recipient countries.

The conflicts intensified in the 1980s, as policy reform became more important in developing countries and U.S. trade policies became more protectionist. Restrictions on textile and apparel exports to the United States under the Multifiber Arrangement (MFA) became more binding (see chapter 6), and many developing countries found themselves increasingly subject to U.S. trade restrictions and administered trade laws.

U.S. authorities urged Brazil, like other highly indebted countries, to promote exports and earn foreign exchange for debt servicing. At the same time, the United States named Brazil an unfair trader under Super 301 provisions, placed Brazil on the "priority watch list" for its violation of intellectual property rights, negotiated a voluntary export restraint agreement with Brazil on steel, restricted Brazilian exports of oranges because of a bumper crop in Florida,[69] restricted Brazilian imports of sugar under the U.S. sugar program, and restricted Brazilian exports of textiles and clothing under the MFA.[70] Brazil entered a steel agreement after U.S. producers filed a number of antidumping complaints against Brazil in the United States; in exchange for the agreement, the suits were dropped.[71] While some of these measures may have been designed to open Brazilian markets, others clearly limited access to the U.S. market.

As one of very few countries named unfair traders under Super 301, Brazil was a somewhat extreme example of a more general pattern. The United States imposed import restrictions on many developing country products, including textiles, apparel, sugar, beef, grains, fruits, and vegetables. These items are major exports in many countries that have received U.S. aid or have been urged by U.S. officials to undertake policy reform. U.S. use of administered protection has also been widely viewed as restrictionist. The United States even imposed a sur-tax on rice imports from Thailand because of an alleged government subsidy, despite the fact that the United States subsidizes its rice farm-ers far more heavily than does Thailand![72] This surtax and other pro-tectionist measures, all of which ran counter to the objective of development, undermined the credibility of U.S. aid officials and their policy recommendations.

Appendix: Definition and Measurement of Foreign Aid

There are many kinds of economic assistance. Private organiza-tions, such as CARE, receive individual contributions and provide goods for people in developing countries. Immigrants from develop-ing countries return a portion of their earnings to their relatives. Gov-ernments lend money to other governments to finance the purchase of military goods, assist with famine or other disaster relief, and sup-port development efforts. Governments provide subsidized export credits, low interest rate loans, and even freely given resources to other governments. Governments also consign individual commodities to other countries as gifts, asking only for partial compensation or a long-term repayment commitment.

Two tasks, therefore, are at hand. The first is merely to define de-velopment assistance, and the second is to devise ways of measuring the value of that assistance.

Conceptually, development assistance is provided to permit larger expenditures on development than would otherwise be possible.[73] Fa-mine and disaster relief, therefore, are not development assistance, important though they may be. Likewise, military assistance is not development assistance. In practice, development assistance is taken to be whatever assistance donor countries say is provided for that pur-pose: food aid, long-term lending, subsidized export credits, and out-right gifts. The U.S. foreign aid program, for example, categorizes military assistance as a separate item, but does not count that assis-tance when reporting its foreign aid totals to the OECD.

Several definitions are useful. Development assistance includes all noncommercial resources provided to support development efforts. Official development assistance (ODA) is that provided by govern-ments and international institutions. Bilateral assistance is provided directly from one government to another, while multilateral assistance is provided through international institutions.

If foreign aid only included outright grants and lending at commercial terms, valuing it would be straightforward. Unfortunately, the bewildering variety of terms and conditions makes the task daunting. In theory, the value of any aid is the difference between the present value of the anticipated repayment stream and the commercial value of the items received.

In practice, the problem of valuing the "aid" part of transactions is overwhelming, and the Development Assistance Committee of the OECD has developed criteria that are used as rules of thumb in measuring development assistance. Governments offer some grants for development purposes, but more frequently they make loans to developing countries. These loans, however, are usually extended at interest rates well below those available in the private international capital market and with significantly longer maturities. Aid from the International Development Association (IDA), for example, carries a "service charge" of 0.75 percent annually, with a grace period of ten years.[74] Such a "loan" is highly concessional and is clearly foreign aid.

In other cases, lending terms are closer to commercial rates, or aid funds at low interest rates are mixed with loans that finance commercial transactions.[75] Moreover, many forms of assistance are restricted. Some restrictions require the recipient to spend funds provided by the donor on items produced in the donor country.[76] In other cases, assistance is provided in the form of commodities, the most prominent example being food aid. The United States was a large donor of food aid during the 1960s and 1970s. Surplus U.S. agricultural commodities were shipped to developing countries in return for either local currency (much of which was not spent, or spent on financing the local cost of development projects) or a low-interest loan with a long maturity. Placing a value on the "aid" associated with these food shipments is difficult for two reasons. First, the price of some food-aid commodities in the domestic market of the donor country is often above the world price. In that instance, the value of the aid to the recipient is clearly less than that stated by the donor. Second, lending terms affect the value of aid. An unrestricted loan or grant is more valuable to the recipient country than one with restrictions. Likewise, given equal restrictions, grants are more valuable than loans, and loans bearing higher interest charges are less valuable than loans with lower interest charges.

From these considerations arises a question of more than academic interest: how should aid be valued? In principle, the value of anything is given by the amount it would cost the recipient to obtain the item on the open market. By this criterion, the value of food aid should be based on the international price, not the price in the donor country. The value of loan aid should be the present value of the difference between the terms of the loan and those that would be obtainable commercially.

In practice, the valuation of all official aid flows to developing countries cannot be based on these principles, because the data are simply not available. Instead, the Development Assistance Committee of the OECD has used three criteria to define ODA: ODA must come from official sources, be for developmental purposes, and have a "grant element" of 25 percent or more.

The first two criteria are straightforward. Flows to developing countries from private agencies intended to support development do not count as ODA because they are not official. Likewise, official flows unrelated to developmental purposes do not count. The "grant element" of a given flow is calculated as the difference between the market rate and the actual rate of the loan. A grant, or gift, clearly has a grant element of 100 percent. At the opposite extreme, if a country makes a loan to another country at 10 percent, the interest rate used by the OECD as the market rate, it is considered to have a zero grant element. When official lending is at rates below 10 percent, the grant element is calculated taking into account both the deviation of the interest rate from 10 percent and the maturity of the loan.

In practice, therefore, U.S. wheat shipped to India and other developing countries in the 1960s in return for local currency was valued at the U.S. domestic price of wheat, which at that time was well above the world price. But the lending terms were so soft that the U.S. valuation of the wheat was counted as part of U.S. ODA.

To obtain figures on ODA, the OECD takes submissions by member governments and converts them to a common basis for purposes of international comparison. OECD data provided in this volume are therefore consistent with the OECD definition, but do not precisely correspond to the theoretical concept of foreign aid outlined at the beginning of this section. As a result, OECD data probably tend to overstate the true value of official assistance.

U.S. data, however, are different. They are based on appropriations made under the U.S. Foreign Assistance Acts of various years and are thus derived from budgetary sources. Within the Foreign Assistance Act, there are allocations for various categories of aid. The major categories are economic and military assistance; only the former is usually regarded within the United States as "foreign aid." Because U.S. data on foreign aid pertain to U.S. budgetary accounts, they are not entirely consistent with OECD data nor with an economist's definition of aid.

In any event, foreign aid is not extended to developing countries in the form of outright unrestricted cash. Although foreign aid can consist of commodities such as food or of direct military assistance, development assistance usually takes the form of either "project aid" or "program aid." As the name implies, project assistance is granted to help finance individual development projects. Eligible projects may seek to build hospitals, roads, dams, or port facilities, improve agricultural research and extension services or educational facilities, or meet many other developmental objectives.

By contrast, program aid is normally provided in support of a country's overall development program. Program aid typically goes to countries whose economic policies are in the process of reform. In these cases, foreign aid permits a higher level of investment during the transition period, keeping the level of short-term dislocation lower than would otherwise be possible.

5 ||| The United States and the Multilateral Lending Institutions

THE MULTILATERAL LENDING INSTITUTIONS are important sources of finance and technical assistance for development projects and policy reform in developing countries. The United States remains their largest shareholder, although its ownership share has declined almost continuously since their establishment.[1] As the largest single contributor, the United States potentially exercises significant influence over the policies of these institutions, which can serve as a major channel for U.S. policy toward the developing countries.

During the first three decades of the multilateral institutions, the United States gave them strong support, recognizing the policy goals they could serve. The IMF and the World Bank were viewed as institutions that could improve the functioning of the international economy and accelerate the growth of the developing countries. U.S. leadership was key in enabling those institutions to mature into highly respected and effective international organizations.

In more recent years, however, the United States at best has failed to display leadership toward the multilateral institutions, and at worst has expressed hostility toward them. Policy has become erratic, and even when the U.S. government has given the institutions support, it has often followed prolonged criticism and acrimonious debate.

Both the legislative and executive branches shape U.S. policy toward the multilaterals. On some occasions, the administration has expressed hostility toward or demanded changes in these institutions; on others, it has sought congressional approval of measures that support the multilaterals only to meet stiff opposition. In some instances, such as during Ronald Reagan's first presidential term, it appeared that the policies of the IMF and World Bank that enjoyed the administration's support were opposed by Congress, and that those with congressional support were opposed by the administration!

While U.S. policy toward the multilaterals has at times been in conflict with other U.S. policy objectives, more often the United States has simply failed to use the institutions in ways fully consistent with their charter objectives and with U.S. foreign policy goals. The U.S. government often indicates its disapproval of the institutions without offering leadership or specifying acceptable policy alternatives. U.S. policy is at cross-purposes insofar as it allocates bilateral foreign aid for development and then fails to support the multilaterals to enhance those efforts. The most notable example of the erratic U.S. approach was its policy during the 1980s debt crisis, which this chapter examines in detail after surveying the multilaterals themselves more generally.[2]

The Multilateral Lending Institutions

Although numerous other international agencies support development in developing countries,[3] their combined impact has been much less than that of the multilateral lending institutions: the World Bank, the IMF, and the regional development banks—the Asian Development Bank, the Inter-American Development Bank, and the African Development Bank.[4] The United States also wields much greater influence in the multilateral lending institutions than in the specialized agencies of the United Nations, so this study of U.S. policy focuses on the former, especially the World Bank and the IMF.[5]

Often referred to as the Bretton Woods institutions, the World Bank[6] and the IMF were conceived as part of the postwar international economic order, with their charters negotiated at the Bretton Woods conference in 1944. The IMF was to be responsible for maintaining orderly exchange rates and an international financial system conducive to the open, multilateral trading system[7] that was to evolve under the auspices of a third institution, the International Trade Organization.[8] The International Bank for Reconstruction and Development (IBRD) was intended to be the institution that would ensure the flow of funds from capital-rich to capital-poor countries, and it eventually became part of the World Bank group.[9] The two institutions initially evolved along the intended lines. Although their missions were distinct, there were strong similarities in their structure and governance, most of which remain.

Governance and Structure

The IMF, the World Bank, and the regional development banks all have their own staffs. Each has its capital subscriptions from member countries,[10] which provide financial resources automatically without the need for regular appeals for funds to cover administrative expenses. The capital subscriptions of member countries, which have been increased at intervals, are approximately proportional to their economic size. Each member country is thus an "owner" of the international institutions, and votes are proportionate to capital subscriptions.

Formally, the owners exercise control over the international institutions through executive boards, which consist of executive directors appointed by the shareholders. These directors reside full-time at the institutions, meeting regularly throughout the year to approve the policy and operations of each organization. The executive boards of the World Bank and the IMF each have twenty-two directors currently. Smaller countries collaborate and pool their votes to elect directors jointly, while large countries, such as the United States, Japan, the United Kingdom, France, Germany, China, and—in the case of the IMF—Saudi Arabia, appoint their own directors to each executive board.

The executive directors are representative of their governments and base their positions and votes on their instructions. The U.S. directors of the World Bank and the IMF report to the Treasury Department, the agency responsible for policy toward the Bretton Woods institutions and the regional lending institutions.

This governance structure provides natural channels for communication between the institutions and their member governments. For the United States, the channels of communication are even more direct because the World Bank and IMF are based in Washington, where the U.S. directors can confer with their government more readily than can the directors of other countries. Moreover, the heads of the two institutions, the president of the World Bank and the managing director of the IMF, often meet with top U.S. officials when major policy concerns arise.

Formal voting rights are not the only means by which major shareholders such as the United States exercise influence within the institutions. In an expanding world economy the resources each institution can potentially employ in its mission will inevitably expand. To generate additional resources, member governments must appropriate funds to increase their capital subscription. Large shareholders, such as the United States, can block or delay such an increase. In 1983, just as the United States urged IMF leadership in the debt crisis, congressional opposition to a capital subscription increase was intense. In 1992, when another IMF increase was proposed to provide sufficient resources to Eastern Europe and the former Soviet Union, congressional opposition again surfaced, causing another delay. The United States withheld a general capital increase for the World Bank for several years in the mid-1980s, as U.S. authorities expressed their displeasure with the Bank's activities. Also at the World Bank, both the administration and Congress have delayed or reduced IDA replenishments in the past. The United States has exercised major influence over the appointments of the World Bank president and IMF managing director. Top IMF officials still remember U.S. opposition to Managing Director Pierre-Paul Schweitzer.

The IMF has an Interim Committee that includes the governors of the Fund from member countries, who are normally finance ministers.[11] For its part, the World Bank has a Development Committee with governors of the Bank and the Fund. These committees meet twice a year, once in the spring and once at the annual meetings of the two institutions in the fall. Because the committees are at the ministerial level, they allow member countries to achieve consensus on key issues and to provide guidance to both organizations.

The International Monetary Fund

The IMF is the international organization charged with maintaining an orderly system of exchange rates to facilitate a smoothly functioning, open world trading system. Although it deals extensively with issues pertaining to developed countries, the IMF also plays a key role with respect to developing countries, the focus of this work.

Many developing countries have maintained fixed exchange rates for substantial periods of time despite inflation rates well above those of their major trading partners. In the typical scenario, exchange rates become increasingly overvalued, import licensing becomes increasingly restrictive, and the export sector becomes less and less profitable. These trends usually continue until the country is unable to meet even its short-term foreign exchange obligations. By then, the country is no longer receiving short-term financing for its imports, and the economic dislocation that results has become a major political problem.

Spurred by the "foreign exchange crisis" and the imperative of maintaining import flows, authorities in the country eventually approach the IMF for assistance in taking measures to end the crisis. Often, of course, the IMF staff have foreseen the likelihood of balance-of-payments difficulties and urged action long before the crisis erupted. In other circumstances, the authorities have previously approached the IMF for support but refused to implement the policy measures deemed necessary by IMF staff to restore balance in international payments.

When representatives of the country in question and IMF staff meet, the Fund staff analyze the country's balance-of-payments difficulties and financing situation and discuss these with the authorities. The parties normally attempt to agree on the financing to be provided by the Fund and on the policy measures that will ensure improvement in the balance of payments so that the country can repay its drawings from the IMF.[12] Fund "conditionality" normally requires the country to move toward an appropriate nominal exchange rate and to enact measures to contain domestic credit and other inflationary pressures.[13]

Since the mid-1980s the IMF and the World Bank have collaborated closely in support of policy reform in developing countries. Technicians from the potential borrower and staff of the Bank and Fund jointly develop a policy framework paper[14] that represents a consensus analysis of major economic problems and key measures that must be taken to address them.

When agreement between the Fund and a member government is reached, the IMF offers a loan to the country in exchange for a commitment to implement a set of policy changes. The IMF also helps finance a renewed flow of imports and the import liberalization that usually accompanies a Fund program.[15] Usually, the country specifies its agenda of policy reform in a "letter of intent" from its finance minister to the IMF.[16]

The reforms to be undertaken by member governments vary according to the underlying circumstances that have produced the crisis.[17] Frequently, inflationary pressures resulting from large fiscal deficits have accelerated and led at fixed exchange rates to increasingly stringent import licensing. In that standard case, the letter of intent normally stipulates ceilings on central bank credit and on the government deficit. In addition, measures to liberalize the foreign trade regime, including changes in the nominal exchange rate, are typically part of the package. In individual countries, agreements are tailored to meet particular circumstances that require attention, ranging from pricing policies in public sector enterprises to interest rate regulations to the structure of the banking system itself.[18]

Until the 1980s most IMF programs were termed "stabilization programs," as they sought to stabilize the balance of payments. As observers gradually recognized that resolution of the debt crisis required a resumption of growth in the heavily indebted countries, the IMF began to use support from its structural adjustment facility and other longer-term financing (see note 12). But the Fund continues to focus fundamentally on exchange and trade relations and on policies that are consistent with an open regime.[19]

The World Bank

In step with ideas about economic development in the 1950s and 1960s, the IBRD was to lend in support of reconstruction and development projects. This support, it was thought, would permit additional capital formation and thus enhance growth prospects.

Until the 1980s most World Bank lending was accordingly for projects. At first many loans went to Japan and Europe,[20] but after the mid-1950s development lending for power, irrigation, transportation, communications, and other projects in developing countries predominated.

IBRD lending, like Fund support, has been at near-market rates of interest, although with a longer maturity—usually in excess of fifteen years—than commercial bank loans. By the late 1950s it was evident that the poorer developing countries could not borrow on these terms. The United States therefore proposed that the IBRD should have a second window for lending on soft terms to low-income countries. This window, the International Development Association (IDA), has been financed by replenishments from IDA contributors, the rich industrialized countries.[21] The IBRD and IDA, together with the International Finance Corporation (IFC), became the World Bank. The IBRD and IDA share one staff and one set of criteria for evaluating projects in individual countries. However, lending terms differ depending on the per capita income of the country. The IBRD lends to developing countries with relatively high per capita incomes; IDA extends concessional loans to low-income developing countries.[22]

World Bank project loans and credits are for specified purposes. Normally, they finance only the foreign exchange costs of a project, and lending is usually for new projects, not for maintenance. The World Bank has lent only to governments and always receives a government guarantee for its loan.[23]

Although World Bank lending was primarily for projects until the 1980s, lending was often contingent on satisfactory economic policies surrounding the project in question. For example, when a project was to improve transportation or increase electrical power generation, the loan conditions would include appropriate pricing of railways or electricity. Such conditions ensured the financial viability of the enterprise, allowing the management of the power company or railroad to finance maintenance and sustain the investment's return over time. In a few instances, the World Bank stopped lending when it determined that the overall policy framework was inimical to growth. By and large, however, project support focused on individual sectors and activities of the economy, and the World Bank did not greatly influence overall development strategy.[24]

By the early 1980s the economic policies that had generated the balance-of-payments crises and inflation addressed by the IMF had also become clear obstacles to economic growth. Moreover, even in the absence of external imbalances and inflation, returns on World Bank projects, like aggregate growth rates, seemed to vary systematically with the overall policy framework. Irrigation projects, for example, had lower returns in countries whose agricultural pricing policies for outputs and inputs were more discriminatory.

As a result, the World Bank initiated a program of structural adjustment lending, under which it provided financial support to countries undertaking policy reforms to resume satisfactory growth. The first structural adjustment loan (SAL) went to Turkey in 1980, in support of the reforms that had begun in January 1980 and were proceeding. Thereafter, the World Bank extended a number of SALs in the context of the debt crisis. Sectoral adjustment loans (SECALs), another innovation, were extended to support policy reform in particular sectors of the economy. SALs and SECALs came jointly to be referred to as the Bank's policy-based lending.

Policy-based lending through SALs and SECALs has supported trade liberalization, public sector restructuring and privatization, agricultural price reform, tax reform, financial market liberalization, and other policy reforms.[25] The precise combination of policy measures included in SALs varied according to circumstances and was by no means uniform across countries, or even in the same country over time.[26]

With the onset of the debt crisis, policy-based lending increased dramatically, rising to 91 percent of total World Bank lending to heavily indebted middle-income developing countries after 1983.[27] Adjustment lending overall increased from 8 percent of IBRD and 4 percent of IDA commitments in 1980–82 to 29 percent of IBRD and 23 percent of IDA commitments in 1989.[28]

This move toward structural adjustment lending represented a significant departure from the project lending the World Bank had specialized in before the 1980s. The shift was grounded in lessons learned about development in recent years (see chapter 3). Experience taught that the World Bank and other aid donors needed to pay greater attention to overall policy frameworks in developing countries. Those in the process of reform, especially heavily indebted countries such as Chile, desperately needed financial support. Given their heavy debt-service obligations and correspondingly low levels of domestic savings available for investment, these countries would not have been able to accelerate economic growth at all rapidly in the absence of support from international donors. For countries such as Chile, it was imperative that the World Bank support the policy changes. World Bank studies suggest that countries undergoing reforms with the support of SALs experienced better growth performance than other similarly situated countries.[29] However, the World Bank also initiated policy-based lending in support of programs that were demonstrably unlikely to produce sustained improvements in economic performance. Nigeria, Tanzania, and Argentina, to name just three, received support even though their policy reform agendas were clearly of insufficient magnitude.

The rise of policy-based lending at the World Bank increased its overlap with the IMF. Until the 1980s exchange rate policy in developing countries had been the sole preserve of the IMF, as exchange rates were viewed as relevant only to macroeconomic stability. As observers began to recognize that exchange rate policy was also inextricably linked to the choice between inward- and outward-oriented development, the precise provinces of the Bank and the Fund became more difficult to delineate.

This issue was one of many on which U.S. leadership could have made a difference. Instead of suggesting a division of labor, the United States and other major donors vocally demanded cooperation between the institutions, failing to recognize that the member governments could have addressed the issue more directly. In the absence of leadership, the two institutions did resolve the issue through cooperation, albeit with more tensions than were probably necessary. In the early 1980s the World Bank did not provide policy-based support unless an IMF agreement was already in place. Even in the late 1980s more than half of all SALs went to countries with IMF agreements already negotiated.[30] In addition, the Bank and Fund undertook many operations only after joint consultation on overall strategy for the country in question. By 1989 they had undertaken 359 concurrent operations.[31]

The Regional Development Banks

Like the World Bank, regional multilateral lending institutions are a source of development finance. These institutions, whose members include the countries of the region and other industrialized countries with an interest in the area, have a governance structure very similar to that of the World Bank, and the United States is a large shareholder in each. Each extends concessional credits to poorer members and offers loans to eligible countries with higher per capita incomes.

The Inter-American Development Bank (IDB), the Asian Development Bank (ADB), and the African Development Bank were the only regional institutions until the late 1980s. Then the European Bank for Reconstruction and Development (EBRD) was established to support the transition of Eastern Europe and the former Soviet Union to market economies. The United States is the largest shareholder in the IDB and controls significant stakes in the other regional banks.[32]

For many years the regional development banks concentrated primarily on project lending, remaining relatively uncritical of borrowers' economic policies. Starting in the mid-1980s, however, the United States began to object strenuously to this practice at the IDB, refusing to consider a request for a general capital increase until the IDB changed its lending policies and emphasized overall economic policies in developing countries. By the late 1980s the IDB had in fact made these changes.

U.S. policy toward the regional development banks, with its emphasis on policy-based lending, does not seem to be dependent on any underlying notion of their role or comparative advantage. Table 5-1 illustrates how small the total lending of the regional development banks is relative to that of the World Bank. As smaller regional institutions, their comparative advantage clearly lies in being able to focus on activities requiring more specialized knowledge of the country or region. Neither the IDB nor the other regional banks have sufficient staff competent in analysis of overall economic policy to carry out the U.S. mandate. Even if they had such a staff, the inevitable duplication of World Bank and IMF activities would be an issue.

The rationale for regional banks would appear to be that they have more knowledge of local conditions in member countries and can act as retail lenders, complementing the World Bank's wholesale activities. This consideration is especially important for small Caribbean countries or South Pacific island states. Yet U.S. policy, among other failures, has failed to recognize the comparative advantage of these institutions.

This lack of perspective in Washington emerged clearly at the time of the EBRD proposal. The United States granted approval without seeming to address why a new regional institution was warranted. U.S. concern centered on issues such as democracy and private sector assistance, not on whether a new institution would provide valuable institutional capacity for assisting countries during the transition to market economies.

Support for Developing Countries from the Multilaterals

Table 5-1 presents net resource flows to developing countries from all the multilateral institutions, which accounted for about one-quarter of all flows by the late 1980s. In 1975 total multilateral assistance equaled U.S. $3.8 billion, or slightly less than U.S. bilateral assistance, which equaled $4.2 billion that year (table 3-4). By the late 1980s the situation had reversed, as U.S. bilateral assistance ranged between $7 and $9 billion, while multilateral flows exceeded $11 billion. This shift alone demonstrates the importance of the multilaterals to developing countries and the importance of analyzing their impact.

Table 5-1 disaggregates multilateral aid flows in the 1980s according to their origin and type. By 1990 concessional assistance from the

Table 5-1. **Net Disbursements of Multilateral Institutions, 1980, 1982–90**
Millions of U.S. dollars

Item	1980	1982	1983	1984	1985	1986	1987	1988	1989	1990
Concessional flows from multilateral lending institutions										
IDA	1,543	2,363	2,336	2,492	2,599	3,327	3,530	3,567	3,266	3,912
IDB	326	366	365	438	351	283	121	134	144	155
African Development Fund	96	122	158	111	210	272	374	351	493	603
Asian Development Fund	149	177	223	304	393	416	540	707	919	1,101
International Fund for Agricultural Development	54	104	144	170	270	286	366	102	117[a]	120[a]
Subtotal[b]	2,274	3,190	3,272	3,556	3,857	4,588	4,931	4,861	4,939	5,891
Concessional flows from UN agencies	2,487	2,755	2,739	2,763	3,047	3,052	3,332	3,776	3,879	3,900
Other multilateral concessional flows[c]	1,347	1,541	1,529	1,434	1,420	1,551	1,753	1,823	2,643	3,052
Total concessional flows[d]	7,790	7,525	7,575	7,638	8,055	8,683	9,853	10,381	12,224	13,204
Nonconcessional flows from multilateral lending institutions										
IBRD	3,166	4,534	5,117	5,648	5,041	5,418	4,395	3,417	3,302	5,009
IFC	295	291	166	127	94	156	208	356	388	1,385
IDB	567	832	957	1,550	1,398	1,224	928	1,093	1,258	1,060
African Development Bank	97	115	145	110	235	282	416	625	815	1,001
Asian Development Bank	328	473	550	513	400	364	253	598	669	1,197
Other	10	13	9	14	306	290	431	458	406	237
Subtotal	4,463	6,258	6,944	7,962	7,474	7,734	6,631	6,547	6,838	9,889
Other nonconcessional flows[c]	385	368	282	271	438	53	29	−45	88	299
Total nonconcessional flows	4,848	6,626	7,226	8,233	7,912	7,787	6,660	6,502	6,926	10,188

Sources: Development Assistance Committee, *Development Cooperation in the 1990s* (Paris: OECD, 1989), table 26, p. 230; and Alexander R. Love, *Development Co-operation: Efforts and Policies of the Members of the Development Assistance Committee, 1991 Report* (Paris: OECD, 1991), table 28, p. 200.
a. Secretariat estimate in whole or in part.
b. This figure includes a small amount from IBRD, which peaked in 1980 and ended in 1987.
c. Primary sources were the European Community and the Arab Funds.
d. The total includes small amounts from the IMF Trust Fund, Structural Adjustment Fund, and Extended Structural Adjustment Fund, as well as the Caribbean Development Bank and the Council of Europe.

multilaterals (of which IDA was by far the most important) totaled $13.2 billion, while nonconcessional flows equaled $9.9 billion. The dominant position of the IDA and IBRD relative to the regional development banks (including the International Fund for Agricultural Development) is clear. Although U.N. agencies accounted for about $4 billion of concessional flows in the late 1980s, their activities were spread across many agencies, including the United Nations Development Program and the World Food Program, the largest, and the United Nations High Commission for Refugees, United Nations Children's Fund, United Nations Trustee Administration, and U.N. Fund for Population Activities, each of which provided assistance in excess of $100 million in 1988.

Because of its shorter-term maturity, IMF lending does not count among long-term flows to developing countries. In the 1980s the net use of IMF funds rose from $3.9 billion in 1980 to $11.1 billion in 1983, fell to $4.4 billion in 1984, and then was negative from 1985 to 1989, as borrowers repaid more than the IMF extended in new support facilities.[33] Unlike resource flows from other multilateral development institutions, resource flows from the IMF clearly diminished in the late 1980s following its massive support of heavily indebted countries earlier in the decade. This decline in part reflects the shorter maturity of IMF loans.

U.S. Financial Support for the Multilaterals

As noted, the United States held a 41 percent share in both the World Bank and the IMF at their inception. As other members joined, the U.S. share declined, reaching about 19 percent in the World Bank and 20 percent in the IMF by 1990. When the World Bank proposes a general capital increase (GCI), Congress must approve it. The most recent GCI in the late 1980s left the United States with $1.8 billion of paid-in capital and a total subscription of $24.9 billion.[34]

Whereas the World Bank borrows extensively on private capital markets to finance its operations, the IMF relies much more heavily on its paid-in capital. Of total IMF subscriptions of 90.1 billion special drawing rights (SDR) as of April 30, 1990, SDR68.8 billion was paid-in capital. At that time the World Bank had taken loans worth more than $75 billion, while the IMF had borrowed only about $3 billion.

U.S. contributions to the IDA have been considerably larger because of the need for replenishments to finance concessional loans. As of June 1991, the cumulative U.S. subscription and contribution stood at $18.1 billion, out of a total contribution from all Part 1 members of 65.9 billion.[35] The ninth replenishment, covering the period from July 1, 1990, to June 30, 1993, totaled $15.4 billion at June 30, 1991, exchange rates.

Although U.S. contributions to the World Bank and the IMF have declined as a fraction of the total, the United States was highly supportive of the two institutions until the 1980s. U.S. replenishments for IDA were normally on time, and Washington encouraged both organizations, especially the World Bank, to expand in the 1970s. To a degree, the World Bank and the IMF even had to labor under the perception that they were U.S. institutions doing Washington's bidding, an impression that still prevails in some developing countries. Although the World Bank focused almost exclusively on project lending, it did insist on appropriate pricing policies for its projects. This insistence was interpreted as a sign of U.S. domination in an era when markets were suspect in much of the developing world. The chief criticisms of the World Bank and the IMF regularly came from left-wing critics, who argued that both institutions concentrated too much on markets.[36]

When Ronald Reagan entered office, U.S. policy changed markedly, as the administration held considerable suspicion about both institutions, but especially the World Bank. One of the first initiatives of Reagan's Treasury Department was to commission a report on the performance of the multilateral development banks. The purported intent was to develop a critical document, but the final report generally endorsed the performance of the World Bank, relegating minor criticisms to an appendix. The concluding chapter, however, contended that funding for the IDA should be reduced and that the real resources of the multilateral lending institutions should not be increased.[37]

U.S. opposition to the World Bank appeared to be grounded in the "anti–big government" view of the Reagan administration. The U.S. executive director voted more frequently against loan proposals brought to the board by World Bank staff. By 1984 the United States had opposed more than fifty loan proposals, most of which passed with support from other shareholding governments. Table 5-2 lists some of the loans the United States opposed in 1984 and the reasons for its opposition. U.S. opposition was based on a variety of reasons, such

Table 5-2. **U.S. Opposition to Selected World Bank Loans, 1984**
Amounts in millions of U.S. dollars

Country	Amount of loan	Reason for loan	U.S. objection
India	242.5	Petroleum development	Potential displacement of foreign private capital
India	220.0	National cooperative development	Potential displacement of foreign private capital
Philippines	150.0	Agriculture	Insufficient conditionality
Colombia	130.0	Petroleum development	Potential displacement of foreign private capital
China	100.3	Petroleum development	Potential displacement of private foreign capital and inappropriate sector policies
Hungary	90.0	Petroleum development	Potential displacement of private capital
Ethiopia	70.0	Education project	Past expropriation of U.S. investments
Ethiopia	40.0	Telecommunications	Past expropriation of U.S. investments
Nigeria	25.0	Technical assistance	Potential displacement of private capital
Ethiopia	25.0	Telecommunications	Past expropriation of U.S. investments
Madagascar	10.1	Cashew nut agricultural industrial complex	Doubtful economic and financial viability
Ethiopia	4.0	Technical assistance for economic management	Past expropriation of U.S. investments
Ethiopia	1.4	Irrigation study	Past expropriation of U.S. investments

Source: Clyde H. Farnsworth, "U.S. Votes No at World Bank More Often under Reagan," *New York Times*, November 26, 1984, p. D14.

as that U.S. legislation prohibited support,[38] that the loan would strengthen the role of governments, that the private sector could fund the World Bank project,[39] or that proposed loans did not require sufficient policy reform in the recipient country.[40]

Until the onset of the debt crisis, the United States resisted any change in World Bank policies, insisting that its nonproject lending not exceed 10 percent of the total, opposing any increase in the resources of the Bank (or the IMF), and objecting to numerous individual loan proposals. The seventh IDA replenishment was for $10.4 billion, a sum less in both nominal and real terms than the sixth ($12 billion) thanks to U.S. pressure.

At U.S. insistence, the World Bank had refused for years to lend at a rate that could not be sustained without a general capital increase. Each level of capital subscription thus implied a maximum rate of sustainable lending. By the mid-1980s it was evident that the Bank would soon reach its maximum level of sustainable lending. Yet, in the midst of the debt crisis, the United States continued to oppose any general capital increase. Moreover, when discussions of the eighth IDA replenishment began in January 1986, the United States staunchly opposed the efforts of other major countries to increase IDA funding. That replenishment, in the amount of $12.4 billion, finally took effect in March 1988. This sum only allowed real IDA commitments to remain at their 1984–87 levels, which themselves had been lower in real terms than those of 1981–84.[41]

The pattern of reluctant U.S. funding has continued. In the summer of 1990, the Bush administration opposed a proposed capital increase for the International Finance Corporation (IFC), stating that the World Bank must first shift its lending toward the private sector. Interestingly, lending to governments can support the private sector when it seeks to improve infrastructure, enhance the legal framework, and relax government controls over foreign trade and the domestic economy, all changes that only governments can make. Ironically, direct lending to the private sector is open to charges frequently made by the Reagan administration—that is, that private capital would finance private sector projects if they were worthwhile!

When U.S. administrations have supported funding increases for the World Bank or the IMF, Congress has often delayed approval, sometimes generating enough opposition to place the proposal in doubt.[42] U.S. funding has eventually been forthcoming in every case. But the United States, as the largest shareholder and contributor, is seen to be grudging and confrontational in its approach to funding proposals. Aside from substantive issues of policy, this pattern of delay, uncertainty, and reluctant support has diminished the effectiveness of U.S. resources allocated to the multilateral institutions.

U.S. Policy toward the Multilaterals during the Debt Crisis

In August 1982 the government of Mexico announced its inability to continue servicing its debt without external support. That announcement marked the beginning of a period of protracted difficulties for developing countries. In contrast to the preceding era, when the real per capita incomes of most developing countries were growing, many heavily indebted developing countries experienced falling real per capita incomes and mounting debt-service burdens.

The U.S. government itself reacted directly to these events, but U.S. leaders also came to recognize the potential importance of the World Bank and the IMF in addressing the debt crisis. Despite recognition of that potential, the U.S. response to the multilaterals was slow and begrudging. Because debt was central to the policy discussions of most developing countries in the 1980s, analysis of that crisis illustrates well both the potential role of the multilaterals and the failure of the United States to capitalize on that potential in a way consistent with U.S. policy objectives.

Scores of books and articles have examined the debt crisis from all perspectives.[43] The purpose here is to analyze the U.S. policy response. Doing so, however, requires some analysis of the debt crisis itself and its background.

The Background of the Debt Crisis

Early in the postwar era, observers generally assumed that private markets would not provide long-term capital flows to developing countries. A major argument for foreign aid was that the private capital market would not function well for low-income countries in the early stages of development, because gestation periods were too long and private profitability was too low. Only aid would supplement domestic savings and finance the major infrastructure investments needed to provide a basis for development.[44]

This assumption proved largely correct between 1945 and 1960. Some private foreign firms invested directly in extractive industries in developing countries or in import-substitution industries in countries such as Brazil, and private banks provided some short-term credit for trade finance, but official development assistance was the largest source of funds for developing countries.[45] Early U.S. policy on private capital flows to developing countries, especially foreign direct investment, was supportive, but few observers expected these flows to become a major source of finance.

In the 1960s, however, first Korea and Taiwan and then Singapore began to access private capital markets, borrowing for longer maturities and encouraging foreign direct investment to permit a rate of investment in excess of the domestic savings rate. In Korea, capital flows, which consisted largely of commercial bank borrowing, reached magnitudes of almost 10 percent of GNP in the late 1960s and 1970s. Because real rates of return on investment were very high, the borrowers had little difficulty servicing their debts or financing the repatriation of profits and capital. Their debt-service ratios rose little, if at all, as the growth of exports and GNP kept pace with the value of outstanding debt and interest payments.

After the 1973–1974 oil price increase, however, the liquidity of international capital markets soared, and the bankers took their favorable experience with Korea and Taiwan to mean that other developing countries were creditworthy. Consequently, many oil-importing developing countries discovered that they could borrow with ease. To finance their increased current account deficits, they borrowed heavily, attempting to maintain growth in the face of a sharp deterioration in their terms of trade. For most countries, these policies were unsustainable in the long run. The commercial banks, however, were more than willing to lend—they had found the developing countries of East Asia highly creditworthy, and they were highly liquid, as oil exporters deposited large amounts in short-term assets. By and large, developing countries were able to sustain these policies throughout the 1970s, as worldwide inflation reduced the value of outstanding debt relative to the debtors' exports, and as most loans were at fixed interest rates that turned out to be below the rate of inflation.

In some countries, to be sure, economic policies were so inimical to good economic performance that major difficulties emerged during the late 1970s.[46] Each year, several countries found themselves unable to service their debt and approached the IMF for assistance. An IMF program was then installed, policies were adjusted, and the difficulties were addressed for each country individually.

When in 1980 the price of oil increased again, worldwide conditions were not so forgiving. The major OECD governments adopted anti-inflation policies, and world real interest rates increased sharply. The international economy entered a prolonged recession, with nominal commodity export prices dropping. Initially, developing countries borrowed to finance their greatly increased current account deficits, and outstanding indebtedness increased in step.

Yet not until Mexico announced its inability to continue servicing its debt did international attention focus on the issue. The announcement was startling, because not only was Mexico an oil exporter, but major oil discoveries had recently driven Mexico's export volume up sharply. Six months earlier, the commercial banks had even urged Mexican officials to borrow, and syndicated lending had been oversubscribed.[47] The immediate reaction of the commercial banks was to curtail their lending to all developing countries severely. As a result, many other developing countries, whose net borrowing had constituted 3 to 5 percent of GNP until that time, found themselves unable to service their debt, and the debt crisis had truly begun.[48]

The Challenge of the Debt Crisis

The debt crisis was perceived as a crisis because debt-service problems struck a large number of countries in a very short period of time. Although debt-service problems were specific to each country, the magnitude of the commercial bank claims in apparent jeopardy and the large number of countries involved required a global policy response.

Economic history did include periods of widespread bankruptcies, most recently in the 1930s,[49] but the multilaterals had no precedent for coping with the debt problem. The IMF had negotiated individual stabilization programs, but only a few per year, and the magnitude of resources needed now was much larger.

The issue was complex. The heavily indebted countries, cut off from new lending by the private banks, were suddenly unable to service a large volume of debt. The private creditors were primarily commercial banks of many nationalities—American, Canadian, Japanese, German, British, French, Swiss, and others. Developing country debt was owed both to official agencies—individual governments and the multilaterals—and to commercial banks. Within the developing countries, both governments and private sector entities had incurred debts, sometimes with government guarantees and sometimes without. Clearly, international cooperation was necessary on a variety of issues.

Although the severity and duration of the worldwide recession of 1980–83 contributed to the debt-service problems of developing countries, the major difficulty lay in the policies of those countries themselves. The fact that some countries—primarily the East Asian

NICs, but also Colombia and Turkey[50]—with relatively heavy debt burdens were able to continue servicing their debt without resorting to rescheduling demonstrated the importance of policy.[51] No across-the-board solution was therefore possible; policy reform and debt rescheduling would have to be on a case-by-case basis.

Despite some alarmist reports, almost no heavily indebted countries seem to have seriously considered repudiating their debt, probably for two reasons.[52] First, despite import-substitution policies, most heavily indebted countries were integrated enough with the international economy and had benefited enough from that integration to make the costs of economic isolation and sanctions too large and too immediate to contemplate. Second, the mechanisms available for debt rescheduling made it a far more attractive short-run measure than debt repudiation.

Because their leaders were committed to maintaining international economic ties and honoring debt, heavily indebted countries had to reverse their economic policies sharply (see chapter 3). Given the levels of indebtedness and debt-service obligations, the crisis could only be resolved after growth resumed. Governments could not reduce imports sharply enough to service the debt at existing export levels.[53] To resume growth and service the debt, developing countries had to tighten fiscal and monetary policies and reduce the high levels of import protection given to domestic industries. The simple arithmetic of debt service implied that export growth would have to be rapid if debts were to be serviced and imports were to be able to grow as they must if economic growth was to resume.[54]

It was thus clear that the only way out of the morass required governments in heavily indebted countries to undertake significant policy reforms. That the challenge was primarily to these governments did not, however, imply that there was no role for the international community.

The potential support role of the international community had four major components. First, it had to devise a mechanism for debt rescheduling when countries faced insurmountable debt-service obligations. Second, it had to take measures that resulted in lower worldwide interest rates and to spark renewed growth in the international economy; both goals would lower the costs of debt servicing to developing countries, increase the nominal and real value of their exports, and possibly improve their terms of trade, or at least prevent their deterioration. Third, open markets to permit the exports of goods and services once policy reform had begun were essential if there was to be any hope of resolving the debt crisis. In this regard, measures to reduce protectionism and improve the access of developing countries to markets in developed countries would clearly benefit both developed and developing countries.[55]

Fourth, once strategies for policy reform had been devised in individual debtor countries, foreign capital inflows permitting greater rates of investment than domestic savings alone could be highly productive. Some of the capital stock in import-competing industries would become obsolete and uneconomic after policy reform, and the absence of supplementary external resources was likely to constrain export expansion in newly profitable industries. Moreover, additional resources could ease the pain of adjustment, facilitating a more rapid, and therefore more credible, transition process. In many cases, the collapse of voluntary lending created a macroeconomic problem so great that even draconian measures could not have brought current account deficits quickly into line with available sources of finance. This crisis differed from earlier balance-of-payments episodes in that it required additional financing in amounts much greater than the IMF could provide out of its existing or prospective resources.[56]

The policy challenges were multiple. The initial reaction of the international financial community was to fear an international liquidity crisis and to take measures to insure the stability of the system. Early economic analyses suggested that the crisis was more of liquidity than of solvency.[57] It quickly became apparent, however, that coordination among the central banks of the major OECD countries could prevent the debt crisis from spilling over into international financial markets.

The central problem was to find ways to assist developing countries in their transition to more sustainable economic policies.[58] One obvious way was to reduce the trade barriers confronting developing countries' exports; another was to allocate at least some foreign assistance during the policy reform process. The obvious instruments for that support were the multilateral institutions, which were well placed to play a central role in resolving the debt crisis. They had experience in providing support for policy reform programs, both in design and to some extent in financial assistance. Moreover, they could bring together representatives of the various governments that were creditors to the developing countries.

Other dilemmas also confronted policymakers during the debt crisis, even after it became manifest that the international financial sys-

Table 5-3. **External Debt and Debt-Service Obligations of Developing Countries, 1982–91**[a]

Item	1982	1983	1984	1985	1986	1987	1988	1989	1990	1991[b]
Total external debt										
Billions of U.S. dollars	839	889	932	1,005	1,098	1,220	1,235	1,237	1,303	1,354
Percent of total exports	121	135	135	152	173	162	144	130	124	117
Debt by region (billions of U.S. dollars)										
Africa	122	130	134	150	173	199	204	209	225	236
Asia	187	206	227	251	284	316	334	331	354	382
Europe	85	85	87	100	113	130	125	124	134	139
Middle East	114	124	129	137	146	158	163	166	175	182
Western Hemisphere	331	344	360	367	381	418	409	408	414	414
Debt-service payments										
Billions of U.S. dollars	136	120	136	140	142	152	166	153	168	190
Percent of total exports	20	18	20	21	22	20	19	16	16	16
Debt-service ratios by region (percent)[c]										
Western Hemisphere	54	43	42	41	45	39	46	33	37	43
Asia	13	12	13	14	14	14	11	10	9	8
Africa	20	22	27	27	28	23	26	25	27	27

Source: IMF, *World Economic Outlook* (October 1990), table A45, p. 173, and table A46, p. 174.
a. Figures are rounded to the nearest billion dollars.
b. Estimated.
c. Actual debt-service payments (not servicing obligations coming due) as percentage of exports.

tem was not at risk. Most of the heavily indebted countries were middle-income countries.[59] If foreign aid resources were reallocated to the heavily indebted countries,[60] it would seem to reward more affluent countries for profligate behavior at the expense of poorer countries whose fiscal and monetary policies had been more restrained.[61] Also, because the need for policy reform had become so evident, it was clearly undesirable to provide support to developing countries whose governments were unwilling to make the necessary policy adjustments.

The Policy Response

The crisis in the heavily indebted developing countries was so sweeping that the United States had to address it. U.S. policies on foreign aid, trade, and the multilateral institutions should all have been part of a coordinated response. But the debt crisis caught U.S. policymakers by surprise. No central agency was responsible for coordinating debt policy. USAID was responsible for administering foreign aid programs, which were of little use because of their country- and program-specific allocations. USAID officials, moreover, had little experience in macroeconomic policy analysis or in middle-income countries. The lead policy roles instead went to the Treasury Department, which oversaw relationships with the multilateral lending institutions, and the Federal Reserve, which had a strong interest in the commercial banks and directed initial refinancing efforts. The State Department also become involved with the foreign policy implications of the crisis.

Officials in the multilateral organizations tried throughout the crisis to dramatize a "trade-finance" link, emphasizing to OECD governments the crucial importance of market access for indebted countries in the process of economic policy reform. Trade policy, however, continued to be dominated by domestic concerns in the United States and in other OECD countries. U.S. trade negotiators, for example, decried export promotion policies in the same developing countries that officials from the Treasury Department and the multilateral institutions were urging to stimulate exports.[62]

Understanding the statistical scope of the debt crisis and the financial positions of indebted countries facilitates analysis of the policy response. Table 5-3 offers several indicators of the debt that point to

Table 5-4. **External Financing of Developing Countries, 1982–91** [a]
Billions of U.S. dollars

Item	1982	1983	1984	1985	1986	1987	1988	1989	1990	1991 [b]
Deficit on goods, services, and private transfers	84	67	37	35	56	12	29	31	19	25
Nondebt transfers	26	19	21	32	27	36	29	27	34	36
Net assets	-49	-4	-14	-12	-17	-6	-25	-9	-22	-12
Errors and omissions	-26	-18	-7	-1	3	-7	-6	2	2	-1
Use of reserves	35	-3	-10	-17	-4	-54	1	-21	-40	-40
Net borrowing	98	72	48	33	47	43	31	32	46	42
From official creditors	37	41	38	22	29	27	18	26	37	45
From commercial banks	69	39	17	-2	-1	3	-7	-3	-1	-23
Exceptional finance										
Arrears	12	15	4	-11	8	n.a.	11	13	-10	-4
Rescheduling	6	25	31	42	35	48	27	27	36	11

Source: IMF, *World Economic Outlook* (October 1990), table A40, p. 159.
n.a. Not available.
a. Figures are rounded, so totals may not match precisely. Data on arrears and rescheduling do not necessarily agree with data from other sources. The timing of agreements and signed reschedulings differs, and data can vary depending on which criterion is used.
b. Estimates.

the magnitude of the problem between 1982 and 1991. The external debt of the developing countries was increasing throughout the 1980s. From 1982 to 1985 the magnitude of the increase is understated owing to the appreciation of the dollar, which reduced the dollar value of debt denominated in yen, deutsche marks, and other currencies; after 1985 the dollar value of the debt fails to reflect the increased borrowing that occurred (see table 5-4). Overall, debt rose from $839 billion in 1982 to $1,354 billion in 1991. However, debt-service ratios rose far less than outstanding debt, reflecting the fact that many countries were unable to make scheduled payments of principal and interest even though interest rates fell after 1983.

Total indebtedness and debt-service obligations also differed markedly among regions. Asia's indebtedness and debt-service ratios (with the exception of the Philippines) were reasonably low, although its ratios of debt to GNP did not differ significantly from those in Latin America. The difference stemmed from their different policy approaches, most notably the outward orientation of the East Asian economies. Africa's debt-service ratios were very high, although the absolute value of its indebtedness was much lower.

Table 5-4 provides data on the external financing of developing countries during the 1980s. Current account deficits were large in 1982, as they had been in the period following the first oil price increase and worldwide recession. These external deficits gradually declined throughout the decade, as the net voluntary lending of commercial banks virtually ceased. The only financing available came largely from official sources. The most noteworthy aspect of these data is the sharp reduction in credit for developing countries. It forced tremendous economic shifts designed to reduce their current account deficits, shifts that had an enormous impact on economic performance.

Despite the numerous U.S. agencies playing a role in its formulation, U.S. policy toward the debt crisis had several continuities over the decade. First, the United States clearly articulated that policy reform was an essential prerequisite to external support of any kind.[63] Second, the United States formulated and executed debt policy independent of foreign aid and trade policies, never altering the latter two in any significant way to support administration policies on debt. Third, U.S. preoccupation with its own budget and current account deficits precluded any increase in budgetary allocations for foreign aid or other assistance to developing countries. Thus, despite Washington's rhetorical support of policy reform in debtor countries, the United States had few resources to support such reform, leaving the multilateral institutions in a key role.

With these continuities, the U.S. policy response evolved in three distinct phases. The first lasted from the onset of the debt crisis in 1982 until 1985, as the implications of the situation gradually became clear and the entire policy community continuously reassessed its diagnosis of the problem. The second phase began in September 1985, when Treasury Secretary James Baker announced his plan to grapple with the debt problem; it ended in March 1989, when Baker's strategy was abandoned. That date marked the beginning of the third and current phase, with Treasury Secretary Nicholas Brady's announcement of a new policy approach.

As Joseph Kraft and Jesús Silva-Herzog have documented, Mexican officials began discussing their problems with U.S. counterparts in the spring of 1982 as the seriousness of the situation became increasingly apparent.[64] The initial reactions of officials at the U.S. Treasury Department, when informed of the impending financial disaster,[65] were described as "dialogues of the deaf."[66] Finally, an emergency bridging loan was arranged while officials negotiated a longer-term solution under the aegis of an IMF stabilization program. Rescheduling the debt by itself was not a viable option for Mexico or later for other indebted countries that could not meet their obligations once the commercial banks were no longer willing to provide new loans.[67] Mexico's financing needs in 1983 alone exceeded IMF resources. The fundamental problem was that the anticipated size of the financing shortfall in 1983 was large, and unless concerted action was taken with the commercial banks, any monies lent by the IMF or other multilaterals would be offset by the refusal of the banks to roll over outstanding loans. Each commercial bank had an incentive to attempt to recover its money. Thus, even with a significant increase in resources, the World Bank and the IMF could not have supported the heavily indebted countries without a standstill agreement with the commercial banks, unless they were willing to substitute their own credit for that of the banks.

With support from the United States, the IMF convened meetings of private bankers to raise the funds needed to stabilize the situation and to roll over the debt.[68] These meetings were themselves unprecedented, since "advisory committees" of bankers were established for each heavily indebted country that could not voluntarily service its debt.[69] The IMF and World Bank, of course, also increased their lending, but only by limited amounts.[70]

As other countries announced their inability to continue servicing the debt, U.S. policy was based on the premise that the crisis was a short-term liquidity problem that would presumably recede when the worldwide recession ended.[71] The Reagan administration, as noted, had come into office highly suspicious, if not downright critical, of the multilateral institutions. As debtor after debtor announced financing difficulties, however, it became clear that the U.S. position toward the IMF, at least, would have to change. The first major U.S. policy action was therefore to reverse its initial position and reluctantly support additional funding for the IMF's new role as a catalyst for commercial bank financing.[72] Congress passed the increase late in 1983 after a touch-and-go battle. The rallying cry of opponents was that additional IMF funds were being made available to "bail out" the commercial banks. As noted, the United States continued to oppose a general capital increase for the World Bank until 1987, and was even tardier in increasing support for activities of the Inter-American Development Bank.

IMF lending to developing countries rose sharply in 1982 and 1983, providing net credits of about $7 billion and $11 billion in those years. By 1985, however, net repayments to the IMF exceeded its lending, and only in 1990 did the IMF return to a net lending position.[73]

Recovery from the unusually prolonged and severe worldwide recession began late in 1983, and global economic activity and world trade expanded in 1984 much more rapidly than had been anticipated. The official U.S. view was that recovery from the "liquidity problem" was proceeding very well.[74] As the expansion continued in 1985, however, a number of developing countries were still having great difficulty servicing their debt even after reschedulings, and growth in those countries had not resumed. The World Bank summarized the situation in 1985:

> As the pace of global economic recovery slackened during the year, the prospects for an early resumption of full debt servicing faded. Even for most of the problem debtor countries that steadfastly were pursuing efforts to strengthen their economies, a restoration of creditworthiness came no closer; for many others, it receded.[75]

After one reasonably good year in 1984, many of the countries that had undergone debt rescheduling were experiencing stagnant or falling real GDP growth ratios. Investment and savings rates had fallen sharply, inflation had accelerated, and real interest rates had skyrocketed. It became evident that the debt crisis had been triggered by events in the international economy but sustained by more fundamental problems in some developing countries. The debt crisis was primarily the symptom of underlying policy weaknesses that had effectively been concealed by increased borrowing in previous years. By early 1985 most analysts in the development community had concluded that developing countries required serious policy reforms and more financial resources or debt relief than they seemed likely to receive at that time.

The United States, however, continued to assert that existing resources were adequate. Opposing any expansion of World Bank policy-based lending, U.S. officials remained convinced that the problem was short-term.[76] Criticism of the U.S. position was widespread in these circumstances. One group of critics maintained that the "debt overhang" was too great and that at least partial debt forgiveness was necessary if growth was to resume.[77] Others argued that debt relief might be unnecessary, but that more new loans to ease the reform process were essential.[78]

Faced with this criticism and the continuing difficulties of many developing countries, the United States first shifted its policy in the fall of 1985. Treasury Secretary Baker, the U.S. governor of the World Bank, addressed the annual meetings of the World Bank and IMF in Seoul, Korea, and in effect announced a reversal of U.S. policy. Baker continued to insist that growth could be resumed and creditworthiness restored without the commercial banks writing down any debt, implying that the United States still viewed the debt crisis as a temporary problem of liquidity rather than something more fundamental.[79] But for the first time he acknowledged the need for new money to support countries in the process of policy reform, stating,

Despite . . . progress, some serious problems have developed. A number of principal debtor countries have recently experienced setbacks in their efforts to improve their economic situations, particularly with regard to inflation and fiscal imbalances, undercutting prospects for sustained growth. Bank lending to debtor nations has been declining, with very little net new lending anticipated this year.[80]

Secretary Baker then announced his "Program for Sustained Growth," consisting of "three essential and mutually reinforcing elements." These were policy reform in the developing countries, "a continued central role for the IMF in conjunction with increased and more effective structural adjustment lending by the multilateral development banks," and "increased lending by private banks in support of comprehensive economic adjustment programs." His advocacy of increased lending by the World Bank and other multilateral institutions to support policy reforms marked a reversal of long-standing U.S. policy. Baker also urged greater cooperation between the World Bank and the IMF in support of reform programs and reiterated that the United States continued to advocate a case-by-case approach to debtor countries.

Questions immediately arose about the provision of new funds by the commercial banks. Secretary Baker estimated that $20 billion over the next three years in new commercial bank lending would be required and called for "the banking community to make a pledge to provide these amounts of new lending and make it publicly."[81] However, the United States suggested no mechanism whereby the banks could be expected to achieve it. Because the banks were anxious to reduce their levels of exposure in developing countries, it was not evident what was being proposed.[82] That this part of the Baker Plan was nonoperational was evident in the speech itself and in subsequent events. As table 5-4 indicates, the commercial banks did not in fact provide any new funds over the subsequent three years.[83]

From 1986 to 1989 the basic tenets of the Baker Plan remained official U.S. policy. The United States encouraged the multilaterals to support policy reform and pushed them to take the lead in providing new monies themselves and in coordinating activities of the commercial banks. In that regard, U.S. policy toward the multilateral institutions was less hostile than before, and the World Bank actually received a general capital increase in 1988.

Official U.S. statements also strongly encouraged developing countries to adopt policies conducive to attracting new foreign capital through foreign direct investment. The United States also encouraged debt-equity swaps, under which debtor countries exchange instruments of indebtedness for equity in new investments. In one scheme with Mexico the U.S. government permitted its securities to guarantee the principal (but not the interest) on Mexican bonds issued in exchange for earlier bonds.

Table 5-5. **Economic Conditions in Heavily Indebted Countries, 1986–90[a]**
Percent unless otherwise specified

Item	1986	1987	1988	1989	1990
Real GDP growth	4.0	2.6	0.9	2.0	−0.2
Real GDP growth per capita	1.8	0.4	−1.2	−0.1	−1.8
Gross capital formation/GDP	17.8	19.0	19.1	17.9	18.4
Inflation rate	61.8	85.7	164.1	291.5	309.7
Central government fiscal balance/GNP	−8.6	−8.8	−9.1	−14.0	−3.0
Export growth	−0.1	6.0	9.8	5.3	4.9
Debt/exports	306.2	303.0	271.6	251.6	254.4
Debt-service payments/ exports	35.1	30.2	33.2	25.6	28.4
Current account balance (billions of U.S. dollars)	−33.9	−16.2	−18.6	−17.9	−19.6

Source: IMF, *World Economic Outlook*, (October 1990), various tables.

a. Data for current account balance, debt, debt-service payments, and inflation rates are for countries with recent debt-service difficulties; all others are for fifteen heavily indebted countries, known as the Baker fifteen, which were Argentina, Bolivia, Brazil, Chile, Colombia, Ecuador, Ivory Coast, Mexico, Morocco, Nigeria, Peru, Philippines, Uruguay, Venezuela, and Yugoslavia.

Nonetheless, U.S. policy remained hostile to the notion of reducing or forgiving debt.[84] The official position was that new money could support the resumption of growth, after which debt-service ratios would start to decline and voluntary creditworthiness would eventually be restored.

During the four years that followed Baker's announcement, debt-service issues were not as prominent as they had been. Some indebted countries made considerable progress in increasing their foreign exchange earnings, and a few resumed growth. But the progress of the "Baker fifteen," the heavily indebted countries identified by Secretary Baker as most needing assistance, was limited.[85] Table 5-5 gives some data on their economic situation between 1986 and 1989. In those countries, real GDP growth remained sluggish, central government fiscal deficits soared (in part because of interest obligations on domestic and foreign debt), and inflation accelerated sharply. Current account deficits had declined from more than $80 billion in 1982 to $17.9 billion in 1989, but the debt-service burden was dropping only slowly (and the fact that some countries were in arrears understated the magnitude of obligations), and investment ratios remained low.[86]

In these circumstances, the United States once again reversed its position and announced its support of initiatives to reduce the value of outstanding debt. In March 1989 Treasury Secretary Brady announced a new plan that encouraged debt forgiveness. Instead of urging new lending in support of heavily indebted countries, like the Baker Plan, Secretary Brady urged the multilateral institutions to use their resources to support voluntary write-offs of commercial bank debt. His goal was that 20 percent ($70 billion) of the $350 billion debt outstanding to commercial banks should be forgiven.[87]

Equally important, Secretary Brady indicated that the IMF should no longer withhold its own lending until commercial banks had agreed to rescheduling. This move significantly reduced the bargaining power of the commercial banks and gave officials in developing countries somewhat more latitude in dealing with their creditors.[88] The Brady Plan gave official acceptance—so long denied—to the view that the existence of debt itself might be a barrier to the resumption of growth in heavily indebted countries. In that way it officially sanctioned debt reduction, whereas earlier U.S. policy had vigorously rejected that alternative.

Initial reaction to the Brady Plan was skeptical.[89] After protracted negotiations, however, Mexico (one of the countries whose policy reforms had proceeded most rapidly) and its commercial bank creditors struck a deal that was important not only for Mexico, but as a precedent. The banks were to choose among three options: (a) they could continue to receive service at the same terms on existing debt if they made new loans; (b) they could exchange their claims for thirty-year bonds with a fixed interest rate of 6.25 percent; or (c) they could convert their claims into 30-year bonds, with a floating interest rate then equal to about two-thirds of the rate existing claims carried. Most banks chose the second or third options. This arrangement saved Mexico an estimated $4 billion a year in interest.[90] For the Mexican agreement, the World Bank and the IMF provided $7 billion to guarantee the principal and the first year and a half of interest payments. The U.S. Treasury Department was an active participant, both in encouraging the multilaterals to lend in support of debt rescheduling and in urging the commercial banks to accept some debt reduction.[91]

By the middle of 1990 only four countries had successfully negotiated debt-reduction and rescheduling agreements: Mexico, the Philippines, Costa Rica, and Venezuela.[92] However, as other countries began negotiations, the debt problem appeared to be diminishing in magnitude. Some heavily indebted countries questioned whether the Brady Plan was sufficient and whether the complex negotiations needed to reduce debt-service obligations were worth the effort.[93] Whether the crisis would have abated by itself or the Brady Plan was essential to that result is an open question.

For purposes of analyzing U.S. policy, several features stand out. First, the Brady Plan, like the Baker Plan before it, relied on the multilateral institutions—no additional U.S. resources (except through the multilaterals) were to be devoted to the initiative. Second, in initial discussions, policymakers paid little attention to the effects of the World Bank's debt guarantees on its portfolio.[94] Only after careful discussions between Treasury Department and World Bank staff did guidelines emerge that kept the Bank's lending within limits that would maintain its own credit rating and not require reductions in its other lending programs.[95] Third, the United States undertook no other policy initiatives (such as increased foreign aid or reduced trade barriers) that might have made a significant difference to the developing countries.[96] Finally, each shift in U.S. policy toward the debt problem occurred long after most informed observers had agreed that the preexisting strategy was doomed to failure. U.S. policy during the debt crisis may or may not have been too little, but each initiative was clearly too late.

Missed Opportunities vis-à-vis the Multilaterals

Until the 1980s U.S. support for the multilateral lending institutions was a key factor in their ability to serve the world economy. During that decade, however, U.S. support vacillated far more, swerving from issue to issue, apparently without a clear sense of direction.

U.S. ambivalence was perhaps clearest when the multilateral institutions requested funding. The Reagan and Bush administrations often refused to recommend any action to Congress until the multilaterals met certain conditions, and funding battles in Congress were often intense. Such actions on the part of the United States have had the appearance—and sometimes the reality—of hostility or reluctant support. During the debt crisis especially, U.S. policy was reactive, and there was little leadership on issues of direct concern to the multilaterals.

The United States has also appeared to use the multilateral lending institutions for its own short-term political purposes. Not only in U.S. votes against World Bank loan proposals (table 5-2) have short-term political objectives been sought at the expense of any longer-term vision. To protest violations of human rights, the United States has opposed lending to Chile under General Augusto Pinochet and to China after Tiananmen Square.[97] In these and other protests, the United States has used its influence—as have other large shareholders—for political purposes, relying on a political judgment. In other instances, the United States has supported lending to countries whose policy reforms were clearly insufficient, suggesting even to casual observers that loans could not be used productively.

In one highly publicized example, the United States repeatedly pressured the IMF and the World Bank to lend to Egypt during the late 1980s, when their staffs judged lending to be inappropriate. C. David Finch, then the director of the Department of Exchange and Trade Relations at the IMF, finally resigned because of U.S. interference. In his words,

> The most overt conflict-of-interest case came in the case of Egypt. For political reasons, Egypt had been receiving sizable support from the Western allies, much of it in the form of repayable export credits. With very limited cash aid available, servicing this credit became virtually impossible. Yet, debt relief was blocked by Paris Club rules that required that Egypt have an agreement with the IMF before the creditor countries would reschedule their loans. To maintain even a semblance of its traditional concern for timely repayment, the IMF had to insist on major changes in Egypt's economic policies.
>
> But the Egyptian government, fearing a domestic political backlash, refused to take the required action. Instead, it sought protection from other governments. The Fund was told to reach "agreement" with Egypt without insisting on the necessary policy changes. In recompense, undoubtedly the IMF was given assured priority over other creditors.
>
> The result of cases such as the one involving Egypt was to turn the debt strategy on its head. The IMF was brought into Paris Club procedures in the first place because it was able to help debtor countries adopt adjustment policies designed to help them "grow" out of their problems. But in these cases, the IMF was told to *forget* its adjustment standards and instead to give priority to speedy relief.
>
> The change in direction not only damaged the debt strategy, but

it struck at the heart of international cooperation through the IMF. . . . The intrusion of political factors changes the nature of the IMF.[98]

The Egyptian case was far from unique. In the mid-1980s the Argentine economy was confronting severe difficulties, including very high and accelerating rates of inflation, the accompanying problem of lagging foreign exchange earnings, and debt-service difficulties. Argentine authorities approached the IMF and the World Bank for support. Because its staff was convinced that the government's economic policies had not been altered sufficiently to offer promise of improved economic performance, the IMF was initially unwilling to lend to Argentina. But the United States was adamant that the Argentine government, democratically elected, should be supported. The World Bank quickly acceded to U.S. pressure, while the IMF withheld a loan for several months. Among other consequences, tensions between the two institutions rose sharply.[99] In the summer of 1991 the United States again applied strong pressure on the IMF to approve a program for Argentina despite the misgivings of its staff.[100]

The United States has wielded its political influence on other issues as well. In 1991 the U.S. government delayed a general capital increase for the IFC (which supports private sector development) until the IBRD started lending more to the private sector.[101] In that episode, U.S. officials never appeared to address questions as to why private sources cannot finance private sector activities. Recently, the United States has also pressured the Inter-American Development Bank to pay more attention to the policies of recipient countries. Again, U.S. officials did not appear to have considered the overlap that would necessarily be created between the global multilaterals and the regional IDB.

In these and similar cases, the United States has used its influence as a shareholder to secure an outcome it found politically desirable in the short run. It is quite legitimate for any nation to use its influence as a shareholder, and the United States is by no means the only country ever guilty of attempting to influence the multilaterals' behavior for its short-term interests. But one might hope that a country with systemic interests such as the United States would not lose sight of the ways in which well-functioning institutions might be useful in the future.

The United States has lacked a consistent vision of the role of the multilateral institutions. U.S. policy toward them has been reactive, as policymakers perceive a problem (such as a debt) and then consider the policy instruments available to them. The World Bank, IMF, and regional institutions have been among the instruments to which policymakers have turned, but they have done so only on an ad hoc, case-by-case basis. Without clearly defined missions, the multilaterals are subject to fickle political currents in the United States and other major shareholders.

The United States relied on the multilaterals more heavily in the 1980s because of the budgetary and balance-of-payments difficulties it faced. In earlier eras the U.S. government might have used its own resources, not those of the multilateral institutions, to reinforce political support for Egypt or Argentina. But with the constraints of the budget and current account deficits, little or no domestic funding has been available for the United States to address the problems of developing countries bilaterally. These constraints have also in part underlain U.S. reluctance to increase the funding of the multilaterals.[102] The net effect has been to make U.S. policy toward the multilaterals even less consistent. But inconsistency on this score is merely indicative of a broader failure, the absence of a coherent international economic policy vision in the United States. That absence plagues U.S. aid and trade policies as well.

6 ||| U.S. Trade Policies and Their Impact on Developing Countries

TRADE AND DEVELOPMENT are inextricably linked. An open, growing world trading system has proved to be vital to the economic development prospects of all developing countries. During the debt crisis, U.S. officials repeatedly stressed the importance of open trade policies on the part of developing countries as a determinant of successful development and the ability to service debt. The U.S. government has consistently supported policy reforms in developing countries that remove protection and promote exports. The success of such policy reforms greatly depends on the ability of the countries to penetrate international markets, capitalizing on the growth of the international economy.

The "trade versus aid" question first raised in the 1950s is really a red herring. In the process of development, developing countries necessarily allocate their resources between import-competing and export industries. Their growth depends in part on the economic efficiency of that allocation and on the incentives their policies provide for the economic use of resources. Aid, by contrast, can permit a more rapid rate of accumulation of resources; whereas exports require domestic resources, aid provides additional resources. An appropriate set of economic policies, therefore, can foster rapid growth through balanced incentives for production for the international and domestic markets, while at the same time increasing the rate of investment beyond that sustainable with domestic savings through the use of aid and other foreign resources.[1]

Despite the complementarities between trade and aid, the United States has formulated its international economic policies in the two spheres with greatly differing objectives. Foreign aid—both bilateral and multilateral—has historically been the chief instrument of policy toward the developing countries. U.S. trade policies, by contrast, have centered on two primary concerns: U.S. foreign policy with other industrialized countries and domestic economic interests.

In the years that immediately followed World War II, U.S. objectives regarding the industrialized economies and other foreign policy considerations prompted strong support in Washington for an open, multilateral trading system.[2] Spurred by U.S. leadership, successive rounds of multilateral tariff reductions and the dismantling of quantitative restrictions for Europe and Japan greatly liberalized trade among the developed countries.

The remarkable growth of the international economy between 1948 and 1973 was highly conducive to the growth of developing countries, especially for those willing to take full advantage of it. From 1950 to 1973 the real GDP growth rate of the developing countries for which data are available averaged more than 5.5 percent annually, while the exports of those same countries grew almost 10 percent a year. These rates more than doubled those achieved during any comparable time span after 1800 in developed and developing countries alike.[3] For countries with outward-oriented policies during that period, the average annual growth rate was much higher.[4]

Over time, however, the U.S. position on trade began to shift. Foreign policy concerns were of diminishing importance, while special interest politics—with pressure from textile and apparel producers, shoe manufacturers, the steel and auto industries, agricultural interests, and so on—began to play an increasingly significant role. By the 1980s U.S. trade policies were formulated and administered largely in response to domestic economic interests.[5]

In addition, U.S. support for an open, multilateral trading system—the foundation of the successful trade policy of previous decades—diminished, as concerns about "fair trade" eroded the commitment to free trade. As a result, a variety of other trade practices—especially the encouragement of regional trading blocs—emerged, and by the mid-1980s the momentum of multilateral trade liberalization was largely lost. The absence of strong U.S. initiatives and changes in the international economy also threatened the success of the current Uruguay Round of trade negotiations and hence the future of the open, multilateral trading system itself.

To provide a balanced analysis of the panoply of U.S. trade policies is far beyond the scope of this work, which focuses on the impact of these policies on developing countries. But because the same laws and

Table 6-1.   **Exports of Industrialized and Developing Countries and World Exports, Selected Years, 1950–90**[a]
Billions of U.S. dollars, with percents of total in parentheses, unless otherwise indicated

Year	Industrialized countries	Developing countries	Total world	Unit value index (1985 = 100)	World exports (1985 prices)
			Exports		
1950	36.4 (61.1)	23.2 (38.9)	59.6	n.a.	229.2
1960	83.9 (69.9)	36.1 (30.0)	120.1	27.6	435.1
1970	220.0 (75.7)	69.1 (23.8)	290.6	30.8	943.8
1980	1,239.8 (65.5)	632.5 (33.4)	1,892.1	115.8	1,663.9
1990	2,458.0 (73.9)	866.1 (26.0)	3,324.1	132.8	2,503.1
			Imports		
1950	39.8 (65.2)	21.1 (34.5)	61.0	. . .	. . .
1960	85.4 (67.8)	40.1 (31.1)	125.9	. . .	. . .
1970	226.9 (74.6)	75.6 (24.9)	304.1	. . .	. . .
1980	1,370.2 (70.4)	556.4 (28.6)	1,946.3	. . .	. . .
1990	2,573.5 (75.0)	857.8 (25.0)	3,430.4	. . .	. . .

Sources: IMF, *International Financial Statistics, 1988 Yearbook*, and May 1978 and July 1991 issues. The May 1978 issue was used to obtain export unit values for 1960 and 1970, which were then linked to the 1985 base used in later years.
n.a. Not available.
a. The percentage shares of industrialized and developing countries do not add to 100 percent because the trade of the East European countries and the Soviet Union, which the total incorporates, is not included in either category.

procedures shape U.S. trade policies toward both developed and developing countries, this chapter must address the overall stance of the United States vis-à-vis the global trading system. Although the chapter refers to several estimates of their impact, U.S. trade policies are so multidimensional and commodity-specific that generalizations about their effect on developing countries are difficult. Also, the conflict between U.S. trade policy and policies on the multilaterals and foreign aid should readily be evident, even though such contradictions are better illustrated in the concrete case studies that follow.

The Importance of Developing Countries as Trading Nations[6]

During the 1940s and 1950s almost all developing countries were predominantly primary commodity exporters that depended heavily on imports of manufactures for domestic consumption. Because their import-substitution policies discouraged exports, the share of developing countries in world exports declined until the 1970s.

Table 6-1 presents the data. The exports of developing countries

Table 6-2. **Exports of the Newly Industrializing Countries (NICs), Selected Years, 1960–89**
Billions of U.S. dollars unless otherwise indicated

Country	1960	1970	1980	1989
Hong Kong	0.69	2.51	19.73	73.14
Korea	0.03	0.84	17.51	62.33
Singapore	1.13	1.55	19.37	44.66
Taiwan	0.16	1.42	6.89	66.21
Total NICs	2.01	6.32	55.50	246.34
Total exports of all developing countries	36.09	69.14	632.54	765.26
Share of NICs exports (percent)	5.6	9.1	8.8	32.1

Sources: IMF, *International Financial Statistics, 1988 Yearbook* and November 1990 issue for all data except for Taiwan. For Taiwan: data for 1960 and 1970 from IMF, *International Financial Statistics, 1979 Yearbook*; data for 1980 obtained by using growth rate given in Shirley W. Y. Kuo, *The Taiwan Economy in Transition* (Boulder, Colo.: Westview Press, 1983), applied to 1970 data; and data for 1989 from *Financial Times*, October 10, 1990, p. B13.

grew rapidly but did not keep pace with the exceptionally strong growth of world trade. The dollar value of world exports, deflated by an index of export unit values, virtually doubled between 1950 and 1960. In the 1960s world trade growth accelerated, and the real value of world exports more than doubled. Even during the 1970s real world exports grew at an average annual rate in excess of 4 percent.

By 1970 the developing countries' share of world exports had fallen to 23.8 percent.[7] During the 1970s, however, two things reversed that trend. On the one hand, some developing countries experienced major success with outward-oriented growth strategies, as exports rose at phenomenal rates. On the other hand, oil price hikes increased the developing countries' share of world trade, because they were net oil exporters. Their declining share of world exports in the 1980s reflects the decline in the price of oil in the middle of that decade. In 1986 developing countries' share of world manufacturing exports was only 13 percent.[8]

Boosting the export share of developing countries until the 1980s was the rapid export growth of the newly industrializing countries (NICs). Table 6-2 gives data on the four East Asian countries that had outward-oriented trade policies by the 1960s. Those four countries exported only $2 billion in 1960, which was about 5.6 percent of all developing country exports. By 1989 their exports had grown to $246 billion, or 32 percent of the total for all developing countries. That rapid export growth was a major factor in the astonishing growth performance of those countries.[9]

The success of the NICs also affected markets in the developed countries, primarily the United States, that imported their manufactured commodities. The comparative advantage of the developing countries, especially in the early stages of their rapid growth, centered on the export of commodities that were relatively intensive in the use of unskilled labor, a factor they had in abundance. In the developed countries these same industries were under pressure, as the scarcity of unskilled labor pushed wage levels upward, raising production costs.[10]

In the 1970s the NICs were increasing their market shares of some major manufactured goods in the United States, and pressures arose from those industries for protection.[11] By the 1980s other developing countries were also increasing their export capacity, and protectionist pressures arose against them as well. The United States often responded by increasing the protectionist content of existing protectionist instruments. Some protectionist measures have been broadly based, while others have been commodity specific. Some measures target specific developing countries, but most are part of overall U.S. trade policy. The impact on developing countries of these general protectionist policies has often been disproportionate.

Global U.S. Trade Policy: An Overview

U.S. policy became unequivocally supportive of freer world trade in the 1930s, when Secretary of State Cordell Hull enunciated U.S. support of an open, multilateral trading system.[12] Hull's commitment followed the disastrous Smoot-Hawley Tariff Act of 1930, which triggered a spiral of tariff increases widely understood to have deepened the Great Depression. During World War II, the United States took the lead in proposing a multilateral International Trade Organization (ITO) as a complement to the IMF and the IBRD. Although the ITO charter was never ratified, its key provisions were adopted in the General Agreement on Tariffs and Trade (GATT), the organization that emerged in its place.

Signatories to the GATT commit themselves to an open, multilateral, nondiscriminatory trading system and pledge to respect GATT obligations, which limit the use of quantitative restrictions, prohibit discriminatory treatment,[13] and restrict other practices in violation of open, multilateral trade.[14] GATT also sponsored successive rounds of multilateral negotiations for reciprocal tariff reductions.

At least until the 1970s GATT agreements successfully liberalized trade more than could have been anticipated. In the early postwar

Table 6-3. **Average Tariffs, All Products, Selected Dates**[a]
Percent

Area	Pre–Tokyo Round	Post–Tokyo Round	1987
European Community	9.4	6.4	4.8
Japan	10.8	6.0	4.2
United States	11.6	6.3	3.4

Sources: For pre–Tokyo Round and post–Tokyo Round estimates, GATT, *The Tokyo Round of Multilateral Trade Negotiations*, vol. 2, Supplementary Report (Geneva, 1980). For 1987 estimates, Samuel Laird and Alexander Yeats, "Tariff-Cutting Formulas—and Complications," in J. Michael Finger and Andrzej Olechowski, eds., *The Uruguay Round: A Handbook* (World Bank, 1987), p. 92.
   a. Tariffs are simple averages of tariff rates.

years, the U.S. economy was already highly open, with tariffs as the only significant barrier to trade. By contrast, both the European countries and Japan employed quantitative restrictions on trade; over time they successively eliminated these quotas, in part because of U.S. pressure under the Marshall Plan.[15] Quota reductions spurred their economic growth, which in turn permitted further liberalization.

At the same time, tariff levels among the industrialized countries fell sharply. By the late 1960s tariffs had been reduced and "bound" at levels low enough to render them no longer the most significant barrier to trade among advanced industrial countries.[16]

Instead, with tariffs bound, policymakers responded to protectionist pressures by erecting nontariff barriers to trade, such as the Multifiber Arrangement, discussed below. Agricultural trade barriers had also been exempted from GATT rules at the insistence of the United States when the agreement was first negotiated.[17]

As of the early 1970s, however, trade among the industrialized countries was essentially liberalized. The major nontariff barriers— European and Japanese quantitative restrictions—had been eliminated, and tariffs greatly reduced. Table 6-3 gives average tariff levels for the United States, the European Community, and Japan, before the Tokyo Round in the early 1970s, after the Tokyo Round in 1980, and in 1987. The average tariff rate had already fallen to about 10 percent before the Tokyo Round. By 1987 the average tariff rate had fallen to less than 5 percent in all three areas. To be sure, these averages obscured some variation among individual commodity groups. Some of the higher-than-average tariffs that remained applied to exports that came predominantly from developing countries, and nontariff barriers to trade replaced tariffs to a degree. Despite these qualifications, however, successive multilateral tariff negotiations greatly liberalized world trade and accounted in part for its tremendous growth, as seen in table 6-1.[18]

Trade liberalization slowed in the 1970s and then began to stall, if not reverse itself, in the 1980s. In the United States, the loss of momentum was a consequence of several factors. First, the rapid growth of imports of footwear, textiles, clothing, and assembled electronic products intensified protectionist pressures in those industries. Second, and not unrelated to the first, the U.S. dollar appreciated in real terms, which placed increasing pressure on all U.S. industries, including those that were labor-intensive. Third, even as the dollar was appreciating in real terms, a severe recession struck in the early 1980s. Finally, sharp reductions in transport and communications costs made producers increasingly sensitive to practices in other countries and increased the range of goods and services that could be traded. The share of exports and imports in U.S. GNP rose from its level of 5 to 6 percent in the 1970s to about 15 percent in the late 1980s. With the real appreciation of the dollar and the U.S. fiscal deficit, imports surged more rapidly than exports. Americans began to blame the boom in manufactured imports on the practices of other countries, such as subsidies to domestic industries.[19] In some quarters, cries for fair trade, rather than free trade, became the order of the day.

Aggressive Unilateralism

In 1985 protectionist pressure in the United States was intense. The dollar stood at an unprecedented level in real terms, and popular calls for action were strong. In response, President Reagan announced in a speech that the United States would begin acting more aggressively to obtain access to foreign markets. Since then, U.S. trade policy has become more aggressive in a variety of ways. The conditions under which private parties may receive protection from foreign competition under antidumping and countervailing duty laws have loosened. The United States has retaliated against foreign trade practices it has found unfair by imposing punitive tariffs. In tough bilateral negotiations, the U.S. government has also confronted trade partners over practices it deemed harmful to U.S. interests.

This unilateral behavior did have legal precedent. Section 301 of the Trade and Tariff Act of 1974 authorized the U.S. Trade Representative (USTR) to determine whether a foreign act, policy, or practice

was in violation of a trade agreement or was unwarranted *and* bur-
dened U.S. trade. If the USTR so determined, he or she was required
to take action to eliminate the foreign practice, unless GATT authorities ruled that U.S. rights had not been violated or the USTR found
that the foreign country had taken steps to correct the unfair measure.

Since allegations of unfair trade could be taken to GATT for resolution, Section 301 of the 1974 act was in principle consistent with
GATT. By 1989, the United States had retaliated in only nine cases
under Section 301.[20] In 1988, however, new trade legislation strengthened Section 301 in two important ways. First, the Trade Expansion
Act of 1988 required the USTR to act on a greatly accelerated timetable; because GATT rulings would not usually be available in time,
consistency with GATT was no longer assured. Second, an additional
provision, known as Super 301, required the USTR to build invento-
ries of "unreasonable and discriminatory" foreign trade barriers. On
that basis, the USTR was to establish a priority list of those "unreasonable" practices most prejudicial to U.S. exports. The USTR was
then to set deadlines for the removal of these practices. If a country
did not remove them according to the timetable, the USTR was to
determine that the country was an unfair trader and to identify appropriate imports from the country on which to impose retaliatory and
punitive tariffs.

Super 301 goes well beyond GATT in mandating that USTR declare a country (rather than a particular practice) an unfair trader if it
fails to remove the offending practices, even if it has not violated GATT.
Furthermore, the United States applies Super 301 entirely outside of
GATT, as the USTR alone determines what is unfair and what measures the offending country should take to avoid retaliation.

Under Super 301, the USTR declared Japan, India, and Brazil "unfair traders" on May 25, 1989, according to the timetable specified in
the 1988 act. The priority practices targeted were Brazil's use of quantitative import restrictions for balance-of-payments reasons[21] and two
Indian practices: its requirement that foreign investors meet export
performance targets, and its restrictions on foreign insurance sales.[22]
Both Brazil and India condemned the U.S. use of Super 301. India's
official statement asserted that the country could not accept "dicta-
tion" of its economic policies.[23]

In addition to declaring those three countries unfair traders, the
United States also held discussions with a number of others about
their trade practices. The implied threat of U.S. retaliatory action un-

der Super 301 was clearly present and greatly resented by foreign trade negotiators. U.S. discussions with Korea are representative of this new bargaining stick and are covered in chapter 8.

In addition to Super 301 a section of the 1988 law referred to as Special 301 required the USTR to identify countries denying intellectual property rights protection and market access to U.S. firms. As in Super 301 cases, the USTR was to proceed unilaterally, but to identify only those countries that have (a) enacted the "most onerous or egregious acts, policies, or practices"; (b) caused the "greatest adverse impact (potential or actual) on the relevant U.S. products"; and (c) not carried on "good faith" negotiations with the USTR regarding the alteration of those practices.[24] After naming them, the USTR was to begin a regular Section 301 investigation of the practices of priority countries within 30 days. As it happened, the USTR reported to Congress in 1989 that because no foreign country met the standards set forth for intellectual property protection, the United States would not single out any for retaliation. Instead, the USTR would communicate U.S. concerns to each country individually.[25] At the same time, the U.S. International Trade Commission (USITC) was hearing intellectual property rights cases under Section 337 of the 1988 Trade Expansion Act, many of which targeted exporters from developing countries (see table 6-6).

Another provision of the Super 301 legislation required the USTR to note the extent to which U.S. trading partners respected labor rights (organizing collective bargaining units, rights to strike, minimum wages, health and safety conditions), although the final bill authorized the USTR to take into account a country's level of development in acting on this provision.[26] To date, the United States has not used this provision to take retaliatory action, but the law raises a number of questions. From the perspective of policymakers and economists in developing countries, this provision is potentially dangerous. It contains a real threat that the United States might use low wages, often a function of a country's poverty and the major source of its comparative export advantage, as an excuse for restricting imports of labor-intensive commodities.[27] U.S. leaders have already expressed concern over wages and labor practices in Mexico and in the Caribbean.

Both Super and Special 301 received heavy criticism in the United States, and even more abroad. When the USTR held bilateral discussions with many trading partners before its determination of Special and Super 301 targets, the implicit pressure effectively persuaded some countries to change policies. But this form of bilateral pressure generated strong resentment abroad. The United States notified Thailand, for example, that it would lose some major trade benefits under the Generalized System of Preferences if it did not take action by December 10, 1988, to protect U.S. copyrights.[28] In response, Thai textile workers demonstrated outside the U.S. Embassy, and a coalition of business and labor leaders protested the labor rights provisions of the 1988 law. The United States Pharmaceutical Manufacturers Association brought suit against Brazil under Special 301, and the United States raised the ad valorem tariff on a number of Brazilian imports to 100 percent. Brazil subsequently challenged the U.S. action before a GATT dispute settlement panel.

One can debate the wisdom of aggressive unilateralism as a long-term trade strategy,[29] but Super and Special 301 represented clear departures from the principles of GATT. The USTR could find a trading partner guilty even if the allegedly unfair practice was not illegal under GATT. Because of the tight timetable Congress imposed on the USTR, the United States was unlikely to be able to use GATT channels to seek redress against foreign trade practices, including those that might be illegal under GATT. Finally, under the new provisions, the United States aimed to take bilateral, rather than multilateral, action in disputes. Super 301 was clearly designed to make the aggrieved party in a dispute also its judge, disregarding GATT procedures.

Foreign objections to Super 301 were so serious that GATT convened a special council meeting in June 1989, during which the GATT Secretariat identified Super and Special 301 as the trade policy initiative "which could have the biggest [single negative] impact on the multilateral trading system and on the Uruguay Round."[30] Arthur Dunkel, director general of GATT, was reported to believe that Super 301 should be significantly weakened because of the threat it posed to the multilateral system and to the success of the Uruguay Round.[31] The European Community complained that the United States had taken an unfair negotiating advantage. Although the provisions of Super 301 expired on June 30, 1990, after the USTR had removed all three countries named in 1989 from the list of unfair traders, the U.S. use of bilateral bargaining power during the Uruguay Round fueled foreign perceptions that the U.S. commitment to GATT had seriously eroded.

*Antidumping, Countervailing Duty, and Copyright
Protection Measures*

The United States has always resorted to administrative law to a greater extent than other countries. In the case of U.S. trade law, the consequences have been remarkable. In most countries, government officials listen to the complaints of citizens about the unfair practices of trading partners and, if they deem it warranted, implement appropriate responses. In the United States, by contrast, citizens and firms can directly initiate court action under the relevant section of U.S. law. U.S. trade law is thus open to use by individual U.S. producers as a source of protection. Moreover, U.S. officials can negotiate with foreign counterparts, claiming that if grievances are not amicably settled through bilateral bargaining, they cannot guarantee what may transpire under administrative trade laws. Fearful of such proceedings, foreign steel suppliers agreed to voluntary export restraints in the early 1980s, after a large number of suits in the United States alleged foreign subsidization of steel production.[32]

Administrative provisions have been present in U.S. trade law for some time.[33] During the 1980s, however, resort to these provisions was much more frequent. Furthermore, the 1988 Trade Act strengthened these provisions in several ways, making it easier to file a suit and requiring quicker response from government officials.[34]

Many lawsuits seeking administered protection have been brought against developing countries under U.S. trade law. As tables 6-4 and 6-5 indicate, the number of cases actually under consideration at the end of 1989 was fairly small relative to the volume of U.S. trade with developing countries. However, that number has been rising rapidly. Whereas 13 antidumping and 7 countervailing duty cases were initiated in 1980–81, 62 antidumping and 16 countervailing duty cases were initiated in 1988–89.[35] Of the 381 antidumping duty cases investigated between July 1980 and June 1989, 51 were against Japan, 24 against Taiwan, 23 against Korea, and 22 against Brazil. Of these investigations, 194 were in the metals and basic metal products sector, 66 in chemicals, and 22 in agricultural products.[36]

But the number of cases itself or the fraction of trade covered is not necessarily an appropriate indicator of their importance. Administrative provisions clearly have several potential deterrent effects. They may discourage new entrants who fear that, even if (or possibly because) they are successful in the U.S. market, legal actions taken against them will erode their gains. They may also deter exporters to the U.S. market from pricing as aggressively as they would without the threat of antidumping actions.

Moreover, antidumping measures as presently administered have a protective bias. The law states that dumping occurs when commodities are sold in the United States for less than they are sold in the producer's home market. To establish whether dumping has occurred, the USITC constructs a reference price of sales in the foreign market and contrasts it with the prices at which goods are sold in the U.S. market. If the reference price (which includes no "unusually low" prices) abroad is lower than the price of *any* sale in the U.S. market (because selling at a high price cannot offset selling at a low price), dumping is construed to have occurred.[37]

The antidumping procedures were so friendly to protectionists that in 1989 the National Knitwear and Sportwear Association claimed that foreign manufacturers of manmade fiber sweaters were dumping in the U.S. market, despite the fact that quotas already restricted these imports![38] The USITC ruled in favor of the domestic producers, finding "dumping margins" of 1.3 percent for Korea, 5.8 percent for Hong Kong, and 21.4 percent for Taiwan. By contrast, the alleged dumping margins were 44 to 190 percent for Taiwan, 13 to 94 percent for Korea, and 25 to 115 percent for Hong Kong.[39]

The United States perhaps ought to guard against foreign firms that attempt to obtain a monopoly position by pricing below marginal cost and that receive subsidies unrelated to externalities in their home economy. But current U.S. antidumping and countervailing duty laws do far more than that. Their legal provisions and the manner in which they are administered make them highly protectionist in effect.

When the USITC agrees to hear allegations of dumping, the accused foreign firms face a number of immediate consequences. First, the Commerce Department sets temporary duty rates that must be paid until the case is settled. Second, the firms must provide detailed information on their costs and other aspects of their operations to U.S. investigators. If the firms fail to provide the information within a fairly short time period, the best available estimates are used. These estimates normally come from the U.S. producers that entered the

Table 6-4. **U.S. Antidumping Cases against Developing Countries, 1989**

A. CASES ACTIVE DURING 1989

Country	Product	Date of petition	Determination
Argentina	Rectangular pipes and tubes	6/06/88	Affirmative
Brazil	Steel wheels	7/29/88	Negative
	Industrial nitrocellulose	9/19/89	Pending
China	Sewn cloth headwear	5/26/88	Negative
	Industrial nitrocellulose	9/19/89	Pending
Hong Kong	Man-made fiber sweaters	9/22/89	Pending
Korea	Industrial belts	6/30/88	Negative
	12-volt motorcycle batteries	5/17/89	Negative
	Business telephone systems	12/28/88	Pending
	Industrial nitrocellulose	9/19/89	Pending
	Man-made fiber sweaters	9/22/89	Pending
Malaysia	Probe thermostats	4/15/88	Negative
Mexico	Steel pails	5/31/89	Pending
	Portland hydraulic cement	9/26/89	Pending
Singapore	Antifriction bearings	3/31/88	Affirmative
	Industrial belts	6/30/88	Affirmative
Taiwan	Rectangular pipes and tubes	6/06/88	Affirmative
	Business telephone systems	12/28/88	Affirmative
	12-volt motorcycle batteries	1/11/85	Negative
	Probe thermostats	4/15/88	Negative
	Martial arts uniforms	11/15/88	Negative
	Residential door locks	4/24/89	Pending
	Man-made fiber sweaters	9/22/89	Pending
Thailand	Antifriction bearings	3/31/88	Affirmative
Venezuela	Aluminum sulfate	3/29/89	Affirmative

B. ORDERS IN EFFECT AS OF DECEMBER 31, 1989

Country	Product	Date of action	Country	Product	Date of action
Argentina	Rectangular pipes and tubes	5/26/89	Korea (cont.)	Pipe fittings	5/23/86
	Carbon steel wire rod	11/23/84		Photo albums	12/16/85
	Barbed wire	11/13/83		Television receiving sets	4/30/84
Brazil	Disk wheels	5/28/87	Mexico	Fresh cut flowers	4/23/87
	Orange juice	5/05/87		Cookware	12/02/86
	Brass sheet and strip	1/12/87		Elemental sulphur	6/28/72
	Butt-weld pipe fittings	1/07/86	Singapore	V-belts	6/14/89
	Pipe fittings	5/21/86		Ball bearings	5/15/89
	Construction castings	5/09/86		Color picture tubes	1/07/88
Chile	Standard carnations	3/20/87	Taiwan[a]	Rectangular pipes and tubes	11/14/86
	Sodium nitrate	3/25/83		Small-business telephone systems	12/11/89
China	Tapered roller bearings	6/15/87		Rectangular tubing	3/27/89
	Cookware	12/02/86		Stainless steel cookware	1/20/87
	Candles	8/08/86		Butt-weld pipe fittings	12/17/86
	Paint brushes	2/14/86		Cookware	12/02/86
	Barium chloride	10/17/84		Oil country tubular goods	6/18/86
	Chloropicrin	3/22/84		Pipe fittings	5/23/86
	Potassium permanganate	1/31/84		Circular pipes and tubes	5/07/84
	Shop towels	10/04/83		Television receiving sets	4/30/84
	Print cloth	9/16/83		Fireplace mesh panels	6/07/82
Colombia	Fresh cut flowers	3/18/87	Thailand	Carbon steel plate	6/13/79
Dominican Republic	Portland cement	5/04/63		Clear sheet glass	8/21/71
Ecuador	Fresh cut flowers	3/18/87		Ball bearings	5/15/89
Hong Kong	Photo albums	12/16/85		Pipe fittings	8/20/87
India	Pipes and tubes	5/12/86	Turkey	Circular welded pipes and tubes	3/11/86
	Construction castings	5/09/86		Aspirin	8/25/87
Kenya	Standard carnations	4/23/87	Venezuela	Pipes and tubes	5/15/86
Korea	Color picture tubes	1/07/88		Aluminum sulfate	12/15/89
	Stainless steel cookware	1/20/87		Electrical conductor redraw rods	8/22/88
	Brass sheet and strip	1/12/87			

Source: USITC, Operation of the Trade Agreements Program, 1989, 41st Report, 1989, Publication 2317 (September 1990), tables A26, A27, A28.
a. The antidumping order against Taiwanese polyvinylchloride sheet and film, which had been in effect since June 1978, was revoked in 1989.

Table 6-5. **U.S. Countervailing Duty Cases against Developing Countries, 1989**

A. CASES ACTIVE DURING 1989

Country	Product	Date of petition	Determination	Date of completion
Brazil	Steel wheels	7/29/88	Negative	5/24/89
Costa Rica	Portland hydraulic cement	7/18/84[a]	Negative	10/12/89
Korea	Industrial belts	4/15/88	Negative	5/23/89
Malaysia	Steel wire nails	4/18/89	Negative	9/05/89
Singapore	Antifriction bearings	3/31/88	Affirmative	5/08/89
	Industrial belts	6/30/88	Negative	4/18/89
	Software products	9/06/89	Pending	. . .
Taiwan	Probe thermostats	4/15/88	Negative	1/25/89
Thailand	Malleable iron pipe fittings	9/23/88	Affirmative	2/10/89
	Antifriction bearings	3/31/88	Affirmative	5/08/89
	Butt-weld pipe fittings	8/30/89	Pending	. . .
Venezuela	Aluminum sulfate	3/29/89	Affirmative	12/06/89

Country	Product	Date of action
Argentina	Welded carbon steel pipe and tube products	9/27/88
	Textiles and apparel	3/12/85
	Oil country tubular goods	11/22/84
	Cold-rolled sheet steel	4/26/84
	Wool	4/04/83
	Leather wearing apparel	3/17/83
	Footwear	1/17/79
	Woolen garments	11/16/78
Brazil	Brass sheet and strip	1/08/87
	Castings	5/15/86
	Agricultural tillage tools	10/22/85
	Pig iron	4/04/80
	Cotton yarn	3/15/77
	Scissors and shears	2/11/77
	Certain castor oil products	3/16/76
	Standard carnations	3/19/87
Chile	Fresh cut flowers	1/13/87
Ecuador	Certain iron-metal castings	10/06/80
India	Stainless steel cookware	1/20/87
Korea	Porcelain cookware	12/12/86
Mexico	Textile mill products	3/18/85
	Auto glass	1/14/85
	Bars, rebars, and shapes	8/17/84
	Portland hydraulic cement and cement clinker	9/21/83
	Iron-metal castings	3/02/83

Country	Product	Date of action
Mexico (cont.)	Toy balloons and playballs	12/27/82
	Litharge, red lead, and lead stabilizers	12/06/82
	Ceramic tile	5/10/82
	Leather wearing apparel	4/10/81
Pakistan	Cotton shop towels	3/09/84
Peru	Pompom chrysanthemums	4/23/87
	Rebars	11/27/85
	Textiles and apparel	3/12/85
	Cotton sheeting and sateen	2/01/83
	Cotton yarn	1/01/83
Singapore	Antifriction bearings	5/03/89
Sri Lanka	Textiles and apparel	3/12/85
Taiwan	Stainless steel cookware	1/20/87
Thailand	Ball bearings	5/03/89
	Pipe fittings	2/10/89
	Steel wire nails	10/02/87
	Rice	4/10/86
	Pipes and tubes	8/14/85
	Certain apparel	3/12/85
Turkey	Aspirin	8/25/87
	Pipes and tubes	4/07/86
Uruguay	Leather wearing apparel	7/17/82
Venezuela	Aluminum sulfate	12/19/89
	Electrical conductor redraw rods	8/22/88
Zimbabwe	Wire rod	8/15/87

Source: USITC, *Operation of the Trade Agreements Program, 41st Report, 1989*, tables A28, A29.

a. The case had been initiated in 1984, suspended at the request of the petitioner, and then reinstated at the petitioner's request in 1989.

b. The orders against India for certain fasteners, Korea for offshore platforms, and Mexico for lime, bricks, and carbon black were revoked in 1989. Other agreements suspended orders for Argentine carbon steel wire rod; Brazilian forged crankshafts and orange juice; Colombian miniature carnations, textiles and apparel, cut flowers, and leather wearing apparel; Costa Rican fresh cut flowers and cement; Mexican float glass, polypropylene yarn and film, and pectin; Peruvian shop towels; Singaporian compressors; and Thai textiles.

complaint![40] Third, the firms need to hire U.S. defense attorneys who can guide them through U.S. legal processes. Especially for smaller firms and new entrants to the U.S. market, these possibilities constitute awesome threats. For poor countries newly liberalizing their economies, the lack of information and the difficulty of defending against these challenges constitute a significant deterrent.[41]

Tables 6-4A and 6-5A list the antidumping and countervailing duty cases decided during 1989 or under active consideration in that year, while tables 6-4B and 6-5B catalogue those commodities on which duties were in effect at the end of 1989.

An itemization of the number of commodities affected does not indicate the relative importance of these administrative provisions for three reasons. First, some commodities are more important than others in the exports of any given country. Fresh cut flowers, for example, are the only export from Colombia on which any duty was in effect at the end of 1989, but they are one of Colombia's leading nontraditional exports. Orange juice is a major export for Brazil, but some items listed for other countries are relatively unimportant. Second, the fact that a duty was imposed does not indicate the duty's magnitude or its impact on a country's exporters. When the duty is relatively high and there are other foreign exporters competing free of that burden, the impact of a duty may be considerable; when there are few direct competitors and the duty is relatively low, it may have little impact. Third, no catalogue of countervailing and antidumping duties provides any indication of how often firms adjusted their behavior in response to the threat of suit.

Nonetheless, the data in these tables provide some indication of the prevalence of these actions in the United States. At the end of 1989, the fraction of manufactured exports from developing countries covered by antidumping or countervailing duty orders was very small. Casual inspection of the orders against developed countries suggests, however, that developing countries proportionately faced a greater number of cases than developed countries relative to the size of their manufactured exports to the United States.[42] Exporters from a few developing countries—Korea and Taiwan most notably, but also Brazil, China, Singapore, and Thailand—were the objects of a vast majority of complaints. Moreover, the number of complaints filed each year increased markedly between 1980 and the early part of 1991.

Actions under Section 337 of the Tariff Act of 1930 have increased even more rapidly.[43] This section, as noted, aims to protect the intellectual property rights of U.S. firms abroad. Table 6-6A lists the cases the USITC considered during 1989, while table 6-6B catalogues those items on which findings had been made. In these cases, administrative actions are against particular types of the commodity in question, so the list suggests the range of commodities covered but does not specify the precise coverage of any particular finding. Interestingly, the list does indicate that Taiwan and Korea are the chief developing countries against which suits have been successfully prosecuted.

In all three types of administrative actions, U.S. law does not distinguish between developed and developing countries. Developing countries may be more adversely affected, however, because their producers are smaller and less able to afford the legal expenses of USITC hearings or because they export goods in industries more likely to seek relief in the United States under administrative trade laws.

U.S. Protection against Imports from Developing Countries

Like other aspects of U.S. international economic policies, U.S. trade policies toward developing countries have been highly schizophrenic. On the one hand, as an aid provider, the United States has urged open trade policies on the developing countries, offering debt relief under the Brady Plan and proposing the Enterprise for the Americas Initiative, a proposal for free trade in the western hemisphere discussed below. In addition, the United States has had a Generalized System of Preferences (GSP), under which the exports of developing countries, subject to certain conditions, may receive preferential tariff treatment in the United States. U.S. tariff laws also allow parts exported abroad for foreign assembly and reimported to the United States to enter duty free, a provision that favors developing countries well endowed with low-cost labor.

On the other hand, protectionist pressures have mounted in the United States against imports, especially of labor-intensive manufactured goods. Responding to those pressures, U.S. officials have implemented a number of measures that, far from encouraging open exchange, actively restrict U.S. trade with developing countries. These restrictions assume a variety of forms, from elevated tariffs to negotiated quotas, each of which is considered in turn after an overview of U.S. policies that have discriminated in favor of developing countries.[44]

Table 6-6. **U.S. Intellectual Property Rights Protection Cases against Developing Countries, 1989**

A. CASES ACTIVE DURING 1989

Country	Product	Determination
Brazil	Pressure transmitters	Pending
Hong Kong	Small aluminum flashlights	Limited exclusion order
	Novelty teleidoscopes	Pending
Korea	Erasable programmable read-only memories, parts and components	Limited exclusion order
	Concealed cabinet hinges and mounting plates	Dismissed
	Cellular radiotelephones, parts	Terminated with settlement agreement
	Key blanks for high-security cylinder locks	Pending
Taiwan	Small aluminum flashlights	Limited exclusion order
	Plastic light-duty screw anchors	General exclusion order
	Venetian blind components	Terminated with settlement agreement
	Electronic dart games	Terminated with consent order
	Track lighting systems and parts	No violation
	Strip lights	General exclusion order
	Straight knife cloth cutting machines	Terminated with consent order
	Concealed cabinet hinges and mounting plates	Dismissed
	Low-friction drawer supports	Terminated with consent order
	Softballs and polyurethane cores	Pending
	Electric power tools, battery cartridges and chargers	Pending
	Insulated security chests	Pending
	Self-inflating mattresses	Pending
	Bath accessories and components	Pending

Country	Product	Patent expiration date
China	Feathered fur coats and pelts	9/23/90
Hong Kong	Exercising devices	7/03/90
	Display devices for photographs	11/30/90
	Electric slow cookers	4/29/92
	Novelty glasses	No patent
	Personal computer parts and components	1/23/96
	Plastic food storage containers	No patent
	Miniature hacksaws	9/04/90
	Small aluminum flashlights and parts	3/18/03
	Reclosable plastic bags and tubing	3/23/93
Korea	Luggage products	11/02/90
	Roller units	5/24/94
	Pump-top insulated containers	9/12/95
	Air-tight cast-iron stoves	No patent
	Sneakers with fabric uppers and rubber soles	No patent
	Caulking guns	3/28/97
	Personal computer parts and components	7/14/98
	Trolley wheel assemblies	8/29/95
	Fans with brushless DC motors	1/15/02
	Feathered fur coats and pelts	9/23/90
	Reclosable plastic bags and tubing	3/23/93
	Erasable programmable memories	Various
	Reclosable plastic bags and tubing	3/23/93
Malaysia	Reclosable plastic bags and tubing	2/13/96
Mexico	Minoxidil powder, salts	No patent
Philippines	Nut jewelry and parts	7/03/90
Singapore	Exercising devices	3/23/93
	Reclosable plastic bags and tubing	7/14/96
	Personal computer parts and components	
Taiwan	Exercising devices	7/03/90
	Luggage products	11/02/90
	Roller units	5/24/94
	Flexible foam sandals	9/07/93
	Pump-top insulated containers	9/12/95
	Rotary scraping tools	5/25/93
	Air-tight cast-iron stoves	No patent
	Adjustable window shades	2/07/94
	Coin-operated audio-visual games, components	No patent
	Cube puzzles	No patent
	Miniature plug-in blade fuses	Various
	Heavy-duty staple gun tackers	No patent
	Caulking guns	3/28/95
	Personal computer parts and components	1/23/96
	Canape makers	3/22/97
	Plastic food storage containers	No patent
	Single-handle faucets	No patent
	Woodworking machines	Various
	Cloisonné jewelry	No patent
	Compound action metal cutting snips	No patent
	Fans with brushless DC motors	1/15/02
	Nut jewelry and parts	No patent
	Miniature hacksaws	9/04/90
	Small aluminum flashlights and parts	3/18/03
	Reclosable plastic bags and tubing	3/23/93
	Light-duty screw anchors	No patent
	Certain strip lights	3/15/00
Thailand	Reclosable plastic bags and tubing	3/23/93

Source: USITC, Operation of the Trade Agreements Program, 41st Report, 1989, tables A30, A31.

Trade Policies That Differentiate in Favor
of Developing Countries

Despite the importance of an open, multilateral trading system to the growth prospects of developing countries, most of them have insisted on "special and differential treatment" under GATT. Although differential tariff treatment for different countries violates the principle of nondiscrimination, the GATT articles were amended to permit such treatment for developing countries' exports. Most economists have viewed this insistence as a mistake on the part of developing countries,[45] and it has certainly weakened those who maintain that open trade policies best encourage the growth of developing countries.[46]

Nonetheless, the representatives of developing countries at the U.N. Conference on Trade and Development managed to persuade the major developed countries to provide tariff preferences to imports from developing countries.[47] The United States initially opposed special treatment but changed its stance because of the strong advocacy of the developing countries and the support they won from most other industrialized countries.[48] GATT amendments to permit special treatment were passed in 1971. At that time the European Community initiated preferences for developing countries, subject to a number of limitations. Not until 1976, however, did the United States introduce its GSP program.[49]

All industrialized countries imposed eligibility conditions on their programs. They also exempted certain commodities from special treatment and limited the value of each commodity that could be imported under preferential terms. The United States excluded from GSP certain commodities such as petroleum and import-sensitive items such as textiles and apparel. The United States also denied special treatment to imported goods in excess of either 50 percent of the value of total imports of the product or a certain dollar amount that is adjusted with the growth of U.S. GNP (starting at $25 million in 1976). The president also has discretionary authority to deny items eligibility under GSP. In 1990 President Bush removed six items, worth $20 million of imports, from the list of GSP eligibility.[50]

Analysts of GSP and its effects have concluded that the same protectionist interests that determined overall U.S. trade policy were able to prevent GSP from having its intended effects on the exports of

Table 6-7.   **U.S. Imports from GSP Countries and from World, 1989**

Item	From GSP countries	From world
	Billions of U.S. dollars	
Total	86.1	466.4
GSP-eligible products	24.4	172.8
Duty-free under GSP	10.1	10.1
GSP program exclusion	9.1	9.1
Other	5.2	153.6
Noneligible products	61.7	293.6
	Percent	
GSP-eligible to total imports	28.3	37.0
GSP duty-free to GSP-eligible imports	41.1	5.8
GSP exclusions to GSP-eligible imports	37.4	5.3
Other imports to GSP-eligible imports	21.5	88.9
GSP duty-free to total imports	11.6	2.1

Source: USITC, *Operation of the Trade Agreements Program, 41st Report, 1989*, p. 149.

developing countries to the United States.[51] Analysis of patterns of protection suggests that the bias against developing countries in the structure of U.S. tariffs remains even after taking GSP into account.

Table 6-7 gives data on the magnitude of the GSP program in 1989. Total exports from GSP countries in 1989 were $86 billion, $10 billion of which entered duty-free. Until 1989 the largest beneficiaries were Hong Kong, Korea, Singapore, and Taiwan. In 1989 the United States denied those four East Asian exporters GSP eligibility, because it was judged that they had reached a stage of development at which preferences were no longer necessary. During that year Mexico (with duty-free imports of $2.5 billion, equal to 24.7 percent of all GSP imports and 9.3 percent of Mexico's exports), Brazil (with $1.2 billion duty-free out of total exports of $8.4 billion), Malaysia, Thailand, and the Philippines had the largest value of exports eligible for GSP.[52]

In light of the quantitative and eligibility restrictions on GSP and the limited number of countries that export significant amounts under its terms, the attachment of the developing countries to the GSP program is puzzling. Because most policymakers in developing countries consider it important, the USTR has been able to use GSP eligibility as a bargaining tool, threatening to revoke it unless market-opening conditions were met. The GSP program thus provides limited benefit to developing countries but gives the USTR additional bargaining leverage on issues as diverse as worker rights, intellectual property protection, treatment of service industries, and nontariff barriers to trade.

Although GSP does not provide sizable benefits to developing countries, another provision of the tariff code does significantly benefit some of them. The Harmonized Tariff Schedules (HTS) Subheadings 9802.00.60 and 9802.00.80 (which replaced Articles 806 and 807 of the previous tariff schedule without substantive changes) permit commodities assembled abroad from U.S. parts and components to be imported with duty paid only on the value added in assembly. This provision has permitted the rapid expansion of foreign assembly of electronic, automotive, and other commodities. While the schedules are not restricted to developing countries,[53] the fact that assembly has historically been intensive in the use of unskilled labor has meant that developing countries have benefited from these provisions. In 1989 an estimated $74 billion of imports entered under the two headings, out of total U.S. imports of $468 billion.[54] Mexico's exports to the United States under the foreign assembly provision rose from $6.4 billion in 1986 to $11.8 billion in 1989, representing 44 percent of Mexico's total exports to the United States in that year.[55]

Tariff Levels on Commodities of Particular Interest to Developing Countries

With the exceptions of GSP and the provision for overseas assembly, U.S. trade law tends to affect developing countries negatively. Although average U.S. tariffs are fairly low and have been declining over the past several decades (table 6-3), tariff levels vary widely among commodity categories, and the variance often operates to the disadvantage of developing countries.

Table 6-8 gives the average U.S. tariff rates in 1988 by category of imports. Despite a low overall tariff average, U.S. duties on commodities most important to developing countries—animal and vegetable products and textile fibers and products—are clearly above average. Other miscellaneous products of particular interest to developing countries, including most electronic assembly, are also subject to above-average tariffs.

If tariffs were the only form of protection, the costs, while significant, would be of a known magnitude. In fact, a variety of nontariff barriers are even more damaging than tariffs. Three deserve special

Table 6-8. **U.S. Tariff Rates and Import Values, by Commodity Group, 1988**

Commodity group	Value of imports (millions of dollars)	Average tariff rates (percent)	
		Simple	Weighted
Animal and vegetable products	26,776	8.0	8.0
Textile fibers and products	25,269	9.9	17.2
Wood and paper products and printed material	18,325	2.7	2.0
Metals and metal products	229,148	4.3	3.8
Nonmetallic minerals and products	11,565	5.1	4.8
Chemicals and related products	60,545	5.6	2.8
Miscellaneous products	54,689	7.5	6.3
Subtotal	399,541	. . .	. . .
Total imports	426,316	6.6	4.9

Source: GATT, *Trade Policy Review, United States*, March 1990, p. 224.

attention: the Multifiber Arrangement, protection of U.S. agriculture, and various voluntary export restraints (VERs). Each is considered in turn.

The Multifiber Arrangement

In the mid-1950s protectionist pressures from U.S. textile and apparel manufacturers led to the inauguration of a short-term agreement on these industries, which was essentially a voluntary export restraint against Japan. That agreement expired but was replaced in the early 1960s by a long-term agreement, which covered only textiles and natural fiber apparel. During the 1960s Hong Kong, Korea, and Taiwan entered the U.S. market, and manmade fibers emerged as a competitor to cotton and other natural fibers. Protectionist interests in the United States lobbied to have those items also covered under the agreement. By the late 1960s apparel imports from developing countries were perceived as the "main problem" in the U.S. textile industry.[56]

In the early 1970s the Multifiber Arrangement (MFA) was negotiated to cover global textile and apparel trade, covering many manmade and natural fibers. Europe and the United States were signatories to the agreement, which was negotiated under the auspices of GATT.[57] Under this umbrella agreement, the industrialized countries then negotiated bilateral VERs on textile and apparel imports from developing countries, but not from each other. Umbrella agreements specified the approximate magnitude by which imports were permitted to increase in quantitative terms. During the 1970s this growth ceiling was set at 6 percent annually. Because the limit was quantitative, exporters were able to expand the value of their trade by upgrading production to higher value-added items.

Until the late 1970s the intention was that the industrialized countries would share (and to some degree limit) the expansion of textile and apparel imports. By the early 1980s, however, the MFA was becoming more restrictive.[58] Expansion of imports had been greatly slowed by the late 1980s, and even more restrictive measures were proposed before Congress.[59]

By the late 1980s the United States restricted imports in 127 separate categories of textiles and apparel and had bilateral agreements with ninety-eight countries. Some countries, to be sure, did not use all their quotas. Indeed, the mean-weighted average utilization rate was 84 percent.[60]

Textile prices in the United States are estimated to be 28 percent higher than they would be without the MFA, while clothing prices are 53 percent higher. This price difference amounts to an average cost per U.S. household of $238 and implies an average annual consumer cost per job saved of $134,686 for textiles and $81,973 for clothing.[61]

Despite quotas, the textile and clothing exports of developing countries have grown rapidly. As the MFA has tightened, however, observers have expressed concerns about whether that growth can continue, as growth rates have already shown a tendency to decrease. Textile and clothing imports under the MFA into the United States fell from $19.1 billion in 1987 to $18.5 billion in 1988, a decline of 3 percent, supporting those that claim the agreement is becoming more restrictive.[62]

Perhaps the most comprehensive recent analysis of the impact of the MFA on developing countries is that of Irene Trela and John Whalley. Using a carefully specified general equilibrium model, they estimate that as of the mid-1980s the loss to developing countries from the MFA and the tariff protection of all industrialized countries, not just the United States, was about $8 billion in 1986 dollars.[63] According to their estimates, countries losing more than $1 billion (Hicksian equivalent variation) included Brazil, China, Korea, and Taiwan. Their findings suggest that even countries such as Korea and Taiwan that receive rents from existing quotas would benefit in net terms from gains in export volume if the MFA and tariff protection on textiles and apparel were dismantled.

One of the primary concerns of the developing countries going into the Uruguay Round of trade negotiations was that a plan be established for phasing out the MFA. When the June 30, 1991, expiration date for the MFA arrived, however, the agreement was extended for seventeen months to allow additional time for bargaining.[64] The United States had proposed gradual phase-out, replacing country-specific quotas with global quotas as a first step.[65] The developing countries, however, advocated greater liberalization of country-specific quotas, claiming that those countries not already under quota would be adversely affected by the imposition of global quotas and that the initial period would not represent liberalization.[66]

Voluntary Export Restraints

On several occasions in the 1950s—including the first textile arrangement—the United States asked Japan to limit the volume of Japanese exports to the U.S. market for particular products judged to be particularly sensitive politically. Over time, the frequency of U.S. resort to VERs has increased. Although Japanese exports were the original target, the United States has increasingly negotiated VERs on commodities of special interest to developing countries.

VERs have effects similar to tariffs in that quantitative import restrictions also produce higher prices in the U.S. market. However, unlike tariffs, which permit the government to collect revenue, VERs permit the exporter of the commodity to collect the "tariff equivalent" of the quota in the form of a higher price. Established exporters, especially those whose costs are rising relative to new market entrants, thus gain with guaranteed market access and a higher price for some of their exports, although they lose to the extent that they are unable to export in quantities that they would otherwise find profitable.[67] Potential market entrants, however, are at a disadvantage with quotas. While they are not initially subject to restrictions, potential exporters are aware that success may lead to VERs, and that knowledge can discourage the necessary investments.[68]

Table 6-9 lists the major commodities (other than textiles and apparel) with VERs in the mid-1980s and the estimated extent to which the VERs raised prices to U.S. consumers. These agreements primar-

Table 6-9. **U.S. Voluntary Export Restraints (VERs) and Their Estimated Tariff Equivalents, 1980s[a]**

Industry	Nature of VER	Estimated tariff equivalent of VER (percent)	Comments
Automobiles	Agreement with Japan	15.3	United States lifted VERs in 1985 but Japan continued to abide by their terms
Nonrubber footwear	Series of VERs and other measures	9.7	In effect from 1977 to 1981; there is also an 8.8 percent tariff
Heavyweight motorcycles	Tariff-quota	25	Tariff-quota imposed in 1983 after USITC finding
Food products made of sugar	Series of restrictions	n.a.	To protect manufacturers using high-cost sugar
Color television sets	VERs with Japan, Korea, Taiwan	15	In effect from 1979 to 1982
Semiconductors	Voluntary import expansion with Japan	0	Japan agreed to give United States 20 percent of Japanese market
Machine tools	VERs with Japan, Taiwan	17	Imposed for 5 years starting in 1987
Specialty steels	Series of VERs	15	In addition to 10 percent tariff
Coastal shipping	U.S. carriers only	60	Foreign carriers not permitted
Ocean shipping	Subsidies and requirements to ship minimum percent of goods in U.S. carriers	0	Domestic costs are subsidized

Sources: Gary Hufbauer, Diane T. Berliner, and Kimberly Ann Elliott, *Trade Protection in the United States, 31 Case Studies* (Washington: Institute for International Economics, 1986); GATT, *Trade Policy Review, United States*, 1989; and for machine tools, Elias Dinopoulos and Mordechai Kreinin, "The U.S. VER on Machine Tools: Causes and Effects," in Robert E. Baldwin, ed., *Empirical Studies of Commercial Policy* (University of Chicago Press, 1991), pp. 113–28.

n.a. Not available.

a. This table does not include textiles and apparel, which are subject to the Multifiber Arrangement and are quantitatively the most important VER.

ily covered commodities in which East Asian exporters have been highly competitive. Although many were initially aimed at Japan, their focus has shifted over time toward the newly industrializing countries. Negotiations over these commodities have generated considerable trade frictions, as the Korean case discussed in chapter 8 demonstrates.

A recent study by Jaime de Melo and David Tarr gives some indication of the relative importance of quantitative restrictions. The authors estimate the direct welfare costs of quantitative restrictions and the losses associated with the capture of quota rents by foreigners. They found the direct cost of quantitative restrictions to be much larger than the loss of rents. For automobiles, the combined total gain without quotas from additional imports and the recapture of rents was estimated to be $15.5 billion, while that for steel was $1.6 billion.[69] Since much of the protection on automobiles and steel affects developed countries, other VERs clearly have an impact on developing countries smaller than that of the MFA.

Agricultural Protection

For many agricultural commodities, such as wheat and other cereal grains, the United States has a comparative advantage and is a natural exporter. Because of its interest in export markets, the United States has strenuously advocated a phase-out of Europe's subsidies for grain production, which impede U.S. exports. The United States is not a producer of tropical agricultural commodities, such as coffee and cocoa, and does not protect against those imports. But for many other agricultural products, U.S. protection is strong.

Administrative trade laws apply to agricultural imports just like other commodities. To name just one example, a case that dramatically illustrated the unilateral approach of U.S. trade policy, the United States imposed a countervailing duty on Thai rice imports in 1986 on the grounds that the Thai government was subsidizing its rice growers.[70] Yet the government subsidy to U.S. rice growers was more than 100 times greater than the Thai subsidy that it countervailed![71]

In another form of trade barrier, the United States protects a number of agricultural commodities with both commodity price-support programs and restrictions on imports. These commodities include sugar, cotton, tobacco, peanuts, and livestock, all of which are also produced by a number of developing countries.

Table 6-10 estimates the producer subsidy equivalents (PSE) on U.S. crops and livestock products, as estimated by the OECD and reported by GATT. The PSE is the percentage amount by which the price of a commodity or group of commodities would have to be subsidized to leave the revenues and incomes of farmers unchanged. For example, a PSE of 25 percent implies that if all domestic programs for the item in

Table 6-10. **Producer Subsidy Equivalents for U.S. Agriculture, 1984–88**
Percent

Product	1984	1985	1986	1987	1988
Crops (gross)	21	26	45	42	34
Livestock products (net)	34	36	41	40	33
All products (net)	28	32	43	41	34

Source: GATT, *Trade Policy Review: United States* (1989). Derived from OECD estimates.

question were removed and the commodity was freely imported, domestic producers would be unaffected if they received a subsidy equal to 25 percent of the world price. As the table indicates, these rates varied considerably from year to year during the 1980s but were on average higher than estimates of tariff and tariff-equivalent rates for all categories of goods except textiles and apparel. For some individual commodities, the PSEs were even higher. The PSE on sugar, for example, is more than 60 percent, while that for milk ranges between 59 and 81 percent.

Estimates of losses to developing countries caused by agricultural protection in developed countries vary, both because the impact of protection changes markedly from year to year and because economists make different assumptions about the manner in which agricultural protection would be phased out. In 1986 the World Bank estimated that if all agricultural protection in developed countries were cut by 50 percent, the exports of developing countries would increase on net by $5.8 billion, and the costs of importing cereals and other commodities for countries that are net importers would fall by $1.4 billion. If selected commodities of major importance in international trade were fully liberalized, the worldwide efficiency gains would be about $41 billion, of which the developing countries would realize $18 billion.[72]

For some countries, the impact of U.S. agricultural policies has proportionately been far greater than even these numbers suggest. The supported price of sugar in the U.S. market during the 1980s ranged between two and five times the world price. As the domestic price of sugar rose, U.S. consumers switched to nonsugar sweeteners, primarily high fructose corn syrup, reducing their consumption of sugar substantially. The result was that U.S. sugar imports fell from more than 5 million tons annually in the 1970s to less than one million tons by the late 1980s, causing most major exporting countries to lose export markets and earnings. Because sugar is produced primarily in developing countries,[73] the U.S. price supports had a major impact on many of them. Chapter 8 shows that the effect of U.S. sugar quotas and price supports has been enormous in the Dominican Republic. For other sugar exporters, as well, the U.S. sugar program has hurt more than U.S. foreign aid has helped.[74]

The Uruguay Round and Regional Trading Arrangements

The developing countries benefited greatly from the rapid growth of the international economy in the postwar years, despite their own trade and exchange rate regimes that were often highly inward-oriented. The developed countries tended to view trade policy as primary among themselves and foreign aid as their chief policy instrument toward the developing countries. Yet as long as the developed countries were liberalizing trade and growing rapidly, the developing countries were major beneficiaries, even though they remained on the fringes of U.S. trade negotiations and policy.

In recent years that situation has changed dramatically for three important reasons. First, the developing countries have recognized the importance of a rapidly growing international market for the success of the outward-oriented policies they have begun to adopt. Second, the successful NICs have become major trading partners of the United States. Third, the U.S. commitment to a global economic system based on open, multilateral trade has eroded in significant ways. That erosion must be addressed in any discussion of U.S. trade policy toward developing countries.[75] The shift has two significant manifestations: U.S. demands in the Uruguay Round of trade negotiations, and increasing U.S. support of bilateral and regional trading arrangements.

The U.S. Position in the Uruguay Round

U.S. policy toward the Uruguay Round—built on a complex and sometimes contradictory set of positions—has left some observers wondering how strong the U.S. commitment to GATT remains. The legislative provisions of Super 301 represented a shift from multilateralism toward unilateralism in U.S. trade policy, a shift dangerous enough to prompt the director-general of GATT to single it out as the most unfavorable development for the Uruguay Round during 1989. The failure of the United States to commit itself unequivocally to GATT procedures, regardless of the reasons for that failure, has itself reduced the round's prospects. U.S. leadership was crucial in earlier rounds, and the fact that the leader has appeared less than fully committed to GATT principles in its actions has impaired the negotiations.

U.S. negotiating positions have themselves had mixed effects on the Uruguay Round—truly the most vital concern for the developing countries—and on prospects for an improved global trading environment. In essence, the United Sates has taken a very hardline position on agricultural subsidies, demanding that the European Community abolish or significantly slash its Common Agricultural Policy (CAP). The U.S. government blames Europe's recalcitrance on agricultural subsidies for the failure of the round to move forward toward a conclusion. Although U.S. insistence that Europe dismantle the CAP should favor the agricultural producers of developing countries, it will not if the extremity of the U.S. position does not win credibility and instead undermines the round's prospects.[76]

Likewise, Washington's commitment to trade liberalization in the round has been less than wholehearted. The United States signaled its desire very early to exclude shipping,[77] civil aviation, telecommunications, and banking from the GATT principles established in Geneva[78] and even failed (temporarily) to sign the Telecommunications Code to which U.S. negotiators had earlier given consent.[79] The United States also argued for item-by-item negotiation of tariff reductions, whereas the European Community advocated across-the-board cuts. The reported reason was that the United States wanted to maintain its relatively high tariffs on textiles and clothing.[80] Moreover, certain items of great potential interest to developing countries—construction services, for example—have not been open for discussion thanks in part to U.S. opposition.

Although the official U.S. position fully supports the Uruguay Round, U.S. actions outside the GATT and even some of its negotiating positions within the GATT have raised questions. Without a doubt, the United States has not supported the reduction of trade barriers as wholeheartedly as it did in earlier rounds.

Regional Trading Arrangements

Even before the start of the Uruguay Round, the official U.S. position was that the United States would hedge its bets on the multilateral trading system by being open to bilateral free trade agreements with "like-minded" countries. This approach was to be both "carrot and stick" for the Uruguay Round negotiations and also for talks with individual trading partners.[81]

A first agreement was signed with Israel in 1985, and the U.S.-Canada Free Trade Agreement was signed in 1988. Quite independent of those initiatives, the United States had in the early 1980s understandably declared a Caribbean Basin Initiative, designed to provide assistance to Caribbean countries and to give them preferential access to the U.S. market. It became clear that more free trade agreements were possible, but the U.S.-Canada relationship seemed warranted because of their proximity and importance to each other, while the U.S.-Israel agreement seemed grounded in special political relationships. Most observers believed that few, if any, developing countries would be interested in pursuing free trade discussions. Speculation ranged widely over a number of possibilities, with many observers believing the East Asian countries to be the most likely partners, although negotiations were far from probable.[82]

Mexico, with its history of inward-oriented trade policies and strong nationalism, seemed very unlikely to contemplate free trade with the United States. U.S.-Mexican relations changed drastically, however, when early in 1990 President Carlos Salinas de Gortari announced Mexico's desire to negotiate a free trade agreement with the United States as rapidly as possible. The possibility of a North American Free Trade Agreement (NAFTA) suddenly appeared to become a probability, and many issues surfaced.

Authority for all trade negotiations must be delegated from Congress to the administration. The Bush administration requested "fast-track" legislation for this purpose from Congress in the spring of 1991 to cover extension of the Uruguay Round and negotiations with Mexico. By granting fast-track authority, Congress empowers the president to negotiate trade agreements within a limited time period and agrees to vote yes or no on any treaty without an opportunity to revise it. The latter condition gives U.S. negotiators real credibility; otherwise Congress could conceivably amend any agreement to death.

The policy debate over fast track raised a number of thorny issues that are illustrative of the cross-currents at work in the formulation of U.S. trade policy. On the one hand, many concerns were specific to Mexico: oil, immigration policies, phytosanitary regulations on U.S. imports of Mexican fruits and vegetables, and integration of the maquiladora industries that developed under the assembly provisions of the U.S. tariff act. On the other hand, U.S. labor and environmental groups voiced more general concerns. U.S. labor leaders vocally opposed any pact that did not include an agreement on "minimum standards of wages, benefits, safety and environment."[83] Labor's insistence on a sufficiently high minimum wage in Mexico could render any agreement ineffective and, if enforced on the local economy, could frustrate all Mexican attempts to expand through trade. Environmental groups also opposed the pact, fearing that U.S. industries would move to Mexico to escape environmental regulations in the United States. Although many labor leaders and environmentalists were genuinely concerned about these issues, other protectionist forces seized upon their fears to forge a "potent coalition" opposing the initiative.[84] The staunch opposition of these groups places in question the ability of the U.S. government to negotiate a genuine free trade agreement with any developing country.

The prospect of a U.S.-Mexico free trade agreement also raised questions about its impact on other countries. The first question centered on the relationship of Canada to any such pact.[85] Canadians were naturally concerned for two reasons. If the agreement with Mexico became the first in a series of bilateral agreements between the United States and other countries, U.S. producers would enjoy an edge over Canadian competitors when obtaining raw materials and intermediate goods from partner countries. Also, Canada had bargained extensively with the United States in the expectation of gaining preferential access to the U.S. market. To the extent that Mexico or other countries received the same preferences (or even worse, better ones) the value of Canada's hard won special access would diminish.[86]

Canada's concerns about a potential series of bilateral U.S. agreements only multiplied in June 1990 when President Bush announced his Enterprise for the Americas Initiative. This proposal contemplated the extension of free trade, along with debt relief, to other Latin American countries. According to Bush, all Latin American countries were to be eligible, after policy reform, for membership in a hemisphere-wide free trade area. This initiative immediately focused attention on the potential inconsistencies between various U.S. bilateral arrangements and on the future relationship of the United States to the open, multilateral trading system. Within the western hemisphere, Caribbean countries expressed concern about the potential erosion of their preferential margins if U.S.-Mexico and other agreements came into force. Chile quickly applied for an agreement with the United States to avoid losing ground to Mexico and to take advantage of its open trade policies. In other parts of the world, U.S. trading partners expressed concern about the potential effects of free trade in the western hemisphere on them. East Asian countries, in particular, strongly objected to potential discrimination against their goods in the U.S. market.[87] Out of this concern, Malaysia proposed an Asian regional trading arrangement to offset losses they might experience in the U.S. market.[88]

Questions persist about the extent to which regional agreements will truly promote free trade, given protectionist opposition, and about their impact on excluded countries. A larger question, however, concerns the effect of a bilateral approach to trade negotiations on the world's open, multilateral trading system under GATT. If a strong free trade bloc emerges in the western hemisphere, pressures in Europe for more protectionist trade policies would surely intensify. Should those result in greater restrictions on foreign trade with Europe, the negative impact on developing countries, not to mention Japan and other excluded industrialized countries, would be profound. Such an outcome would certainly diminish the growth prospects of the international trading system and thus of the developing countries as well.

Under GATT rules, a free trade agreement is acceptable if the contracting parties adhere to the principles of multilateral trade and dismantle trade barriers among themselves across the board, not just in certain sectors. Article 24 of the GATT charter specifies the terms that free trade agreements must meet. Most observers agree that the U.S.-Canada treaty meets GATT criteria. Whether additional pacts would do so remains an open question. All contracting parties in a free trade area should surely sign the same agreement—in the western hemisphere, separate agreements between each country and the United States appear undesirable from every viewpoint.

If the Bush administration's vision of hemispheric free trade becomes a reality that is consistent with GATT and that accepts all other countries that adhere to the "GATT-plus" principles, the arrangement could substantially enhance the welfare of its developing country members and probably of the United States as well. If, however, NAFTA and the Enterprise for the Americas Initiative degenerate into a regional trading bloc and a substitute for GATT in part or in whole, its members, along with the rest of the world, could become much poorer.

7 ||| The Caribbean Basin Initiative

THE WAYS IN WHICH U.S. international economic policies are at cross-purposes with each other appear in U.S. policy toward almost any developing country.[1] U.S. trade policy has singled out Brazil as an "unfair trader" under Super 301 while simultaneously urging that heavily indebted country to expand exports. The United States offers strong political support to Turkey as a NATO ally and urges the liberalization of its economy, yet Turkey's textile and apparel exports to the United States are very restricted, despite the great comparative advantage it enjoys in these products. While Mexico was discussing a free trade agreement with the United States and opening up its economy, the United States accused Mexican exporters of dumping cement in the U.S. market.[2]

U.S. policies toward Caribbean countries offer a useful case study of the crosscurrents that emerge even when U.S. policy objectives are clearly articulated and strongly supported by the president.[3] U.S. interests in the Caribbean are reasonably straightforward, free of the political complexity of the Greek-Turkish, Arab-Israeli, and Pakistani-Indian disputes. Moreover, the economic structures and interests of most Caribbean countries are readily understandable, lending a sharp focus to the issues. The Caribbean Basin Initiative (CBI), a major development program launched by the United States during the 1980s, showcases the interaction of policy instruments and illustrates how complex and self-defeating bilateral policies and relations can be.

U.S. Interests and Caribbean Development

In the early 1980s events in Central America and the Caribbean alarmed the Reagan administration. Cuba's government had long been hostile to the United States, and it was thought that some other countries were giving Cuban diplomatic initiatives increasingly receptive responses. A revolution had occurred in Nicaragua, and civil war was ongoing in El Salvador. Jamaica's government was avowedly socialist, and an insurgency movement was growing in Guatemala. Most Central American and Caribbean countries had been experiencing very slow per capita income growth in the 1970s and had been hurt by the oil price increase of 1979–80 and the ensuing worldwide recession.

In that dismal environment, President Reagan announced a new initiative for the economic recovery of Central America and the Caribbean before the Organization of American States in February 1982. The clear intent of the CBI was to improve the economic performance of the region, in the belief that continuing stagnation would be conducive to insurgencies, civil wars, and Marxist governments. In Reagan's initial formulation, the CBI agenda was to have several components. It was to provide eligible countries with preferential duty-free access to the U.S. market, tax incentives for U.S. foreign investment,[4] and increased foreign aid, conditioned on certain policy reforms that would foster free enterprise.[5]

Congress passed the foreign aid component ($350 million) of the CBI in September 1982, slightly reducing the portion the administration had earmarked for El Salvador. However, Congress failed to act on either the investment incentives or the trade proposals at that time. Opposition to the trade provisions principally arose from senators and congressmen from states with labor-intensive industries. After the invasion of Grenada focused attention on the Caribbean, Congress finally passed the Caribbean Basin Economic Recovery Act (CBERA) in July 1983, extending duty-free access to the U.S. market.[6] As passed, however, the act had major limitations. On the trade side, a number of items were not eligible for duty-free importation, including sugar and textiles and apparel subject to the Multifiber Arrangement.[7] The proposed incentives for U.S. foreign direct investment in the Caribbean never passed, although CBERA did make the expense of some business meetings in eligible countries tax-deductible in the United States. This provision was designated the CBERA tourism incentive, as it was to encourage the tourism industry in the region.[8]

To be eligible for duty-free treatment, 35 percent of the value added of the imported product had to originate in CBI countries as a group. However, as much as 15 percentage points of that amount could be U.S. materials assembled in the Caribbean. A safeguard provision empowered the president to withdraw duty-free treatment if Caribbean imports caused domestic injury.[9]

The act authorized the president to designate individual Caribbean and Central American countries as eligible for CBI treatment, provided they met seven mandatory criteria. Designation was in order as long as the country did not have a communist government; enacted certain regulations to prevent the expropriation of U.S. property; cooperated with U.S. authorities in antinarcotics activity; recognized arbitration awards to U.S. citizens; did not provide preferential treatment to the products of developing countries that adversely affect U.S. trade; abstained from the illegal broadcast of U.S. copyrighted material; and had an extradition treaty with the United States. In addition, the act encouraged the president to consider eleven additional criteria, such as the use of subsidies, respect for worker rights, compliance with GATT rules, and so on.

Initially, the United States designated twenty countries as eligible for CBI benefits. Later, four more were added. Panama was placed on the initial list, removed in 1988, and reinstated in 1990. Table 7-1 lists the countries covered by the CBI initiative at the end of 1990 and gives some background data about each. The CBI countries are highly diverse. Some are English-speaking (the eastern Caribbean islands and Belize), while others are Spanish-speaking. Some have strong ties with the United Kingdom, France, or the Netherlands. Some, such as Aruba, are oil-exporters with high living standards. Others, especially Haiti, Guyana, and Nicaragua, have very low living standards. Many of the Caribbean islands have very small populations with less than a million inhabitants (table 7-1); their open trade regimes and economic structures reflect that fact. By contrast, many of the Central American countries, with populations of at least several million, chose to protect some domestic industries in earlier years.

The record of growth in the region before the CBI was also mixed. As noted, U.S. concern centered on the generally poor economic performance of the region, which itself was attributable in part to civil unrest and the worldwide recession of the early 1980s. Economic success stories were not entirely unknown. Costa Rica, for example, experienced sustained growth and political stability during the 1960s and 1970s, but by the 1980s it was heavily in debt. At the other extreme, Jamaica's real per capita income had been falling for two decades before the impact of the worldwide recession was fully felt in the early 1980s.[10]

The data on exports and the U.S. share of exports in table 7-1 include only merchandise exports and thus overlook services, which are

Table 7-1. **Countries Eligible for CBI Benefits, 1990**

Country	Population, 1988 (thousands)	GDP per capita, 1988 (dollars)	Annual growth rate, 1965–83 (percent)	Exports, 1988 (millions of dollars)	U.S. share of exports, 1988 (percent)
Antigua and Barbuda	800	3,520	−0.4	20	n.a.
Aruba	600	10,000	n.a.	30	64
Bahamas	240	9,660	−1.8	274	90
Barbados	250	6,060	3.8	170	30
Belize	180	1,500	3.6	120	47
British Virgin Islands	n.a.	8,900[a]	n.a.	2[a]	n.a.
Costa Rica	2,850	1,760	2.1	1,250	75
Dominica	80	1,410	−0.4	50[a]	5
Dominican Republic	6,900	670	3.9	890	74
El Salvador	5,000	1,070	−0.2	570	49
Grenada	100	1,540	0.9	30	4
Guatemala	8,700	900	2.1	1,030	29
Guyana	1,010	450	n.a.	230	12
Haiti	6,240	380	1.1	180	77
Honduras	4,800	930	0.6	1,000	52
Jamaica	2,400	1,330	−0.5	830	40
Montserrat	n.a.	3,780	n.a.	3[a]	n.a.
Netherlands Antilles	190	5,500	n.a.	1,300	55
Nicaragua	3,620	470	−1.8	240	0
Panama	2,300	1,960	0.5	280	90
St. Kitts–Nevis	40	3,240	2.4	30	44
St. Lucia	150	1,330	3.1	119	18
St. Vincent	110	1,310	1.8	90	10
Trinidad and Tobago	1,200	3,070	3.4	1,410	61

Sources: For exports, U.S. export share, and per capita income, State Department, *Report by the Department of State on the Caribbean Basin Initiative (CBI)*, November 1990. For population, IMF, *International Financial Statistics, 1991 Yearbook*. For growth rates from 1965 to 1983, World Bank, *World Development Report, 1985*, pp. 174–75, 232.
n.a. Not available
a. 1987 data.

very important for some CBI economies. Tourism, for example, has been a major source of foreign exchange in Jamaica, the Bahamas, and many other countries. Moreover, it is likely that the United States accounts for a higher percentage of total foreign exchange earnings in CBI countries from goods and nonfactor services than of exports alone. The small U.S. share of some countries' export markets is a result of their historical ties with a European country, usually the United Kingdom or France.[11]

The exports of many CBI countries are concentrated in primary products. Four countries are oil refiners or exporters (Aruba, Bahamas, Netherlands Antilles, and Trinidad and Tobago), but the rest depend on petroleum imports. Among the other primary product exports are a variety of tropical agricultural commodities, the most predominant being sugar.

The initial CBERA gave eligible imports duty-free treatment for twelve years. However, some of the bill's limitations rapidly became evident, and in 1987 a bill to extend and expand CBERA was introduced.[12] It passed as part of the Customs and Trade Act of 1990 and is often referred to as CBI II. The most important provision of CBI II extended duty-free treatment indefinitely. Other provisions prohibited the president from designating as eligible any country that had not taken steps to conform to internationally recognized worker rights standards; exempted CBI countries from worldwide cumulation of imports in determining injury in countervailing duty and antidumping cases; required Puerto Rico to insure that at least $100 million of tax-exempt section 936 funds was invested in CBI countries during each calendar year;[13] expressed the sense of the Congress that Andean countries could be eligible for CBI benefits; and extended to Puerto Rico the same duty-free treatment that inputs of U.S. origin enjoyed. The new bill also included a number of minor changes that do not merit attention.

Provisions of the Initiative

The sections that follow describe the CBI as it operated during the late 1980s. The changes enacted in 1990 with CBI II have not, as of the time of writing, materially affected CBI benefits, other than indirectly creating greater incentives for investment in the region with the assurance that preferences will continue indefinitely.[14]

Foreign Aid

The CBI increased U.S. economic assistance to the region by $350 million in 1983, bringing total assistance in that year to $900 million.[15] Economic assistance, including Economic Support Fund, development assistance, and food aid, rose to a peak of more than $1.5 billion

Table 7-2. **U.S. Quotas on Sugar Imports, 1983–88**[a]
Thousands of short tons

Country	Average, 1975–81	1983	1984	1985	1986	1987	1988	Net change, 1983–88
Barbados	37.5	19.6	21.3	17.8	12.5	7.5	5.8	– 13.8
Belize	53.0	30.8	33.5	27.9	18.9	10.0	7.7	– 23.1
Costa Rica	83.0	42.0	62.4	52.3	34.7	17.6	13.1	– 28.9
Dominican Republic	815.3	492.8	535.4	447.0	302.0	160.2	123.2	– 369.6
El Salvador	129.1	72.8	89.2	74.5	50.0	26.0	19.7	– 53.1
Guatemala	217.0	134.4	146.0	121.9	82.4	43.7	33.6	– 100.8
Haiti	6.4	16.5	16.8	12.5	12.5	7.5	5.8	– 10.7
Honduras	42.8	28.0	59.5	50.0	32.7	15.9	11.5	– 16.5
Jamaica	47.9	30.8	33.5	27.9	18.9	10.0	7.7	– 23.1
Panama	130.9	81.2	88.2	73.7	49.8	26.4	20.3	– 60.9
St. Kitts–Nevis	19.1	16.5	16.8	12.5	12.5	7.5	5.8	– 10.7
Trinidad and Tobago	31.6	19.6	21.3	17.8	12.5	7.5	5.8	– 13.8

Source: Ralph Ives and John Hurley, *United States Sugar Policy: An Analysis* (U.S. Department of Commerce, April 1988), p. 74.
a. Agriculture Department data on quotas for 1988 and subsequent years were increased in response to drought conditions in the United States. Years refer to those ending in October.

in 1985, then declined to about $1 billion in 1989. El Salvador received the most assistance, equal to $100 million in 1981, $250 million in 1983, and $400 million in 1985, and then fell gradually to just under $300 million in 1989. Guatemala and Honduras were the next largest recipients, with Costa Rica not far behind. Each received more than $100 million annually from 1983 to 1989. Jamaica also received sizable assistance. The eastern Caribbean countries as a group never received more than $50 million. Not all CBI countries qualified for assistance under USAID guidelines because of their high per capita incomes.[16]

Not only did aid totals increase, but USAID administered more assistance through the Economic Support Fund for balance-of-payments support and import financing. The emphasis on private sector development also increased, consistent with the overall thrust of USAID financing in the 1980s.

For many CBI countries, foreign aid was an important source of resources. For the countries included by the World Bank in its World tables, official development assistance as a proportion of GNP in 1988 was 5.9 percent in Haiti, 2.5 percent in the Dominican Republic, 7.3 percent in Honduras, 4.1 percent in Guatemala, 7.7 percent in El Salvador, 6.0 percent in Jamaica, and 4.0 percent in Costa Rica.[17]

Trade Policy: The Case of Sugar

The CBERA did not affect sugar imports into the United States, because the overall U.S. sugar program in effect was more restrictive than any CBERA measures would have been. To be eligible for duty-free exports of sugar, beef, and veal to the United States, CBI countries had to file an acceptable staple food production plan. Entirely ignoring the principle of comparative advantage, the CBERA stated that importing agricultural commodities was undesirable unless the country had produced enough food to feed its own population![18]

The CBI provisions for sugar were irrelevant because the United States reinstated sugar import quotas in 1981. As U.S. sugar production increased more rapidly than consumption, the quantity of imports permitted under quota began declining rapidly, a decline that did not stop in 1983 with CBI's introduction. Table 7-2 presents data on sugar exports from CBI countries to the United States between 1983 and 1988, with data on average imports between 1975 and 1981 for comparison. Sugar imports from each country listed fell sharply

Table 7-3. **Exports of CBI Countries to the United States, Selected Years, 1980–88**[a]
Millions of U.S. dollars

Item	1980	1983	1984	1985	1986	1987	1988
Traditional exports	1,988	1,501	1,763	1,446	1,775	1,376	1,263
Nontraditional exports	1,064	1,295	1,602	1,770	1,963	2,339	2,878
Apparel	242	350	447	579	748	1,049	1,383
Other manufactures	444	496	623	678	686	786	920
Primary products	378	449	531	513	528	564	575
Total	3,051	2,796	3,364	3,216	3,738	3,775	4,141

Source: James W. Fox, "Is the Caribbean Basin Initiative Working?" USAID/LAC/DP, October 1989, p. 7.
a. These statistics, originally presented by USAID officials to Congress, include only those Caribbean countries with per capita incomes low enough to qualify for U.S. foreign aid. They include the vast majority of CBI countries.

during these years.[19] Since the price paid for sugar under quota was fairly constant throughout the period, losses in earnings were roughly proportional to losses in export volume for Caribbean producers. Although these exporters could sell sugar on the world market, prices were sharply depressed largely because reduced U.S. quotas greatly increased supply in the world's "free" market. Whereas the price for sugar imports under quota in the United States was about $0.20 per pound, the world price fluctuated between $0.05 and $0.10 per pound.

The economic consequences of quota reductions and declining exports to the United States varied widely for the countries in the region. In the Dominican Republic, sugar export earnings fell from $533 million in 1981 and $300 million in 1983 to $142 million in 1988 and $217 million in 1989. Haiti's sugar export earnings fell from $25 million in 1980 to $32 million in 1990.[20] The impact was not uniform across all countries in the region, however, and sugar producers in some countries suffered less dramatically.

Comparing the gains from aid with the losses from sugar quotas is difficult, because the resources employed in sugar were available for use in other lines of activity. Reduced quotas were thus not a complete loss, although they contained sizable rents. To the extent that countries continued to produce sugar and sell it at lower prices in world markets, quota losses and aid receipts are directly comparable. USAID presented to Congress its estimate of the net effect of aid gains and quota losses between 1983 and 1987, and table 7-3 reproduces the numbers. For the Dominican Republic and Panama, the reduction in sugar export revenue was greater than the foreign economic assistance authorized in 1987. For Belize, the sugar loss was equivalent to five-sixths of foreign assistance. For other countries, the impact was significantly smaller.

Nonetheless, the net impact of U.S. quota reductions for many CBI countries was that foreign exchange earnings from sugar fell so sharply that overall export earnings actually decreased during the initiative's first five years. Whatever positive economic impact additional aid and preferential trade access might have had was offset to varying degrees by protectionist U.S. sugar policy.

Manufactured Export Incentives

The most significant characteristic of the CBI was the U.S. grant of duty-free status to imports from eligible countries. The CBI was unique among U.S. trading arrangements in that preferential treatment was conferred unilaterally in the absence of any agreement with the beneficiaries. To be sure, GSP was extended to individual commodities, and thus bore a great similarity, but CBI was a one-way regional trading arrangement.

Manufactured exports were thought to be key to the economic fortunes of the Caribbean countries. Part of the theory underlying the CBERA was that trade was preferable to aid as a means of fostering economic development. Although the bill exempted a number of commodities from duty-free status, all others were eligible for duty-free importation if 35 percent or more of their value came from CBI countries, 15 percent of which could also come from the United States.[21]

Table 7-3 provides summary data on the exports of CBI countries to the United States across different categories between 1980 and 1988. The decline in traditional exports, a consequence of both U.S. sugar policy and the drop in oil prices in the middle of the decade, was pronounced. Nontraditional exports, however, increased significantly.

After CBI exports to the United States failed at first to respond to the initiative, the president announced in February 1986 a new Special Access Program for U.S. imports of some textile and apparel products from eligible Caribbean countries, provided the imports were assembled entirely from parts made and cut in the United States. The arrangement is complex, but it has provided additional incentives for some textile and apparel imports and is partly responsible for the increase shown in table 7-3. Since the value added to these products is significantly less than that in many other export categories, the rapid increase in apparel exports reflects in part the reexport of textile and fiber products made and cut in the United States.[22]

Because CBI countries depend heavily on nontraditional exports, especially labor-intensive manufactured goods, the U.S. initiative arguably increased export growth more than would otherwise have been possible. CBI countries exported about 35 percent of their total exports to the United States from the mid-1960s to the early 1980s; yet by 1990 the United States accounted for 43 percent of total exports.[23] Moreover, CBI exports of nontraditional goods to the United States in 1988 were 2.7 times their 1980 value; total U.S. nonpetroleum imports, by contrast, in 1988 were only 2.4 times their 1980 value. Nonpetroleum imports seem appropriate for comparison because among the most rapidly expanding CBI exports were nontraditional agricultural commodities.[24]

Despite that aggregate success, export and real GDP growth has been spread unevenly among the CBI countries since 1983. Costa Rican exports to the United States virtually doubled between 1985 and 1989, rising from $489 million to $967 million. Other countries whose exports to the United States increased more than 50 percent during those years included Guatemala, Grenada, St. Lucia, the Dominican Republic, and Jamaica. By contrast, El Salvador's exports fell from $396 million in 1985 to $243 million in 1989 (in part because of the civil war), and those of the eastern Caribbean islands as a group declined from $297 million to $180 million. Likewise, the oil-exporting countries of the region experienced a decline in export earnings from $2,764 million to $1,601 million over the period.[25]

The extent to which the increase in exports was a consequence of preferential access to the U.S. market under CBERA remains unclear. Before the CBI, some exports from developing countries already enjoyed duty-free treatment in the United States under the GSP (see chapter 6). Consequently, many CBI countries were already receiving duty-free treatment under GSP on a significant volume of exports (table 7-4). To be sure, treatment under CBERA was somewhat more favorable in that GSP rules of origin applied to individual countries, whereas CBERA applied to groups of countries, and GSP preferences were limited to an upper bound of $25 million, whereas CBERA had no such limitation. Even so, the existence of GSP reduced considerably the value of CBERA preferences to the eligible countries, especially because CBERA did not reduce the heavy trade restrictions on

Table 7-4. **Tariff Status and Value of U.S. Imports from CBI Countries, 1986–90ª**
Millions of U.S. dollars

Item	1986	1987	1988	1989	1990
Customs value of all imports from CBI countries	6,064	6,039	6,061	6,637	7,525
Dutiable value of imports from CBI countries	1,916	2,110	1,975	2,101	2,574
Duty-free value of imports	4,148	3,928	4,085	4,536	4,951
CBERA duty-free	671	768	791	906	1,023
GSP duty-free	476	301	353	416	472
Assembly duty-free	612	757	907	1,089	1,153
MFN duty-free	2,340	2,056	1,927	1,854	1,968

Source: USITC, *Operation of the Trade Agreements Program*, Annual Reports, various years.
a. Assembled goods entered duty-free under TSUS 806.30 and 897 until 1989, then under HTS 9802.00.60 and 9802.00.80 plus the special arrangement for apparel exports (807A and then 9802.00.80.50). Total imports under these categories are greater than the values shown because a fraction (about 25 percent) entered with duties. Individual items do not add to totals because of rounding and because of a small "other" category not separately recorded here.

some imports ineligible for GSP, such as textiles and apparel. In 1989, for example, $905.8 million of exports from CBI countries entered the United States under CBERA provisions; another $415.9 million entered under GSP provisions. The first category increased 84 percent from 1985 to 1989, while the latter declined by 22 percent.

Also limiting the value of CBERA was the fact that provisions already permitted the duty-free entry of goods whose parts were manufactured in the United States and assembled abroad (see chapter 6). The existence of these provisions, officially known as HTS Subheadings 9802.00.70 and 9802.00.80, meant that CBERA did not improve the status of many Caribbean countries that could already export assembled goods duty free. In 1985 CBI countries reexported $547 million of commodities under these HTS provisions; by 1989 their assembly exports equaled $1,090 million. Because the assembly exports of other countries, notably Mexico (with its maquiladora industries), also increased rapidly during the same period, it is difficult to believe that the CBI accounted for much of the export increase.

Furthermore, CBERA's promise of duty-free import status simply did not extend to a number of Caribbean manufactured goods.[26] Among the items Congress excluded were sugar, canned tuna, luggage, handbags, flat goods, some leather products, rubber and plastic gloves, footwear, watches or watch parts, and, most important, goods subject to the Multifiber Arrangement.[27] Since the low-wage CBI countries presumably have a strong comparative advantage in labor-intensive

Table 7-5. **Largest U.S. Imports Entering under CBERA, by Commodity, 1990**
Millions of dollars unless otherwise indicated

Commodity	Total imports from CBI countries	Duty-free imports under CBERA	Ratio of duty-free imports to total (percent)
Cane sugar, raw	205.6	94.5	45.9
Nonretail cuts of meat, frozen boneless	85.4	84.3	98.8
Medical instruments and appliances	83.4	55.2	66.1
Fresh nonretail cuts of meat, chilled, boneless	45.6	45.5	99.7
Cigars, cheroots, and cigarillos containing tobacco, valued at more than $0.23 each	36.9	35.4	96.2
Pineapples in crates	40.4	34.2	84.5
Baseballs and softballs	43.2	33.6	77.7
Jewelry with precious or semiprecious stones	54.3	27.1	49.9
Footwear uppers, other than formed, of leather	116.7	25.1	21.6
Cantaloupes, fresh, if imported between September 15 and August 1	23.6	22.5	95.0
Switching electrical apparatus	35.8	21.8	60.8

Source: USITC, *Operation of the Trade Agreements Program, 42nd Report, 1990*, Publication 2403 (July 1991), p. 176.

activities, the ineligibility of these products significantly limited the CBI's potential benefits. Despite this limitation, U.S. apparel imports from CBI countries grew significantly between 1983 and 1989 (table 7-3).[28]

The overlap between CBI preferences, the assembly provisions of U.S. trade law, and the GSP has been considerable. Table 7-4 provides data on the provisions under which manufactured imports entered the United States from CBI countries in the late 1980s. Between 1986 and 1990 total imports from those countries were between $6 and $7 billion a year. Of that total, duty-free imports under CBERA accounted for less than $1 billion each year until 1990, when they first exceeded that level.

Table 7-5 lists the largest commodity imports entering under CBERA privileges in 1990. The leading items remained largely the same from year to year, with the exception of ethyl alcohol. Of course, after the initiative and all its restrictions became law, other U.S. trade policies continued in effect. A team from the USITC visited some eastern Caribbean islands in 1989 and interviewed local exporters, many of whom pointed to domestic problems that discouraged exports.[29] In addition, however, the USITC team noted in its report that

> processed agricultural products do not escape bureaucratic delays. These products must meet USFDA [U.S. Food and Drug Administration] regulations before they are sold in the United States. Many producers lack the financial resources to make their products conform to those regulations. Those who have the resources must be extremely persistent to get the product to market. A relatively sophisticated producer of jellies, tropical fruit syrups, and sauces elaborated at length on the problems it experiences in gaining USFDA approval. The difficulty arises not from actually meeting the regulations, but rather from getting a clear explanation on what is required not only of the product, but of the labeling on the container. Producers describe the process as a bureaucratic nightmare that is characterized by inconsistent, legalistic explanations from U.S. agencies as well as inconsistent advice and poor communications among various U.S. agencies. Some producers state that part of the problem is a result of attracting greater scrutiny by U.S. Government agencies than is given to U.S. producers. The decision to export to the United States may require many months if not years of delays, they said. Such delays require extreme patience on the part of their U.S. buyer, they added, who often abandons the business venture when delays become prolonged.[30]

The report also described the failure of U.S. officials to communicate changes in regulations or the variance of regulations in different parts of the United States. When asked to compare the difficulties of exporting to the European Community and to the United States, respondents reported that it was "much easier" to gain access in Europe.[31]

Evaluations of the CBI have not all been negative. One observer credits the success of nontraditional Caribbean exports (table 7-3) under the initiative "to the extremely active implementation of the policy by U.S. government agencies, not the legislated duty-free provisions. . . . The result was not only wide-spread government support and involvement but unusually positive inter-agency coordination."[32]

Such praise, of course, suggests that bureaucratic difficulties normally present a significant barrier to imports from developing countries.

Other evidence, however, indicates that the CBI, like the GSP (see chapter 6), failed to offset the protection inherent in standard U.S. trade regulations. Edward John Ray provided statistical estimates of the levels of protection faced by CBI countries relative to other developing countries without special preferences. These tests suggested that preferences did not offset the protection inherent in the underlying pattern of U.S. trade policy.[33]

The case of ethanol illustrates how one protectionist pressure can dilute the effects of another and how both in turn can substantially weaken any intended trade liberalization.[34] Ethanol was one of the first Caribbean industries to attract large (relative to the size of the economies involved) new foreign investment from the United States in response to CBI incentives. As noted, the law required 35 percent domestic content (including labor, capital, and local materials) for duty-free entry. Ethyl alcohol imports into the United States were routinely taxed at a 3 percent ad valorem duty plus $0.60 per gallon starting in 1977.[35] Because ethanol distilled in CBI countries would not be subject to such a duty, several companies established refineries in the Caribbean, building factories that would have employed 12,000 people in Jamaica, several thousand in Costa Rica, and 1,200 in the Virgin Islands. Local feedstock was in limited supply, but enough was available to meet the 35 percent criterion.

U.S. companies in the business of distilling ethyl alcohol first brought suit with the Customs Service, arguing that ethanol was ineligible for CBI duty exemption. When the Customs Service ruled that ethanol imports were eligible for duty-free importation under the CBI, these U.S. producers brought a second suit, which was again denied. At that juncture, the interested parties began to lobby Congress to alter the law, arguing that duty-free entry through the Caribbean was really a loophole that permitted surplus wine to enter the United States as a substitute for corn in ethanol, thus threatening U.S. jobs and farm income. They also argued that avoidance of the $0.60 per gallon tax undermined the intent of the exemption for gasohol that had been written into the 1978 energy tax law. Although proponents of the CBI argued vehemently that the magnitude of ethanol imports was insufficient to affect the prospects of U.S. industry, Section 423 of the 1986 Comprehensive Trade Policy Reform Act stated that ethyl alcohol could be regarded as an indigenous product from the country exporting it only if it had been both dehydrated and fermented entirely within that country. Although temporary exemptions were given to factories already existing in the Caribbean, the effect of the act was to prevent any expansion of production in the region (because locally produced feedstock was insufficient), and to leave idle several factories already built. Ethyl alcohol imports from CBI countries were first listed in USITC publications as one of the largest exports under CBERA: in 1987, $28.7 million; in 1988, $17.1 million. Thereafter, their value must have fallen off, because they were no longer listed.

As the case of ethanol indicates, CBI eligibility in no way exempted Caribbean countries from the concerns of U.S. protectionists, nor did it give additional security against the trade actions they often pursued. Between 1987 and 1990 countervailing duty or antidumping orders were issued or in effect for the Dominican Republic (portland cement since May 1963) and Trinidad and Tobago (carbon steel wire and rods from November 1983). A suspension agreement was in effect between the United States and Costa Rica for fresh cut flowers and cement, until the USITC rejected a complaint that Costa Rican cement had been dumped in the U.S. market.[36]

The CBI in the Context of U.S. Trade Policy

The effects of the trade provisions of the CBI have been very mixed. The impact on the earnings of oil and sugar exporters was strongly negative, while the impact on other countries that managed to increase their exports was somewhat positive.

The invasion of Grenada in 1983 was the political impetus for whatever reduction in U.S. protection against imports from developing countries the CBI produced. The fact that GSP preferences and the assembly provisions of U.S. trade law were already in existence substantially lowered CBI's value to Caribbean countries. Moreover, the fact that items such as beef, sugar, and textiles and apparel remained restricted further reduced the initiative's potential impact. The negative effects of U.S. sugar policy offset much of the increase in nontraditional exports, some of which would have occurred without the CBI.

Even from the narrow perspective of trade flows, therefore, the value of CBI preferences is questionable. Moreover, granting these privileges involved a cost for the United States. The designation of imports from Caribbean and Central American countries as eligible for duty-free entry into the U.S. market represented a departure from traditional U.S. trade policy. The set of preferences may not have been consistent with GATT, as the CBI countries did not reciprocate with benefits for the United States. Without reciprocal privileges, it was not a free trade area.[37]

Other questions also plagued the initiative. Because benefits accruing to CBI countries were enjoyed, in part, at the expense of other countries, questions arose about the mechanics of preferential trade policy. For example, the United States inserted additional provisions for Puerto Rico once observers recognized that the CBI reduced the value of Puerto Rico's special access to the U.S. market. With the recent announcement of a free trade agreement between Mexico and the United States, the value of Caribbean preferences has been called into question. If the agreement with Mexico is ratified, Mexico will have preferences equal to, if not greater than, those the CBI countries now enjoy, a prospect that certainly diminishes the value of the CBI for Caribbean countries. Investments located in the Caribbean to take advantage of special access to the U.S. market may again be diverted to Mexico.[38] President Bush's announcement of the Enterprise for the Americas Initiative, with prospective free trade agreements for other Latin American countries, introduces still further questions. How will any concessions granted to Mexico be treated in the negotiation of subsequent agreements? The interaction of preferential U.S. trade policies remains unclear and promises to be a source of continuing controversy.

U.S. Coordination with the Multilaterals in Facilitating Policy Reform and in Debt Policy

In its initial announcements of the CBI, the United States stressed its support for policy reform in CBI countries, urging the shift to a market-oriented system and the removal of protection for domestic industries. Despite those pronouncements of principle, USAID was limited in the extent to which it could work with domestic policymakers, in part because of the political imperative to provide CBI aid whatever the policy framework, and in part because its staff had focused on microeconomic analysis since the 1974 foreign assistance act.[39]

The multilateral institutions, however, were genuinely supporting

policy reforms in the region, so U.S. policy toward them was important. The CBI countries were caught up in the debt difficulties of the
1980s and were thus affected by U.S. policies toward the multilaterals
and debt. Given the number of CBI countries, tracing multilateral and
U.S. support of policy reform in all of them would be impossible.
Instead, this section focuses on macroeconomic policy in Jamaica and
debt relief in Costa Rica in the hope that these two cases provide some
idea of the ways in which U.S. policy toward the multilaterals and
debt functioned.

Both Costa Rica and Jamaica were of major political interest to the
United States. Costa Rica was the one Central American country that
had apparently maintained stable democratic institutions and reasonable growth rates when the rest of the Central American countries
were demonstrating great instability. Real per capita income grew at
more than 3 percent annually in the 1960s and 1970s, and this growth
appeared to benefit all groups in society, as expenditures on education
and social welfare helped produce a distribution of income better than
that of other countries in the region. Jamaica was one of the larger
Caribbean countries. In the 1970s its elected government had chosen
a policy regime of extensive government participation in the economy
and controls over private economic activity. When an election over-
turned that government in 1980 and brought to power Prime Minister
Edward Seaga, an advocate of a return to a market economy, the Reagan administration was eager to support the new government.

As seen from a Washington perspective, therefore, Jamaica had
economic problems originating from policies in the 1970s and was
needful of support from that time. By contrast, Costa Rica was of
political interest because of its history of democratic institutions in an
isthmus otherwise torn apart by conflict.

Jamaica

The Jamaican case is of particular interest for two reasons. First, it
illustrates the relative importance of bilateral and multilateral aid. Second, it shows how the U.S. political commitment to the Caribbean
that espoused policy reform in fact undercut the policies of the multilaterals and achieved the opposite result.

A full analysis of the difficulties confronting the Jamaican economy
in the early 1980s is beyond the scope of this volume.[40] But a few

Table 7-6. **Economic Indicators for Jamaica, 1974–90**

Year	Real GNP growth (annual percent change)	Government finance (percent)			Consumer price index (annual percent change)	Nominal interest rate (percent)	PPP exchange rate[a]
		Expenditures/ GNP	Revenues/ GNP	Deficit/ GNP			
1974	−5.4	28.5	20.8	−7.6	27.0	9.0	3.02
1975	−1.1	31.4	24.2	−7.9	17.8	8.0	2.83
1976	−6.3	35.4	21.5	−14.6	9.3	9.0	2.74
1977	−2.4	38.5	25.6	−15.0	11.2	9.0	2.62
1978	0.7	39.7	23.7	−17.4	33.3	9.0	3.90
1979	−1.9	42.7	27.9	−16.2	29.0	9.0	3.45
1980	−5.8	48.6	27.4	−21.7	27.1	11.0	2.97
1981	2.6	49.6	33.1	−17.4	12.9	11.0	2.88
1982	1.2	43.3	28.2	−16.1	6.4	11.0	2.88
1983	2.2	41.6	27.3	−13.9	11.6	11.0	5.62
1984	−0.9	43.0	27.6	−15.2	27.7	16.0	6.02
1985	−4.6	48.5	27.8	−20.5	25.6	21.0	5.48
1986	1.6	41.1	31.3	−10.9	15.1	21.0	4.88
1987	6.2	35.9	n.a.	n.a.	6.7	21.0	4.74
1988	1.6	n.a.	n.a.	n.a.	8.2	21.0	4.51
1989	4.5	n.a.	n.a.	n.a.	14.3	21.0	4.85
1990	n.a.	n.a.	n.a.	n.a.	21.7	21.0	5.14

Source: IMF, *International Financial Statistics Yearbook*, 1991, Jamaica country pages for Jamaican data. U.S. pages for U.S. GNP deflator.
n.a. Not available.
a. The purchasing price parity, or PPP, exchange rate is the price of a U.S. dollar in Jamaican dollars deflated by the differential in the U.S. and Jamaican inflation rates. The U.S. inflation rate was taken as the GNP deflator; the Jamaican inflation rate is the consumer price index, the only price series given by the IMF.

salient facts serve to set the stage. Table 7-6 documents the rate of change of real GNP and some important policy variables from 1974 to 1990. Jamaica's real GNP was already falling in 1974 and continued falling after worldwide recovery was well underway in 1975. During those years, Prime Minister Michael Manley began increasing real government expenditures and shifting to greater reliance on direct government action as well as to greater control over private economic activity. The economy was deteriorating rapidly, as accelerating inflation and foreign exchange difficulties (resulting both from declining bauxite prices and from overvaluation of the Jamaican dollar) caused major economic dislocations.

By 1980 Jamaica's per capita income was 79 percent of its 1974 level, after six years of declining real incomes. In that environment Seaga managed to defeat Manley at the polls, promising the electorate to reverse previous economic policies and move toward a "free enterprise" system. This election platform appealed greatly to the Reagan administration, which committed itself to providing assistance to insure the success of the new prime minister's policies.

The U.S. commitment took several forms. On the one hand, the United States provided bilateral support for Jamaica through the Caribbean Basin Initiative and increased allocations of foreign aid. On the other hand, the Reagan administration strongly supported IMF and World Bank lending to Jamaica. In the early 1980s, when the Jamaican government was undertaking some microeconomic reforms but still incurring large fiscal deficits, support was thus forthcoming from the multilateral institutions.

The details of World Bank and IMF support for Jamaica appear in tables 7-7 and 7-8. The IMF was active in the early 1980s, providing sizable Extended Fund Facilities in June 1978 and again in April 1981 that lasted until 1984. In that year the Fund followed those facilities with a Standby Agreement. The World Bank, similarly, offered three Structural Adjustment Loans to Jamaica in the early 1980s. Yet, as table 7-6 indicates, the Jamaican government was unable to reduce its expenditures and raise sufficient revenues to achieve the necessary reduction in the fiscal deficit.

Total official aid received by Jamaica appears in table 7-9. The multilateral institutions' support for Jamaica peaked in the early 1980s when Prime Minister Seaga first came to power, but when macroeconomic excesses were continuing. Until the CBI, U.S. official development assistance to Jamaica was less than one-quarter of the total official

Table 7-7. **IMF Loans to Jamaica, 1978–90**
Amounts in millions of SDR

Date of loan	Date of maturity	Type of loan	Outcome	Amount of principal available	Amount remaining at expiration
June 1978	June 1981	EFF[a]	Canceled in June 1979	200	130
June 1979	June 1981	EFF[a]	Canceled in April 1981	260	175
April 1981	April 1984	EFF[a]	Taken to maturity with augmented funding to SDR 478 million	238	75
April 1981	…	CFF[b]	…	37	0
August 1982	…	CFF[b]	…	19	0
June 1984	June 1985	Standby 4	Taken to majority	64	0
June 1984	…	CFF[b]	…	73	0
July 1985	May 1987	Standby 5	Canceled in July 1986	115	74
March 1987	May 1988	Standby 6	Taken to maturity	85	0
March 1987	…	CFF[b]	…	41	0
September 1988	May 1990	Standby 7	Canceled in March 1990	82	41
1989	…	Emergency credit tranche	…	36	0
March 1990	May 1991	Standby 8	Taken to maturity	82	0

Source: IMF, *Annual Report*, all years, 1980–89.
a. Extended fund facility.
b. Compensatory financing facility.

Table 7-8. **World Bank Loans to Jamaica, 1981–89**
Millions of U.S. dollars

Fiscal year	Project lending	Structural adjustment lending
1981	44.5	. . .
1982	56.9	76.5
1983	60.0	60.2
1984	44.6	. . .
1985	9.0	55.0
1986	. . .	. . .
1987	104.0	60.0
1988	26.3	. . .
1989	45.0	. . .

Source: World Bank, *Annual Report*, all years, 1981–89.

Table 7-9. **Net Official Development Assistance Received by Jamaica, 1980–89[a]**
Millions of U.S. dollars

Year	Total	Bilateral All	Bilateral U.S.	Multilateral
1980	131.0	83.5	16.0	32.5
1981	169.7	110.1	63.0	44.6
1982	180.3	152.5	110.0	29.1
1983	180.7	156.2	109.0	24.5
1984	170.3	156.0	99.0	14.3
1985	169.2	158.2	101.0	11.0
1986	177.8	161.1	104.0	16.5
1987	167.7	146.4	89.0	20.7
1988	192.6	173.0	60.0	19.2
1989	262.8	225.9	90.0	35.9

Source: OECD, *Geographical Distribution of Financial Flows to Developing Countries: Disbursements, Commitments, and Economic Indicators* (Paris, 1984, 1987, and 1991).
a. Data for multilaterals include only concessional assistance and not official lending at market interest rates.

development assistance it received and about equal to that provided by the multilateral agencies. Once the CBI was under way, U.S. official development assistance increased sharply, but then fell off again in the late 1980s.

Any analysis of the Jamaican economy must begin by noting that external circumstances were not favorable during the 1970s and 1980s. Oil price increases and falling prices for Jamaica's exports both contributed to worsening terms of trade. Jamaica's sugar exports to the United States were adversely affected by the decreases in U.S. sugar quotas; Jamaica's sugar export earnings declined along with those of other countries.

Despite these unfavorable external conditions, economists reached a consensus conclusion about Jamaica's troubles, neatly captured by DeLisle Worrell:

> Poor economic policies wrecked the Jamaican economy in the 1970s and 1980s. . . . The mistakes began with Mr. Manley's change of course in mid-1974. The precipitate fiscal expansion would have created absorption and adjustment problems for all but the most affluent and underpopulated developing countries. . . .
>
> Mr. Seaga acknowledged the need for corrective fiscal action. But he failed to appreciate the dimensions of the problem. . . . Other major policy initiatives in the 1980s may have prejudiced the chances of real economic growth.[41]

As Worrell's analysis makes clear, Jamaica could not reasonably expect to improve economic performance without undertaking a more concerted set of policy reforms than it did. The IMF spearheaded a first major effort at reform in 1978, but in light of the worldwide recession and the 1980 election, further difficulties—including an unrealistic exchange rate and highly expansionary fiscal and monetary policy—superseded it. Withholding bilateral assistance or multilateral lending may or may not have reversed these economic policies, but would certainly have diminished their excesses and reduced the level of indebtedness facing Jamaica when it finally restored a greater degree of fiscal balance in the late 1980s, since Bank and Fund lending was not on concessional terms.

Officials at the multilaterals recognized the inadequacy of Jamaican fiscal policy reforms and were reluctant to proceed with lending. The multilaterals even canceled several loans. But these officials could not suspend lending easily because of U.S. pressure to support the new administration of Mr. Seaga. Despite U.S. rhetoric supporting policy reform in developing countries, Washington's enthusiasm for a change of government outweighed any balanced assessment of the actual policy mix in Jamaica.[42]

Jamaica was not among the Baker fifteen of heavily indebted countries. Nonetheless, Jamaica's external debt rose to 227 percent of GNP in 1985, with interest payments constituting 12.4 percent of GNP. Debt had increased from $1.74 billion in 1980 to $3.41 billion in 1985.

Almost that entire increase came from official lending. Jamaica owed private creditors $521 million in 1980 and $555 million in 1985, a nominal increase. Yet Jamaica's debt to the multilaterals rose from $441 million in 1980 to $1.02 billion in 1985, while its debt to bilateral creditors rose from $775 million in 1980 to $1.84 billion in 1985.[43] These creditors have thus far taken no concerted action regarding Jamaican debt.[44]

Costa Rica

Costa Rica's economic difficulties became apparent with the worldwide recession of the early 1980s. In the late 1970s government expenditures had been rising sharply, and the fiscal deficit was already more than 5 percent of GNP in 1978. These expenditures continued rising in the early 1980s, while government revenues fell as a consequence of the worldwide recession and other factors. Costa Rica's current account deficit soared, and the government had to borrow from abroad to finance it. By the mid 1980s Costa Rica had begun to undertake policy reforms, supported by structural adjustment lending from the World Bank and by bilateral U.S. assistance.

As noted, Costa Rica was among the countries eligible for benefits under the CBI. Costa Rican exports could thus enter the United States duty-free, with the exception of certain agricultural products (especially sugar and beef), manufactured items not eligible under CBI, and other goods against which antidumping and countervailing actions had been taken.

Table 7-10 gives data on official development assistance received by Costa Rica during the 1980s. U.S. bilateral assistance constituted less than 10 percent of official development assistance received by Costa Rica before the CBI. Thereafter, U.S. bilateral assistance was large (although that increase was offset in part by declining sugar exports to the United States).

In Costa Rica, policy reform efforts effectively restored growth in the mid-1980s, but failed to resolve debt-service difficulties. Although its real GNP and nontraditional exports began to grow rapidly in response to these reforms, Costa Rica was unable to continue servicing its debt. External debt had reached 166 percent of GNP by 1983; in that year, debt service absorbed 59 percent of foreign exchange earnings from the export of goods and services.[45] Two reschedulings of

Table 7-10. **Net Official Development Assistance Received by Costa Rica, 1980–89**[a]
Millions of U.S. dollars

Year	Total	Bilateral		Multilateral
		All	U.S.	
1980	64.8	22.8	3.0	42.1
1981	54.7	29.7	5.0	25.0
1982	80.3	59.4	42.0	20.9
1983	252.1	217.1	200.0	35.0
1984	217.6	185.7	166.0	31.9
1985	280.1	238.9	199.0	41.2
1986	195.7	164.8	128.0	30.8
1987	228.5	208.2	160.0	20.3
1988	186.8	163.7	107.0	23.1
1989	226.0	205.6	144.0	20.3

Source: OECD, *Geographical Distribution of Financial Flows to Developing Countries* (Paris, 1984, 1987, and 1991).
a. Data for multilaterals include only concessional assistance, and not official lending at market interest rates.

debt to commercial banks had taken place by 1986, but they did little more than postpone and capitalize interest payments, while increasing the size of the debt; no new lending was forthcoming from commercial banks. Costa Rica finally suspended debt service in 1986, but continued with its policies of economic reform.

After the suspension, the Costa Rican government offered proposals to settle its debt with commercial banks. Costa Rica, unlike Jamaica, had undertaken some policy reforms, although a number of questions about the country's fiscal balance persisted. Regardless of those reforms, U.S. opposition to IMF lending to countries that were not in agreement with their commercial bank creditors produced a standoff between Costa Rica and its creditors until the late 1980s and delayed debt buy-back arrangements for several months.[46] Although Costa Rica's debt buy-back proposals were initially rejected by the banks, Costa Rica eventually received IMF support despite the fact that commercial bank debt was in arrears. Having strongly opposed such support,[47] the U.S. Treasury Department finally reversed its position. Once the Brady Plan was announced, Costa Rica negotiated the buy-back of 60 percent of its debt, cutting its debt from about $1.8 to $1 billion.[48] The World Bank and the IMF agreed to lend for this deal, consistent with the mandate received under the Brady Plan. As a result, Costa Rica's debt-service obligations fell sharply.[49]

In the case of Costa Rica, CBI trade preferences for manufactured exports marginally facilitated policy reform and resumed growth, although U.S. restrictions on agricultural exports were a negative factor. Likewise, official development assistance received under the CBI undoubtedly increased the resources available to Costa Rica, although U.S. opposition to debt write-downs before the Brady Plan implied that debt-service obligations would absorb a considerable portion of Costa Rica's foreign exchange earnings.

The fact that Costa Rica undertook policy reforms in the mid-1980s provides perhaps the sharpest contrast between the impact of U.S. economic policies in Jamaica and their impact in Costa Rica. In Costa Rica, unlike in Jamaica, official development assistance supported policy reform and was thus consistent with fostering the country's overall growth. The cases of Jamaica and Costa Rica are representative of overall U.S. international economic policy. On the one hand, some U.S. policies were designed to facilitate growth through the CBI. On the other hand, political considerations led to U.S. pressure on the multilaterals to lend and to continue bilateral aid, regardless of the state of economic policies. The conflicting objectives of U.S. policies in these cases generated confusion and even impeded development, not unlike contradictory U.S. approaches to developing countries more generally.

8 ||| U.S. Economic Policies toward Korea

IN CONTRAST TO U.S. EFFORTS to encourage economic growth in the Caribbean during the 1980s, which were largely offset and rendered ineffective by other policies, U.S. international economic policies toward the Republic of Korea in the 1950s and 1960s were spectacularly successful. U.S. aid was essential to Korea's reconstruction in the years following the Korean War and laid a foundation on which rapid growth could take place. Policy dialogues between U.S. and Korean officials contributed substantially to Korea's decision to undertake reforms and to the technical competence of the reform process. Because the United States was not resorting to protectionist trade policies at that time, the U.S. economy was open to Korean exports in the 1960s and 1970s, a fact that was crucial to Korea's success. By the 1980s, however, the situation had changed, as acrimonious trade relations marked the latter part of that decade. The United States even threatened to name Korea an unfair trader under Super 301. Bilateral disputes over Korean macroeconomic policies, especially regarding the won-dollar exchange rate and the bilateral current account balance, were often bitter.

Even as bilateral relations with Korea were becoming acrimonious, U.S. and other officials who advocated policy changes in developing countries were nonetheless touting the Korean example as a showcase of successful development. The Korean experience, like the Marshall Plan, remains a proud achievement of U.S. international economic policy in the postwar period. This chapter sketches the evolution of the U.S. policies toward the Korean economy, from the aid flows of the 1950s to the trade and macroeconomic policy disputes of the 1980s. Korea's development strategy is also a subject of focus, as is the importance of the open U.S. market in that strategy's remarkable success.[1]

U.S. Aid to Korea

From 1910 until the end of World War II, Korea was a Japanese colony. When U.S. forces arrived in 1945, inflation was rampant, and Korea's economy was devastated by the aftermath of colonial rule and by the departure of the Japanese, who managed and owned almost all the large enterprises. Although reconstruction began almost immediately, economic dislocations continued for several years. Quite aside from the effects of war and Japanese colonization, the partition of Korea was itself an economic disaster.

In the years immediately following 1945, the United States directed most of its aid toward emergency relief measures, although it funded some reconstruction activities. Among the accomplishments of the period were a land reform that disposed of Japanese-owned land and produced a very egalitarian distribution of land and an education reform (the Japanese had run the system) that began providing Korea with a highly motivated and well-educated labor force a decade later. Foreign assistance consisted largely of commodities deemed essential, including fertilizers, food, clothing, and medicines. The Republic of Korea, also known as South Korea, was established in 1948.[2] However, even before Korea had reattained the output levels of the late 1930s, the outbreak of the Korean War in June 1950 resulted in still further destruction and dislocation. By the war's end in 1953, Korea was economically devastated. At that time, Korea was estimated to have one of the lowest per capita incomes in Asia, not significantly different from that of India and Pakistan, and the highest density of population on arable land of any country in the world.

Again the most urgent needs were for emergency supplies of essential consumer goods and for imported materials to reconstruct the transport and communications systems. The situation was so extreme that foreign aid[3] exceeded total domestic savings in several years and was equal to more than 10 percent of GNP. Korean exports were minuscule, accounting for 3 to 4 percent of GNP. Aid was therefore crucial to finance imports and capital formation.

In the chaos of the immediate postwar years, the Korean government was naturally unable to raise tax revenues equal to its expenditures. Despite foreign aid, inflation was rampant. At the same time, the limited availability of foreign exchange led to quantitative restrictions on imports. Negotiations between U.S. and Korean officials

Table 8-1. **Foreign Aid to Korea, 1953–60**
Millions of U.S. dollars unless otherwise indicated

Item	1953	1954	1955	1956	1957	1958	1959	1960
U.S. bilateral aid	12	108	206	271	369	314	220	245
Total aid	201	180	237	294	383	321	222	245
Total imports	345	243	342	386	442	378	304	343
Aid as percent of imports	58	74	69	76	87	85	73	71
Imports as percent of GNP[a]	13	7	10	13	12	11	10	13
Current account deficit as percent of GNP	n.a.	6	9	12	11	9	8	9

Source: Anne O. Krueger, *The Developmental Role of the Foreign Sector and Aid,* Studies in the Modernization of the Republic of Korea: 1945–1975 (Harvard University Press, 1979), p. 67.
n.a. Not available.
a. Measured in current prices.

centered on the appropriate level of foreign aid and its utilization.[4] Key issues in the discussions were Korean economic policies on the exchange rate, import controls, the trade regime, and credit rationing.

At first Korea's need for reconstruction investment was so dominant and its lack of resources so evident that U.S. officials offered high levels of aid despite their inability to persuade Korean leaders to undertake economic policies more conducive to efficient resource allocation and growth. The United States was so committed to military objectives in Korea that withholding aid, given Korea's lack of other resources, was not feasible for any extended period of time. U.S. support for the development of the transport network, communications facilities, basic agriculture, and other infrastructure laid the basis for Korea's rapid economic growth in the 1960s.[5]

By 1957 Korea's early reconstruction objectives had been largely attained, but its economic policies had hardly changed. The rate of economic growth to that point had been very moderate in light of Korea's great opportunities for high-yielding reconstruction investments.[6]

Table 8-1 sketches the magnitude and importance of aid receipts in the 1950s. Korea's aid receipts increased every year between 1954 and 1957 and financed an increasing fraction of imports. With reconstruction largely completed and Korean authorities continuing to pursue inward-oriented policies, U.S. officials notified the Koreans in 1957 that they could not expect aid to continue increasing or even to hold steady in the future.

Starting in 1958 Korea began to alter its economic policies. A first step was an IMF-supported stabilization program. That program included provisions for a sizable devaluation of the currency and a sharp reduction in the fiscal deficit. The short-term consequences were a reduction in the growth rate of real GNP—from 3.9 percent in 1959 to 1.9 percent in 1960—and also an abrupt drop in the rate of inflation. Inflation had proceeded at an average annual rate of 36 percent from 1953 to 1957, but from 1957 to 1960 that rate dropped to 3.8 percent.[7]

In 1960 the government of Syngman Rhee was overthrown in a "Student Revolution."[8] The government that replaced it lasted only eighteen months, at which time General Park Chung Hee became president. Starting in 1960, the new regime enacted policy changes that went beyond the stabilization measures of 1958. A hallmark of these reforms was the abandonment of import substitution and greater reliance on an outward-oriented trade strategy for growth.[9]

Three points from the Korean case are important for analyzing the effectiveness of U.S. international economic policies in general. First, officials, primarily from USAID, engaged the Korean government in an ongoing discussion of economic policies during the 1950s, lobbying actively for policy reform. Some Korean officials in charge of economic policy in the 1960s had even worked for the United States in the 1950s. Second, Korea undertook reforms with strong support and often technical assistance from the United States, adopting policies generally consistent with those described in chapter 3 as conducive to economic growth. Third, although analysts disagree as to the precise role of the Korean government in the economy during the subsequent two decades,[10] all agree that very rapid export growth was key to Korea's success.

The U.S. foreign aid program in Korea was thus largely successful in supporting reconstruction and infrastructure investments in the 1950s and policy reform in the late 1950s and early 1960s. Although the multilateral institutions also gave assistance to Korea, their role was clearly secondary to the enormous scale of U.S. aid at that time. Even so, IMF support of stabilization in 1958 and World Bank lending in support of reconstruction did contribute to Korea's recovery and

Table 8-2. **Indicators of Korean Economic Performance, Selected Years, 1960–85**

Year	Real GNP (billions of 1985 won)	Average annual GNP growth (percent)	Real per capita income (thousands of 1985 won)	Exports (millions of dollars)[a]	Imports (millions of dollars)[a]	Exports as percent of GNP
1960	9,594	n.a.	388	33	306	3.4
1965	13,860	6.3	489	175	416	9.0
1970	22,698	9.9	704	882	1,804	14.8
1975	34,527	7.2	979	5,003	6,674	30.5
1980	50,069	7.4	1,313	17,214	21,598	38.3
1985	74,978	8.1	1,837	26,442	26,461	42.4

Source: IMF, *International Financial Statistics Yearbook, 1987*, for 1960 data; *1991* for all other years.
n.a. Not available.
a. Includes goods and nonfactor services.

growth in the 1950s and 1960s, but far less than bilateral U.S. assistance.

Korea's Growth after Policy Reform

Table 8-2 gives data on Korea's economic performance between 1960 and 1985. The country's economic growth was very rapid and sustained, reaching almost 10 percent a year from 1965 to 1970. Koreans even claim to have achieved the highest real growth rate of any country in the world from 1963 to 1973. This expansion resulted in very rapidly rising per capita incomes (table 8-2); by the mid-1980s per capita income was almost five times what it had been a quarter century earlier.[11] In the postwar era Korea went from one of the poorest countries in Asia to one of the richest.

The trade statistics in table 8-2 indicate the importance of exporting and of the tradable sector for economic growth. In 1960 Korea's exports constituted only 3.4 percent of GNP. Between 1960 and 1965, exports of goods and services increased more than fivefold, and export earnings grew at over 40 percent annually over the following decade.[12] Exports were clearly "the engine of growth," as their share of GNP increased to over 40 percent by the mid-1980s. It is in that context that U.S. trade disputes with Korea (discussed below) must be viewed.

The U.S. market was a major destination for Korean exports.[13] In 1960 the United States accounted for only 6.7 percent of Korea's exports, while Japan received 63.4 percent. These percentages were to be expected because 88 percent of Korea's exports at that time were raw materials, and their magnitude—$33 million—was in any event very small. By 1965 the United States received 35 percent of Korea's exports and by 1970 almost 50 percent. Total Korean exports rose $997 million in the 1960s, and the United States accounted for more than half of that increase. To be sure, Korea's exports to the rest of the world also rose dramatically in that decade: those to Europe from $4 million to $91 million, those to Japan (whose share of Korean exports fell dramatically) from $22 million to $283 million, and those to the rest of the world from $5 million to $138 million.[14]

Thus Korea's export drive was broadly based, encompassing all geographic regions of the world. Korea clearly benefited from Europe's growth in that era and from the rapid growth of world trade, which was in part the fruit of U.S. leadership in the GATT on behalf of trade liberalization. Moreover, at that time the U.S. market was so large and the United States so affluent relative to the rest of the world that a very large portion of Korean exports had to target the U.S. market if the export drive was to be successful. The open U.S. market and the absence of trade frictions in the 1960s and early 1970s were important enabling factors in Korean development.

Korean imports also grew very rapidly during the period after 1960; the value of imports remained higher than that of exports throughout the 1960s and 1970s (table 8-2). Exports grew more rapidly than imports largely because export growth started from a much lower base. The value of exports of goods and services finally caught up with the value of imports in 1985. U.S. aid initially supported the change in Korea's policy regime, and the United States later benefited by having a new, prosperous trading partner.

Over the first twenty-five years of Korea's rapid growth, foreign financing was very important in permitting rapid response to profitable new investment opportunities. Table 8-3 indicates that gross capital formation, or investment, rose from 12 percent of GNP in 1960 to more than 35 percent by 1980. The excess of imports over exports initially financed more than two-thirds of all investment, but domestic savings rose rapidly with growth in real incomes. Some foreign financing came from the multilateral institutions, especially the World Bank. By 1965, however, Korea was borrowing from private commercial banks on the international capital market.

As the data on investment indicate, foreign lending was used to finance capital formation. That capital formation, in turn, was highly

Table 8-3.   **Korean Macroeconomic Indicators, Selected Years, 1960–90**

Year	Investment as percent of GNP	Current account balance as percent of GNP	Inflation rate (percent)[a]
1960	12.1	−9.9	11.1
1965	15.7	−7.7	21.1
1970	24.3	−10.1	15.4
1975	27.2	−9.3	25.0
1980	36.2	−8.3	28.6
1985	34.3	0.7	2.4
1986	31.9	6.9	2.8
1987	32.8	9.1	3.0
1988	33.1	9.3	7.1
1989	35.6	3.2	5.6
1990	40.9	−0.6	8.5

Source: IMF, *International Financial Statistics Yearbook,* various years.
a. The rate of increase of the consumer price index for the year indicated.

productive. Thus, when the debt crisis was preventing other developing countries from servicing their debt in the early 1980s, the Koreans were well positioned. Although high world interest rates and the 1979 oil price increase, whose impact on Korea was very negative, made servicing the debt more difficult, Korean authorities were able to finance their outstanding debt during that difficult time. In 1980 Korea's long-term debt was $18.5 billion and its short-term debt was about $10 billion, giving a total of $29.8 billion, including outstanding IMF credit. By 1985 Korea's total debt had increased to $48 billion.[15] Managing the debt and debt-service payments in the early 1980s was a challenge for the government. A public outcry about the magnitude of the debt pressured the authorities to take measures to reduce it, and table 8-3 reveals their success in doing so. In the mid-1980s the current account swung into surplus, and the government was able to begin repaying the debt. By 1989 Korea's outstanding debt had fallen to $33 billion.

One might imagine that creditors, especially the United States, would have held up Korea's achievements with debt repayment as an example to other developing countries. To the contrary, U.S. officials engaged in prolonged and acrimonious negotiations with the Koreans in the late 1980s, insisting that Korea take measures to reduce or eliminate the current account surplus and thus stop reducing its outstanding debt.

U.S. Pressures on Korean Macroeconomic Policies in the Late 1980s

As table 8-3 indicates, until the early 1980s Korean policymakers were less successful in attaining macroeconomic and price stability than in achieving rapid real economic growth. By the early 1980s government officials perceived price stability as an important prerequisite for continuing healthy economic growth, and the inflation rate plummeted.

As inflation collapsed in the mid-1980s, economic growth accelerated in Korea, while world interest rates and the world oil price tumbled. Korea's savings rate rose in response to rapidly rising incomes.[16] Meanwhile, the U.S. dollar began depreciating in world markets in 1985. The Korean won was closely linked to the dollar, so it also depreciated vis-à-vis the yen and other major currencies. All these phenomena contributed to the current account surpluses Korea began experiencing. That surplus rose dramatically after 1985, reaching $14.2 billion in 1988.

During the early 1980s the United States incurred large current account deficits, which were the consequence of U.S. macroeconomic policy, with its combination of tight monetary policy and easy fiscal policy. With the large U.S. fiscal deficit, tight money resulted in high nominal and real interest rates. High interest rates in turn induced a large capital inflow, which prevented fiscal deficits from being even more inflationary than they in fact were. That capital inflow, however, had as its necessary counterpart an appreciated dollar, which in turn induced the necessary current account deficit.

Although the dollar began to depreciate in February 1985, the large current account deficit was a source of major concern to policymakers in Washington. The inflow of imports induced by the highly appreciated dollar placed considerable pressure on a number of domestic manufacturing industries and made it more difficult for traditional manufacturing export industries to compete with their foreign counterparts.

A major part of the U.S. policy response was to insist that countries with current account surpluses adopt measures to reduce those surpluses. Although Japan was the chief target of that policy (its current account surplus reached $87 billion in the late 1980s), Korea was also affected.

From 1985 onward U.S. officials threatened their Korean counterparts with a variety of actions if Korea did not let the nominal exchange rate of the won appreciate and open its market to imports. These negotiations proceeded parallel to others on trade policy disputes. U.S. authorities pointed to Korea's current account surplus in arguing for improved market access. They also pushed for appreciation of the won.

Pressures from the United States were mounting just as the Korean political system was undergoing major changes. Political opposition to U.S. pressures was intense, while popular pressure to reduce the value of Korea's outstanding debt was strong. As Byung-Nak Song has written,

> Economic relations between Korea and the United States since 1986 have increasingly turned on the trade-balance issue. . . . Many Americans believe that Korea's *embarras de richesse* is due chiefly to the maintenance of unfair trade barriers and an undervalued currency. Conversely, many Koreans see the large United States trade deficit as being mainly of America's own making, and feel that the United States is blaming Korea for its own shortcomings. Many Koreans also believe that the United States fails to recognize that Korea is still a developing country with a large foreign debt, and still undergoing rapid and difficult socioeconomic transformation and political democratization. As a result, economic relations between Korea and the United States have become increasingly contentious.[17]

In an effort to avoid both direct confrontation with the United States and the appearance of bowing to U.S. pressures, Korea finally agreed in April 1987 to have the IMF "arbitrate" the exchange rate dispute during Korea's annual consultation with the Fund. An IMF panel urged Korea to accelerate currency appreciation, but it failed to specify how much. It also urged Korea to accelerate its removal of import restrictions, a move that was probably preferable in economic terms to currency appreciation.[18] The USITC described Korea's reaction as follows: "Acceptance of the IMF recommendations was a politically sensitive issue in Korea. Although the Government's decision to consult with the IMF was reportedly prompted in part by the desire to avoid appearing to capitulate to U.S. pressure, the Korean press described the IMF as 'a typical organization in which U.S. influence is absolutely dominant.' Strong criticism was also voiced by Korean exporters. . . U.S. dissatisfaction with the pace of change [in the appreciation of the exchange rate] continued, making currency revaluation one of the most contentious issues between the two countries in 1987."[19]

Over the next two years, appreciation of the won continued, and by the end of 1988 it had nominally appreciated 29 percent against the dollar.[20] In the Omnibus Trade and Competitiveness Act of 1988, Congress required the Treasury Department to issue two reports a year on the trade and exchange rate policies of U.S. trading partners. In its reports on Korea, the Treasury focused largely on obtaining increased market access for banks and insurance companies. In response to other U.S. demands, Korean authorities agreed to refrain from using Article 18 of GATT (which permits import restrictions for development purposes) beginning January 1989 and to phase out all quantitative import restrictions by 1991. In April 1990 the U.S. government released a report acknowledging Korea's exchange rate reforms. A senior Treasury Department official was later quoted as saying that "since the introduction of the new exchange rate system, there is a lack of evidence of continued direct government 'manipulation' of the exchange rate."[21]

By 1990 Korea's trade and current accounts were once again in deficit. In early 1991 the volume of Korean exports stopped increasing. Whether exchange rate policy or other macroeconomic phenomena were responsible for this outcome is not yet clear. On economic grounds, it was clearly in Korea's self-interest to open its markets. Depending on the pace of trade liberalization, some currency appreciation may also have been warranted for macroeconomic balance. Although it is not clear that they would have improved the bilateral trade balance between the United States and Korea, appropriate economic policies along these lines would clearly have benefited Koreans.

Nonetheless, U.S. pressure on Korea with regard to the exchange rate and the current account imbalance was inappropriate in at least five respects. First, while Korean trade liberalization was no doubt beneficial to the Korean economy, it was unlikely to reduce the size of the U.S. current account deficit. As Korea's bilateral surplus with the United States fell, its bilateral deficit with Japan rose, suggesting that there was little net change for Korea and that Japan's surplus with the United States would simply increase as an offset. Second, the United States did not urge import liberalization or exchange rate policy changes on Korea because they would benefit the Korean economy: the United

States explicitly wished to reduce its own current account deficit. Third, import liberalization in Korea (as in other countries) was politically contentious. On net, U.S. bilateral pressures probably increased the resistance of Koreans to trade liberalization, especially when reports conveyed the impression that such opening was beneficial to the United States. Fourth, the United States had consistently championed Korea as a "model" to other heavily indebted developing countries. The U.S. position was that policy reforms and subsequent economic growth would permit those countries to service their debts voluntarily. To insist that Korea should focus on appreciating the won instead of repaying its debt was completely inconsistent with U.S. pronouncements to other countries. One cannot help but wonder why developing country leaders who opposed continued debt servicing did not use the Korean situation to support their positions. Fifth, as the next segment illustrates, U.S. officials were pressing Korea to open its markets at the same time as they were taking trade actions to protect U.S. markets from Korean products.

U.S.-Korea Trade Relations in the 1980s

While the United States was pressuring Korea to alter the won exchange rate and reduce the size of the bilateral current account surplus, a number of trade issues led to difficulties. The problems centered on U.S. attempts to open Korean markets, U.S. restrictions against Korean imports, and the U.S. decision to negotiate a free trade agreement with Canada and Mexico.

U.S. pressure on Korea to open its markets was intense and its bargaining power was considerable, especially after the passage of the 1988 Omnibus Trade Act, which gave U.S. negotiators the ability to threaten Korea with being named an "unfair trader" under Super 301 provisions. The asymmetry of trade flow between the two countries gave the United States additional bargaining leverage. As it was in the early years of Korea's export expansion, the United States remains Korea's largest trading partner: 30 percent of Korea's exports went to the United States in 1990. In sharp contrast to that figure, only 4.3 percent of U.S. exports went to Korea in that year.[22]

Before Korea's presidential campaign ended in December 1987, U.S. pressures on Korea were somewhat muted because of the political sensitivity of the transition.[23] Thereafter, however, bilateral relations became highly acrimonious and remained so for the rest of the 1980s.

Largely in response to U.S. pressures, Korea did substantially liberalize import regulations overall between 1986 and 1990. This liberalization included the removal of quantitative restrictions, the reduction of tariff rates, and the abolition of a surveillance system that had been intended to guard against "harmful" import surges.

In the specific cases discussed below, Korea's response reflected concern about the possibility of being named an unfair trader under Super 301, fear of other U.S. trade instruments that could damage Korean exports, and recognition of unequal bargaining power. Korean newspapers reported U.S. pressures widely, and the public expressed considerable resentment over trade liberalization, which it perceived as something good for Americans, undertaken in response to U.S. pressure.

Among the most contentious issues to arise was Korea's "market diversification" plan, which encouraged more imports from Japan. U.S. negotiators perceived this plan as directly inimical to the interests of U.S. exporters and strongly advocated some limit on its scope and its ultimate elimination.[24] Korea's initial response was to announce a "trade diversification" program that would encourage expenditures in the United States.

The United States also pressed strongly for liberalization of Korean beef imports. Korea banned imports in 1985 on the grounds that there was a domestic surplus. U.S. negotiators proposed that Korea initially permit beef imports for luxury hotels and then gradually expand the level of imports. Korea allowed beef imports for luxury hotels only and compensated domestic beef producers by exempting cattle feed from customs duties. The American Meat Institute, however, filed a Section 301 complaint in February 1988, and in March of that year the United States requested GATT arbitration to settle the beef dispute.[25] In response to a domestic shortage of beef, Korea lifted the import ban in June 1988. By the end of 1988 the United States had exported $37 million of high quality beef to Korea.[26] In April 1989 a GATT panel found that the Korean restrictions were inconsistent with GATT. Bilateral negotiations then produced a settlement under which the United States did not retaliate and Korea pledged to open its beef market fully over the following three years.[27]

The United States also pressured Korea to liberalize its market for cigarettes. Korea initially responded by making cigarette imports legal in 1986, but they were subject to a 100 percent duty. After further pressure, Korea lowered the duty to 70 percent in 1987. The U.S.

Cigarette Exporters Association filed a Section 301 petition in January 1988, and the USITC began an investigation in February 1988. Negotiations regarding wine followed a similar pattern. The Wine Institute and the Association of American Vintners filed a Section 301 petition in April 1988, claiming that Korean practices had caused U.S. wine producers losses of $45 million in the preceding five years. The USTR began an investigation in July of that year, and Korea agreed to open her market fully after a transition period.[28] Similar petitions by the Motion Picture Export Association of America caused Korea to relax restrictions in that market.

Korea was also subject to a Section 301 investigation of her restrictions on the insurance industry. That dispute was settled in 1986 when Korea permitted a specified number of U.S. firms to enter the market for various insurance transactions.[29] Likewise, the United States pushed for relaxation of a law that prohibited foreign direct investment in advertising. In August 1987 the law was changed to permit up to 40 percent equity investment. In 1989 the United States began pressing for an opening of Korea's telecommunications market. The result was the same as in other cases: Korea began liberalizing slowly in response to the pressure, with considerable acrimony.

Ironically, these market-opening measures by Korea, undertaken in response to U.S. pressure, resulted in little gain for U.S. exporters. The largest beneficiary was not the United States but Japan, whose exports to Korea increased rapidly despite the appreciation of the yen against the won.[30]

In 1989 a different sort of trade dispute erupted, with Korea as the complainant. In June of that year Korean dockworkers claimed that U.S. grapefruit (whose import had been liberalized after earlier U.S. pressures) had been grown with the chemical alar. The news sparked a scare in Korea, and sales of U.S. grapefruit fell sharply before the government announced in October that it was a false alarm. In December the U.S. Food and Drug Administration detained Korean pear imports in the United States because they contained a residue of a prohibited pesticide. The Korean government asserted that the U.S. action was in retaliation against the scare in Korea, and acrimony mounted on both sides.[31]

Pressures regarding intellectual property also intensified sharply in 1989. In May the United States placed Korea on the priority watch list of countries whose protection of intellectual property rights was deemed inadequate.[32] In 1990 the USTR finally pronounced that there had been a "dramatic" improvement in the situation, as the Korean government took stronger measures against counterfeit items. Nonetheless, U.S. pressure did not subside as procedures concerning the protection of trade secrets, the protection of pharmaceutical patents, and generic drug testing were subject to discussion in 1990.[33]

Also in 1990 there was a great deal of controversy between the United States and Korea over an "anti-import" program in Korea. The program was designed to induce Korean consumers to refrain from purchasing imported goods. The Korean government claimed that public promotion of the program was a result of consumer group activities, and not a government effort. The United States claimed that the Koreans were not honoring the market-opening obligations they had pledged earlier in the year to avoid being named an unfair trader under Super 301.[34]

From the U.S. perspective, pressures to open foreign markets are arguably preferable to increased protection at home. Despite that observation, the United States gained little economically from the pressure it applied on Korea and soured bilateral relations. Because the Koreans were acutely conscious of U.S. protection with the Multifiber Arrangement, other trade restrictions, and antidumping and countervailing duty findings, they viewed U.S. pressures for market-opening with considerable hostility. They were sophisticated enough to recognize that changing their bilateral trade and current account balances with the United States would not necessarily change the overall U.S. balance and that U.S. officials advocated certain measures without regard to their impact on the Korean economy.

The United States not only aggressively sought to open Korean markets for imports, it also took measures that affected Korean exports. Tables 6-4 and 6-5 list the countervailing duty and antidumping cases against Korea. Chong-Hyun Nam has analyzed the impact of these and other U.S. nontariff barriers on Korean trade. He estimates that, as of 1989, 20 percent of Korean exports to the United States were under some form of restriction, compared to 43 percent in 1985.[35] Korea's commodity exports to the United States subject to restriction increased during the 1980s from $2.4 to $4.1 billion, while its overall exports rose from $5.7 billion to $20.6 billion. Restricted exports might have grown more slowly than total exports in any event, but their share of the total probably fell because U.S. import restrictions prevented more rapid growth.[36]

Table 8-4 provides a breakdown of nontariff barriers on Korean

Table 8-4. **Korean Exports Subject to U.S. Nontariff Barriers, 1984, 1989**
Millions of dollars unless otherwise indicated

Item	1984	1989
Voluntary export restraints		
Textiles	2,166	3,135
Steel	975	652
Antidumping duties[a]	1,106	270
Countervailing duties	249	0
Safeguard duties	0	11
Sections 337 and 232[b]	35	4
Percent of total Korean exports to the United States	44.5	19.7

Source: Chong-Hyun Nam, "Protectionist U.S. Trade Policy and Korean Exports," paper prepared for Second NBER–East Asian Conference on Economics, rev. version, August 1991, p. 20.
 a. Exports subject to both antidumping and countervailing duties were counted in this category. Exports under investigation at the end of the year were included.
 b. Section 337 covers unfair importing practices; Section 232 covers imports restricted under the National Security Clause.

exports to the United States in 1984 and 1989. Voluntary export restraints for textiles and clothing (under the Multifiber Arrangement)
and steel accounted for about two-thirds of exports subject to restriction in 1984 and more than 90 percent in 1989. To some extent, Korea
continued to expand its textile exports in the 1980s by product diversification and quality upgrading.[37] As noted in chapter 6, however,
the estimated cost to Korea of the Multifiber Arrangement was more
than $1 billion in the late 1980s.

Table 8-5 details the number of administered protection cases initiated in the United States against Korean exporters in the 1970s and
1980s. In the 1970s twenty-nine cases were initiated, fourteen of which
had affirmative findings. In 1980 and 1981 alone sixty-three cases were
initiated, with twenty-nine affirmative findings. Antidumping cases
were the most frequent and, along with Section 337 cases, appeared
to have the highest incidence of affirmative findings.

U.S. plaintiffs won affirmative findings in less than half of all cases.
However, Nam noted that there were few negative findings on preliminary investigation: most cases dragged on for several years. Of the
antidumping and countervailing duty cases initiated against Korean
exports between 1980 and 1988, Nam noted that in only eight were
there positive findings, with an average antidumping margin of 18 per-

Table 8-5. **U.S. Administered Protection Cases against Korean Exports, 1970–89**

Time period	Cases[a]											
	Antidumping		Counter-vailing duty		Safeguard		Section 337		Section 232		Total	
	I.	A.	I.	A.	I.	A.	I.	A.	I.	A.	I.	A.
1970–79	6	2	9	4	10	6	4	2	0	0	29	14
1980	0	0	0	0	1	1	0	0	0	0	1	1
1981	1	1	0	0	1	1	0	0	0	0	2	2
1982	2	0	1	1	0	0	0	0	0	0	3	1
1983	5	3	0	0	1	0	3	2	1	0	10	5
1984	3	0	2	1	3	0	0	0	0	0	8	1
1985	5	3	3	1	3	0	0	0	0	0	11	4
1986	4	3	1	1	0	0	4	3	0	0	9	7
1987	0	0	0	0	1	0	5	3	1	0	7	3
1988	2	1	1	0	1	0	1	0	1	0	6	1
1989	3	2	0	0	0	0	3	2	0	0	6	4
1980–89	25	13	8	4	11	2	16	10	3	0	63	29

Source: Nam, "Protectionst U.S. Trade Policy," table 6, p. 23.
a. I. = number of cases initiated; A. = affirmative finding.

cent and an average subsidy margin of 2.6 percent.[38] In five cases alternative arrangements were negotiated, with an average antidumping margin of 3.35 percent and subsidy margin of 1.17 percent.

The industries with the most cases were iron and steel (six antidumping, of which five were affirmative; two countervailing duty, both of which were affirmative; two safeguards, of which one was affirmative; and one Section 232 that was negative), metal products (four antidumping, of which two were affirmative; five countervailing duty, of which two were affirmative; three safeguards, all negative; and two unfair trade practices, of which one was affirmative) and electronic products (four antidumping, with two affirmative findings; four unfair trade practices, of which three were affirmative; and one safeguard that was negative).

Estimating the costs of these restrictions is difficult. G. David Tarr, in one estimate, found that Korea had benefited in the short run from the voluntary restraint agreement on steel, because the higher price for exports more than offset the diminished quantity. However, Nam calculated that Korean steel exports to third countries rose by 10 percent in the first three years after the imposition of the agreement, while steel exports to the United States fell by 38 percent.[39] Although U.S. steel prices were 23 percent higher after the agreement than before, the prices Korea received in third markets declined 6.5 percent over the same period. Taking that price loss into account, Nam's estimates imply a much smaller gain even in the short run.[40]

For the Multifiber Arrangement (MFA), estimating the costs and benefits to Korea is highly complex. Until the late 1980s Korean exports expanded considerably despite the MFA. For Korea the arrangements with the United States and other importers under the MFA were always more restrictive for clothing than for textiles. With the fourth MFA, which went into effect in 1986, import restrictions increased markedly. Whereas the previous arrangement regulated forty-one categories of textiles and apparel commodities, the 1986 version regulated seventy-five.[41] Chungsoo Kim analyzed the MFA and concluded that U.S. restrictions against Korea were greater and increased more rapidly than those against other exporting countries.[42] Kim also found that the categories in which Korea's share was most restricted were those in which the relative price of Korea's exports to the United States increased the most, indicating that exporters, when restricted in volume, tended to raise prices and upgrade the quality of their products.[43] By the late 1980s there was increasing evidence that Korea's comparative advantage in textiles and clothing was in any event diminishing, as real wages in Korea were rising very rapidly. At U.S. insistence, Korea gradually removed import restrictions on textiles and clothing until in 1989 imports were fully liberalized. MFA restrictions thus appear to have benefited Korean exporters, although they may have retarded the shift of resources toward other industries in which Korea was gaining comparative advantage.

For other exports subject to administered protection in the United States, Korea is a small enough exporter to take the price as given. Factoring in all the cases in which investigations took place, Korean exports declined in volume by about 10 percent from the year before the investigation to the year afterward. Korean exporters responded in part by sending their goods to third-country markets, where export volumes increased by 50 percent in the first three years after an investigation. For cases that resulted in a positive finding, Korean exports to the United States fell by 50 percent in the first two years after the initiation of the investigation. Electronics exports appear to have been the most adversely affected.

In addition to the cost of lost export markets and revenue, Korean firms also bear the cost of legal defense in the United States when U.S. competitors use administered protection. These legal costs are difficult to project in advance and vary significantly from case to case. Combined with the possible obligation to pay duties for the duration of any case, the high costs of defending against these actions and their uncertain outcomes no doubt constrain the behavior of Korean exporters in the U.S. market.

One final aspect of trade relations between Korea and the United States demands attention: the impact on Korea of U.S. moves toward free trade in the western hemisphere. Given its heavy dependence on trade for the current standard of living and for growth, Korea has a vital interest in the global multilateral trading system. The U.S. initiatives toward Canada, Mexico, and much of Latin America, therefore, have raised important questions for Koreans and the future of their trade. Yung Chul Park and Jung Ho Yoo summarized these issues well:

> To a small economy like Korea, which depends on trade for growth and development and which has developed strong and extensive economic and security ties with the United States, the FTA [free trade agreement] makes the future trading environment more uncertain and makes it more difficult to develop a consistent trade policy. . . . Although the United States is by far Korea's most important trade partner, the Korean public is highly skeptical about the possibility of establishing an FTA between the two countries. Aside from the usual dependency rhetoric, Korea will find it difficult to accommodate U.S. demands on agriculture and services trade. . . . Furthermore, many in Korea have voiced concern that an FTA with the United States could be perceived as a means of correcting the bilateral current account imbalance.[44]

Mexican access to the U.S. market in a free trade area will raise important questions for U.S. trading relationships with Korea and other East Asian countries. Given the importance to Korea of trade with the United States, the issue assumes great importance for Korea's economic future.

Conclusion

Korea presents in microcosm the dilemmas of U.S. international economic policies toward developing countries. U.S. concerns about Korea were initially based in part on strategic issues and in part on idealism. Bilateral U.S. aid, the fruit of those concerns, effectively permitted Korean reconstruction and supported policy reforms in the late 1950s and 1960s.

Moreover, U.S. policy toward the world trading regime reinforced this bilateral assistance. Rapid trade liberalization and growth in the world economy provided an environment in which Korean efforts at growth could thrive. Because Korea was so poor in natural resources, with its comparative advantage so concentrated in labor-intensive activities, it benefited enormously from the openness of the U.S. market and from the rapid growth of the international economy.

Both directly and indirectly, U.S. international economic policies thus proved highly conducive to Korean economic growth. By the 1980s, however, U.S. policy had become more fragmented, as particular U.S. trade concerns and political pressures from the current account deficit led to frictions with Korea over its exchange rate and import policies, as well as to resentment in Korea over administered protection in the United States. U.S. moves toward bilateral and regional trade policies vis-à-vis Mexico and the western hemisphere cast even further uncertainties over Korea's trading future.

The United States still has an interest in the stability and prosperity of Korea. When weighed against the possible gains for special U.S. interests, the damage to U.S. consumers and to U.S. foreign policy caused by administered protection and the trade frictions it sparks appear very large. When one recognizes that Korea's current account balance has little, if any, direct impact on that of the United States, recent U.S. economic relations with Korea appear little short of tragic. Looking back on the vast reservoir of good will between the two countries after the successes of the 1950s and 1960s, one can only conclude that it is time for a fundamental rethinking of U.S. international economic policies.

9 ||| Time for Reform

ALMOST ANYONE WHO EXAMINES the crosscurrents in U.S. international economic policy toward developing countries will agree that much is wrong. Foreign aid alone has ample room for improvements, quite aside from questions about its coordination with policies regarding the multilaterals, trade, and debt. So many mandates encumber bilateral foreign aid that it is a wonder the programs work as well as they do. Aid officials have little latitude to support genuine policy reform or to withhold support when policies are not conducive to growth.

Even the most enthusiastic supporters of aid on humanitarian grounds are disillusioned, largely because they see aid going to countries where there is little concern for the well-being of the poor, with assistance channeled through an unsympathetic government. Supporters of aid concerned about economic development are disillusioned because allocated aid is so circumscribed that officials have little leeway to support those who are committed to painful but necessary measures.

Trade policies are largely uncoordinated with aid, and the two are often at cross-purposes. The simultaneous sugar quota reductions and aid increases for the CBI countries serve as only one example of offsetting policies, but such instances may be more the rule than the exception. In its debt strategy the United States championed policy reform based on outward-oriented policies and rapid expansion of exports as the way for heavily indebted countries to regain creditworthiness. At the same time, the United States sought to restrict quotas under the Multifiber Arrangement and insisted on self-sufficiency in food as a condition for accepting exports. Restrictive U.S. trade policies thus discredited U.S. policy advice, even casting doubt on the intentions behind the pious pronouncements.

U.S. trade policies themselves were often in internal conflict: U.S. initiatives to assist Caribbean countries reduced the value of Puerto

Rico's special status, and free trade with Mexico threatens to do the same to the Caribbean. Moreover, because the inclusion of other countries in the western hemisphere is possible, developing countries have difficulty determining the value of free trade with the United States and the costs of forgoing it.

To confound matters further, U.S. influence in the multilateral institutions has been less constructive and weaker than might have been hoped. With U.S. policymakers under a tight budget constraint, the United States might have been expected to turn to the multilaterals as a low-cost instrument for policy regarding growth in developing countries. Instead, most U.S. policies toward the multilaterals have been incoherent and reactive, born of neglect and suspicion, and amended only when U.S. officials realized that the World Bank and the IMF were crucial in achieving U.S. objectives. Instead of using the multilaterals as a cost-effective alternative at a time of budgetary stringency, the United States has attempted to use the institutions for its own political ends when domestic responses have not been available.

Most observers could probably agree on all this analysis. Disagreements arise when they try to identify changes that might reduce inconsistencies and improve effectiveness. U.S. foreign policy does have a variety of objectives, and measures that satisfy one constituency (for example, those supporting foreign aid on humanitarian grounds) may displease another (those supporting it on national security grounds). In the final analysis, estimates of trade-offs must be made. But regardless of the precise weights attached to foreign policy, humanitarian, national security, and other considerations, U.S. international economic policy toward the developing countries could accomplish more than it currently does with existing resources.

To facilitate that analysis, this chapter addresses three issues. The first is the appropriate balance in U.S. international economic policy between the use of bilateral and multilateral instruments. The second is how individual policy instruments, taken one at a time, could achieve their objectives more effectively. The third and final issue is perhaps the most difficult of all: determining the appropriate objectives and operative constraints of each policy instrument.

Bilateralism or Multilateralism?

The United States emerged from World War II as the most economically and politically powerful nation in the world. With its productive capacity largely undamaged, the United States then produced almost half the world's GNP and was almost the only country with the resources to respond to worldwide emergencies.

At that time, the United States could have used economic and political muscle to pursue bilateral solutions to its major problems. Greatly to the credit of the architects of postwar policies, the United States largely rejected that approach in favor of a multilateral approach. Even for Europe, U.S. assistance helped establish purely European institutions. Even though U.S. resources dwarfed those of other countries and the multilateral institutions, the United States was generally committed to supporting those institutions. U.S. policy was heavily oriented toward free trade, as the United States exercised leadership in the liberalization of the international economy. U.S. support of the World Bank was so strong that it was criticized as being too much an American institution.

While U.S. international economic policies were by and large admirable during the first quarter-century after World War II,[1] the economic, political, and military preeminence of the United States was clearly a fact of life. U.S. attitudes toward the international organizations and multilateral forums took shape when U.S. power was so great that U.S. leaders could presume to have not only veto power but the ability to push through measures to which other countries gave at best wavering support.

By 1990 the United States was still a major world economic power. But instead of being preeminent or dominant, the United States was more like the first among equals. Yet, somewhere in the transition between the circumstances of the 1950s and those of the 1990s, U.S. attitudes failed to keep pace with the new realities. Or, more accurately, when bilateral responses to international problems were no longer feasible, the United States began to shift away from the multilateral solutions that were advisable on pragmatic grounds.

Instead of recognizing that reaching agreement required greater effort in the new circumstances, U.S. politicians and policymakers became increasingly tempted to use U.S. economic power for narrow, short-run objectives. Decades ago the United States could have used its economic power through a Super 301 to force policy changes in other countries and to achieve shortsighted, parochial objectives. Correctly, in the judgment of most observers, the United States instead opted to support a multilateral system. The far-sighted vision of U.S. policymakers in that era permitted the reemergence of an economically strong Europe and Japan and led to the inevitable "diminished giant" of which Jagdish Bhagwati has spoken.[2]

Ironically, the predominant U.S. reaction to this relative decline has not been to rely more heavily on multilateral forums and strive harder to achieve consensus with other countries. Instead, as frustrations have mounted with the effects of the reduced relative importance of the United States and the increased competition it faces, U.S. policy has tended to rely increasingly on bilateral approaches to multilateral problems. This tendency has been most evident in U.S. policy toward the Uruguay Round, but it has also been manifest in U.S. policies toward debt (the United States announced the Baker and Brady Plans without truly consulting other foreign creditors, to whom much of the debt was owed), toward the World Bank and the IMF, toward regional trading arrangements, and toward protectionist measures in U.S. law.

The world *is* multilateral. On few issues can bilateral approaches achieve even second-best results. But the United States often formulates economic and political policies in disregard of that reality. U.S. policies will continue to be less effective in achieving even short-run objectives until those who make them recognize that reality.

The issue is especially critical for the United States as the countries of the former Soviet Union and Eastern Europe emerge as newly independent entities. If some of those countries manage to achieve reasonable economic growth and to build stable, democratic political systems, the number of medium-sized countries with influence on the world stage will increase greatly. In that event, the need for strengthened international mechanisms of cooperation and control will also increase.

No particular policy change can reorient the United States from a bilateral to a multilateral focus. Recognition of the realities of the international economy is not itself a policy, but a necessary precondition for policy formulation. As long as U.S. policy is implicitly based on erroneous assumptions, it will be less effective in achieving *any* U.S. objectives.

It is hoped that the preceding chapters have provided enough evidence of the consequences of bilateralism to advance recognition of the multilateral realities of the 1990s. But until that recognition is more firmly entrenched in the mind-set of all Americans, many of the difficulties described in earlier chapters are likely to persist.

Improving Policy Effectiveness

With many policies at cross-purposes, a fundamental realignment of the mechanisms for policy coordination within the U.S. government may very well be necessary. U.S. leaders, however, have attempted to reorganize the administration of international economic policies on numerous occasions in the past. As noted in chapter 3, several commissions have reevaluated U.S. foreign aid; other initiatives include attempts to establish an International Economic Policy Council in the White House and to centralize the administration of U.S. trade laws within one federal agency. Despite many recommendations and the manifest need for change, the desired coordination has not been achieved.[3]

For that reason, it would be foolhardy to suggest one coherent set of policy reforms that would stand or fall on the implementation of one particular recommendation for reorganization or institutional change. This section therefore focuses on measures that could improve the functioning of U.S. international economic policies within the existing decisionmaking structure. If adopted alone or in combination, these measures could significantly improve the effectiveness or reduce the detrimental impact of U.S. international economic policies. If, in addition to the adoption of these or similar measures, policy formulation was predicated on the fact of multilateralism, U.S. policy would stand dramatically improved. It is unlikely that more can be accomplished in the absence of a greater consensus on the importance of economic support for developing countries and on the role that various policy instruments should play in that support.

Foreign Aid Policy

In regard to foreign aid, the first question is whether the United States should have a bilateral foreign aid program at all. Given the desirability of an increasingly multilateral approach to international economic problems, the value of a bilateral foreign aid program is questionable. Some observers, who acknowledge that aid could be productive if effectively used, believe the U.S. program should be terminated because they despair of ever avoiding the difficulties caused by the political constraints imposed on aid.[4]

The idea that all aid should be multilateral, however, ignores a number of political and economic realities. The most important is that when no resources are available to serve political objectives in the bilateral aid program, the inevitable temptation is to use U.S. influence within the multilateral organizations to achieve U.S. political objectives. Over time, such use erodes the very great potential effectiveness of these institutions for the multilateral objectives they should address.

On the positive side, there are a number of reasons why bilateral aid should and will inevitably be a tool of foreign economic policy. First and foremost, the United States is perceived throughout the world as a rich country. In some circumstances the successful economic growth of a country is itself in the U.S. interest as a foreign policy concern, quite aside from humanitarian or other motives. In such cases the United States has an interest in providing greater levels of support than the multilateral institutions are likely to offer. This motive was important for the Marshall Plan, for aid to Korea and Turkey in the 1950s and 1960s, and for the Caribbean Basin Initiative in the early 1980s, to name just a few examples.[5] To forgo the use of such a policy instrument would deprive policymakers of a tool that can be highly effective and would thus reduce the overall effectiveness of U.S. foreign policy.

A somewhat less important rationale for bilateral aid is that other industrialized countries have their own foreign aid programs. For a rich country such as the United States to appear unwilling to extend assistance would be politically costly even when there are no immediate uses for aid as a foreign policy tool. Even if aid were shown to be totally ineffective in promoting development, it might prove worthwhile to provide some aid anyway, since citizens and officials in developing countries perceive it to be helpful.[6] At times aid can facilitate bargains on other issues of concern to the United States, as it did with the Camp David peace accord in the late 1970s.

Moreover, despite its many pitfalls and failings, the U.S. foreign aid program has had notable successes, as the Korean and Taiwanese cases demonstrate. The real question is not whether aid is at all effective—it is—but how aid might serve more effectively U.S. foreign policy goals and the development objectives shared by people in the United States and the recipient countries alike.

In the United States, there is also a constituency that supports the humanitarian extension of aid—for health, nutrition, and other social services for the very poor. While the United States can and should support multilateral efforts to improve the well-being of the poor, it would be foolish not to have a bilateral program when other major OECD donors do. Most Americans appear to support foreign aid for humanitarian purposes, but are disillusioned with its achievements to date.[7]

These arguments do not imply that bilateral aid should be independent of the support provided by the multilateral institutions. But a premise here is that the U.S. bilateral aid program will continue, as will U.S. support for the multilaterals, and that an enhanced appreciation of the potential role of the World Bank and the regional development banks could improve the effectiveness of both bilateral and multilateral assistance.

A crucial question, therefore, is how to improve the effectiveness of bilateral aid in the context of the existing division of responsibilities for trade, aid, debt, and other issues within the U.S. government. A starting point is to recognize that aid programs have very different purposes. Aid can support policy reform. Aid can also provide support for health, education, population control, agricultural research and extension, and other "basic human needs." Finally, aid can be little more than a gift from the United States in return for a political favor, as in Egypt.

When the U.S. aid program is demonstrably ineffective, the cause is often the conflicting objectives of aid's different constituencies, which hamstring USAID by writing legislation that governs the agency's every action to achieve the relevant political compromise. Conflicting directives have left USAID with a very unclear mandate as to its objectives. Those who support aid on humanitarian grounds are disappointed when aid programs seem to serve national security objectives, promote policy reform in middle-income countries, or support governments whose economic policies are inimical to growth. Others who support aid on national security grounds meanwhile question its effectiveness in support of development. The development community itself has voiced concern over aid's inability to support well-designed policy reforms and has criticized aid programs aimed at "reaching the poor" that arguably fail to promote development as effectively as other initiatives.

Assistance that supports policy reform is fundamentally different from aid that is to help the poor improve their earnings in the context of an unsatisfactory overall policy framework.[8] Moreover, aid based on a political quid pro quo (for military bases, Israeli-Egyptian friendship, etc.) represents a third category of assistance.

Although the three types of aid obviously overlap, they also differ in fundamental ways. When aid is politically mandated, as in the Egyptian case, U.S. aid officials will not realistically be able to use leverage to bring about policy reform. Although they may be able to target and condition some assistance,[9] much will be in the form of general resources. Aid for basic human needs or for reforms in particular ministries can be largely in the form of projects. By contrast, aid in support of policy reform is by definition more general and must be extended only after macroeconomic analysis of the overall reform package. Given these considerations, one obvious way to increase aid's effectiveness is to recognize these three separate missions and to forge a political consensus on the objectives of aid.

Commissions have suggested a number of reorganizations of USAID over the years, and none has solved underlying problems. Their failure may in large part be due to their focus on organization, rather than on the fundamental objectives of the agency. What follows is one suggestion for achieving a consensus on the mission of aid. The proposal addresses organization more because it affects the issue of mission than because organizational change is assumed to be able to improve aid effectiveness.

One possible way to reconcile the different objectives foisted upon USAID would be to restructure the agency. Instead of having one foreign aid agency with numerous political compromises in its budget, the U.S. government could create three bureaus within the agency, each of which would have a separate function. Politicians could then retain control over the allocation of aid between competing purposes, but each bureau would be accountable for administering its particular responsibilities.[10]

The "reform bureau" would oversee U.S. bilateral aid and coordination with the multilaterals when policy reform is deemed to warrant conditional support. Assistance to Eastern Europe, the former Soviet Union, and to most of Latin America would be the responsibility of this bureau. Its officials would assess each reform package's chances for success and would recommend assistance for those they find appropriate.

The "basic human needs bureau" would oversee technical assistance and the administration of educational, health, and other programs aimed directly at improving the well-being of the poor. Whereas the reform bureau would focus on the design and execution of policy reform packages, analyzing macroeconomic phenomena across a range of countries, the basic human needs bureau would be more intimately involved, on an ongoing basis, with poor countries.[11]

The third bureau, which for lack of a better term might be called the "international assistance bureau," would be much less substantively involved in development. Its charge would be to insure that "political aid" is used in support of development (through the other two bureaus) as much as possible and to administer the orderly transfer of other funds politically mandated.

Many arguments support such an approach. The basic human needs bureau could maintain a presence in countries where the United States recognized the need for sizable bilateral aid, providing support and technical assistance for programs designed to improve agricultural productivity, health, education, and nutrition. Such support can improve the economic well-being of citizens in developing countries, even in the absence of a policy framework that permits rapid economic growth. For countries with many poor people and a largely unresponsive government, such as Haiti and the Dominican Republic at different junctures in recent decades, aid projects could and should be designed to reach target groups in ways that do not appear to give political support to the regime in power.[12] By focusing assistance in these cases, the United States would avoid a major criticism of aid while simultaneously providing a basis for more rapid growth when economic policies are finally altered. The objectives of aid in such countries would be clear, and a single bureau would be accountable for performance.

The competence of a reform bureau, by contrast, would be in supporting the design and implementation of an overall policy framework conducive to growth. It would insure that aid was used only in support of economic policy reforms with good chances of improving the overall growth prospects of the country. This bureau could simply support programs already prepared and endorsed in cooperation with the World Bank and the IMF, or it could itself have the competence to engage in policy dialogues and evaluate the merits of reform programs.

Finally, the international assistance bureau would oversee aid destined for countries on political grounds above and beyond that which could be extended in project and policy reform support.[13] It could assess the general economic progress of the countries within its purview and insure accountability for aid funds received. Countries that have received U.S. support of this kind during the past decade include

Egypt, Jordan, and Argentina, during its transition to democracy. Were the United States to make a political decision to provide fungible resources to the republics of the former Soviet Union before economic policy reforms were completely in place, the international assistance bureau could administer whatever nonproject aid was so designated.

Of course, all three motives may be present in U.S. support for any particular country. But when the U.S. foreign policy interest is to support development, and the recipient's policies are appropriate for achieving it, assistance would be largely through the basic human needs and policy reform bureaus. In principle there is no reason why two bureaus could not both finance programs in the same country, although basic human needs would probably go to low-income countries on softer terms than support for policy reform.

If the political compromises now exhibited in the detailed allocations of aid bills could instead occur at the stage of resource allocation among the three bureaus, the hamstringing of U.S. foreign assistance programs would be substantially reduced. The concerns of supporters of humanitarian aid, which may be appropriate for the basic human needs bureau, would not restrict the activities of the policy reform bureau. Nor would those genuinely concerned with economic development view support of particular governments on political grounds as a betrayal of aid's mission.

To be sure, division of the foreign assistance program into three bureaus would require politicians to reach a compromise in the budgetary process. Should each aid constituency fail to support the other two, the budget might include even less bilateral assistance. The current political process, however, reduces the effectiveness of aid so much that the chance of improvement might be worth the risk. Other mechanisms for achieving a clear-cut definition of function might be preferable. The point is that consensus on the purposes of aid would "untie" the hands of aid officials; a clear mandate could do much to improve aid effectiveness.

Trade Policy

Any consideration of U.S. trade policy must recognize overall U.S. international objectives—policy toward developing countries is only one piece of the picture. Fortunately, however, there is little conflict between the policy considerations regarding trade with the developing countries and those regarding trade in general. Two questions of trade policy are crucial and closely related: the extent to which trade policies are or are seen to be a component of foreign policy instead of the province of special interests, and the extent to which trading arrangements are bilateral or multilateral.

From the U.S. perspective, a system of open, multilateral trade is desirable on foreign policy and economic grounds, and it is also in the interest of developing countries. The argument that trade protection reduces the efficiency of resource allocation has been a central tenet of economics for many years.[14] Although one can find theoretical exceptions to the economic case for free trade, examination of actual protectionist practices suggests that there is little relationship between these practices and measures that might be in the public interest.[15]

If trade policy is handled on a case-by-case basis, difficulties begin to multiply. For example, concern over U.S. sugar producers prompts restrictive measures that affect the international sugar market. Those restrictions then cause economic difficulties for countries in which the United States has a special interest. To offset the difficulties, the United States offers a preferential trade arrangement. But that arrangement overlaps with the Generalized System of Preferences, the Multifiber Arrangement, U.S. agricultural programs, and other narrow domestic economic concerns. As a result the preferential arrangement directly accomplishes little, except the provision of additional aid, which could have been extended in any event. This scenario is not far removed from the U.S. experience with the Caribbean Basin Initiative, which prompted objections from Puerto Rico and from U.S. ethanol producers, and which will be of diminished value to its beneficiaries if the free trade agreement with Mexico is approved.

The contradictions of the Caribbean Basin Initiative are illustrative of the more general point that ad hoc preferences for one group are bound to give rise to pressures for ad hoc measures supporting other groups, which will in turn reduce the value of the first set of preferences, all the while with diminishing economic efficiency and a gradual abandonment of leadership for open, multilateral trade. Similarly, most U.S. attempts at bilateral protectionist arrangements have foundered on considerations concerning third countries.[16]

Previous chapters have stressed the importance of a stable, expanding international economy for the developing countries. But the future economic growth of OECD countries, including the United States, also depends on the healthy expansion of the international economy.

Such expansion is consistent only with an open, multilateral trade system. Both because the United States is the world's largest trading nation and as such must assume a leadership role and because the growth of the international economy is in the narrow self-interest of the United States, improving the world's trading system should be a major objective of U.S. foreign and economic policy.

U.S. support of open, multilateral trade is not inconsistent with the negotiation of free trade agreements. However, to make them consistent, the United States must grant membership in a free trade area unconditionally to other countries willing to agree to the specified conditions, and the area must be a "super-GATT" that imposes on members all the obligations of GATT plus additional market-opening measures. The U.S.-Canada Agreement seems to pass this test, and the negotiated North American Free Trade Agreement (NAFTA) that includes Mexico may also qualify. The Caribbean Basin Initiative, as unilateral tariff reduction, did not meet that requirement, nor would extension of NAFTA through bilateral U.S. bargaining with individual Latin American countries. If the NAFTA is to create a genuine free trade area that imposes even stronger obligations than GATT, Japan or any other country willing to accept the conditions of membership should be permitted to join.

As long as U.S. trade policy is organized in ways that are responsive to the concerns of particular producer groups, it will be very difficult to avoid protectionist pressures. Nonetheless, the United States could take some measures that would mitigate, at least in part, the excesses of current arrangements.

First and foremost, fully supporting the GATT, including a greatly strengthened secretariat, is perhaps the single most important step the United States could take in the interest of the international economic system. Failure to complete the Uruguay Round has already been detrimental to world trade. As this manuscript went to press, the outcome was still uncertain. A final agreement that phases out the Multifiber Arrangement and liberalizes trade in individual services and agriculture would greatly benefit the entire world, including the developing countries.

Second, any analysis of the impact of U.S. trade policies on developing countries must note the negative effects of the Multifiber Arrangement and of agricultural policies toward sugar, beef, cotton, peanuts, and tobacco. These policies, of course, also adversely affect U.S. consumers and the efficiency of resource allocation in the United

States. The Uruguay Round may yet permit the orchestration of a reduction of Japanese, European, and U.S. trade barriers to agriculture, textiles, and apparel in ways that would benefit many developing countries and reduce the negative impact on producers in any one of the developed countries alone. Even if a mutual reduction is not possible, however, unilateral abandonment by the United States of the Multifiber Arrangement and of agricultural protection, especially on sugar and beef, would greatly benefit developing countries as a group.[17]

Third, the United States could also recast the antidumping and countervailing duty provisions of U.S. trade law to make them more consistent with their original purposes and to reduce their value as instruments of harassment for U.S. producers threatened by foreign competition. As applied, these administrative trade laws are protectionist in effect. The objective here is not to eliminate antidumping or countervailing duty provisions, but to ensure that they operate only in cases of foreign subsidies and predatory pricing that are also illegal practices for U.S. companies.

A number of measures would mitigate the undesirable protectionist effects of existing laws and procedures. At present, U.S. producers that file suit under antidumping or countervailing duty provisions stand only to gain. Even if the ultimate finding is negative, uncertainty during the investigation deters imports in the meantime. Imposing penalties on those that file suits with negative findings would discourage domestic producers from filing repeated suits essentially to harass foreign competitors. The weakest possible penalty would require the plaintiff to reimburse the foreign exporter for legal costs and the costs of developing the required evidence.

A stronger deterrent to filing that would still allow U.S. producers to combat significant dumping or subsidies would permit foreign firms to offer a defense that their practices were no different from those of their U.S. competitors. If Ford sued to demonstrate that Hondas were being dumped in the U.S. market, proof that Ford's pricing practices were the same as those of Honda would constitute a satisfactory defense. With this as an acceptable defense, the U.S. plaintiff and the foreign defendant would at least share the burden of generating records! Another possible reform would require the magnitude of the alleged dumping or foreign subsidy to be significant. Raising the minimum requirements would reduce the harassment potential of suits. U.S. plaintiffs, for example, could be required to show at least a 5 percent reduction in import price due to the alleged unfair practices.

The United States could also alter the procedures for computing dumping margins to provide a fairer test. Such a move would clearly reduce the chances of an affirmative finding when no dumping in the economic sense has in fact occurred.[18]

Each of these changes, taken separately, could improve the functioning of U.S. trade policies, both from the perspective of efficient resource allocation and consumer welfare in the United States and from the viewpoint of the developing countries. As long as U.S. trade policy remains subject to the great influence of individual producer groups, however, it is likely to reflect disproportionately the importance of their parochial concerns.

Policy toward the Multilateral Institutions

Simply by adopting policies and attitudes consistent with U.S. interests and the development objectives of developing countries, the United States could vastly improve its leadership within the multilateral institutions. By seeking to play a more effective and more constructive role on the governing boards of the multilaterals, U.S. representatives would reduce the extent to which those bodies are the objects of criticism and hostility.

As a first step toward these goals, top leaders in the U.S. administration could simply become more supportive and aware of the potential roles of those institutions. The Bush administration does appear somewhat more alert to the presence and potential of the multilaterals than did the Reagan administration, which itself changed course for the better during the mid-1980s, but more could be done.

One problem confronting the multilaterals is that the U.S. officials responsible for relations with them are also charged with a multiplicity of other functions. For obvious reasons, the multilaterals themselves are not well placed to argue their case and plead for change. To increase the effectiveness of U.S. policy toward the multilaterals, the White House could establish a unit, possibly within the Treasury Department, that would serve as a source of understanding about these institutions and would advocate multilateral approaches to issues within the U.S. government. This unit would not make decisions, but it could at least represent the U.S. interest in maintaining the effectiveness of the multilaterals, playing an "advocacy" role in discussions of international economic policy. How much difference such a unit might make is hard to assess, but with continuing responsibility for information about the multilaterals it could at a minimum raise questions about their role that in the past do not appear to have been addressed.

Policy toward Developing Country Debt

Much of U.S. international economic policy toward the debt of middle-income countries has been appropriate. The United States has insisted that debt be handled on a case-by-case basis, and policy reform has been an essential part of the process.

The IMF and World Bank, however, had to take the lead in organizing assistance for heavily indebted countries. The absence of U.S. support for the multilaterals before the debt crisis left the IMF less well positioned than it might have been in the early stages of the Mexican crisis and its aftermath. The Treasury Department was slow to recognize the need for IMF leadership and to support Structural Adjustment Lending by the World Bank. Had the U.S. government included a unit monitoring World Bank and IMF activities, there might have been less misunderstanding of the role of the multilaterals and thus less delay in the early stages of the crisis.

This same too-little, too-late response characterized U.S. policy at successive stages of the debt crisis. The Baker Plan was put forward in September 1985, long after most analysts had concluded that the preceding strategy was insufficient. And the Brady Plan was introduced long after it was evident that growth was not resuming in the heavily indebted countries.

Had these major policy shifts been made earlier, they would have been more instrumental in achieving the desired objectives. More aggressive alternative policies might also have been consistent with U.S. interests in developing countries, even though the chosen U.S. approach could be justified as making good economic sense.[19] Japan, for example, established an organization that in effect bought the debt of developing countries from Japanese commercial banks. Having done so, Japan was able to grapple with policy toward the developing countries independent of policies toward Japanese financial institutions. Likewise, the United States and other industrialized countries did finally forgive some of the official debt of the very low-income countries. Such a policy, carried out earlier, might have generated greater benefits, and at no greater cost.

Many criticisms of U.S. conduct during the debt crisis reflect the fact that the U.S. concern with the development prospects of heavily indebted countries was insufficiently reflected in policymaking fora. At a fundamental level, change will occur only when the U.S. government recognizes and reaches consensus on the role and importance of developing countries in its formulation of international economic policy.

Changing U.S. Understanding of the Developing Countries and Their Role

Underlying all the preceding discussions of U.S. policy at cross-purposes has been the sheer absence of any consensus understanding of U.S. interests in developing countries. In a sense, the only long-run solution is to reach such a consensus on U.S. interests and to improve understanding of how international economic policies can and do affect them. Without such an awareness, policy performance is unlikely to be significantly improved. If this volume contributes to the understanding of present policy conflicts and their effects, it will have achieved its purpose.

In the aftermath of the dissolution of the Soviet Union, there is widespread discussion about future U.S. foreign policy interests and about how to reach a new national consensus. Among others, questions regarding the desirability of aid to the former Soviet Union and trade relations with Eastern Europe have surfaced. On each of these questions and on the broader issue of long-run U.S. interests, a great deal of confusion has been evident, especially with respect to the objectives of U.S. policy and the capability of various policy instruments to achieve them.

If the new national consensus that emerges is to be realistic, it will have to come to grips with the fact that a very large fraction of the earth's population lives in developing countries, many of which will, one way or another, achieve economic growth and improve living standards for their poor over the next several decades. The more successful among them will become more important trading partners of the United States. As the larger developing countries achieve economic growth, they will become important politically and economically for the world as a whole. U.S. policies during their periods of growth will affect future relations. Countries that do not achieve satisfactory growth will also be important, perhaps as sources of political instability and certainly as eligible recipients of foreign aid and support from the multilateral organizations.

The United States cannot afford to ignore any of the developing countries, neither the more successful nor the less so, and it is probably in the world's interest that more countries fall into the former group than the latter. Any vision of U.S. foreign policy interests after the dissolution of the Soviet Union must therefore incorporate the developing countries. No consensus has yet emerged, and U.S. policy toward developing countries will not become much more effective until one does. Should that eventual consensus ignore the developing countries, it will not serve U.S. interests well over the longer run.

Notes

Chapter One

1. International Trade Administration, *United States Sugar Policy: An Analysis* (U.S. Department of Commerce, April 1988), p. 75.

2. See chapter 2 for a discussion of the growth strategies of developing countries.

3. See World Bank, *World Development Report, 1985* (Oxford University Press, 1985), for an account.

4. For analysis of the political economy of U.S. trade policy, see Robert E. Baldwin, *The Political Economy of U.S. Import Policy* (MIT Press, 1985); and I. M. Destler, *American Trade Politics: System under Stress* (Washington: Institute for International Economics, 1986); for the political context of exchange rate policy, see I. M. Destler and C. Randall Henning, *Dollar Politics: Exchange Rate Policymaking in the United States* (Washington: Institute for International Economics, 1989); and on foreign aid, see Samuel P. Huntington, "Foreign Aid for What and for Whom," *Foreign Policy*, no. 1 (Winter 1970), pp. 161–89.

Chapter Two

1. See chapter 5 for further discussion of the IBRD (World Bank) and IMF and chapter 6 for a discussion of GATT.

2. There were several reasons for the centrality of the industrialized countries. First, the United States, Canada, Europe, Japan, Australia, and New Zealand accounted for a very large part of the world economy. Second, those who designed the postwar international economic order were strongly influenced by the Great Depression and wanted to establish institutions that would avoid the conditions (among the developed countries) they believed had caused it. Finally, many developing countries did not attain independence until the late 1940s or afterward. They therefore had little independent voice in the planning sessions.

3. For an account, see J. Bradford De Long and Barry Eichengreen, "The Marshall Plan: History's Most Successful Structural Adjustment Program,"

paper presented at the Conference on Post–World War II European Reconstruction, Centre for Economic Performance and Landeszentralbank Hamburg, September 5–7, 1991.

4. In addition to the Marshall Plan, the U.S. government spent funds under Point Four and in relief operations. However, the Marshall Plan constituted the bulk of the assistance. Marshall Plan assistance to Europe amounted to $13.2 billion between 1948 and 1951. In 1991 prices, that $13.2 billion equals approximately $55.4 billion, or an average annual $13.8 billion. Marshall Plan statistics are from De Long and Eichengreen, "The Marshall Plan," p. 11; to convert the sum to 1991 dollars, the U.S. 1991 finished producer price index and the annual average of the 1948–51 producer price index were used. Those data are from *Economic Report of the President, February 1992*, table B-61, p. 367.

5. Among the U.S. conditions for extending aid under the Marshall Plan was that the European countries form a European Payments Union, which would permit multilateral (as opposed to bilateral) clearing among the European countries. This initiative was the first step toward trade liberalization among the developed countries. The United States also provided strong impetus and support for the first rounds of tariff negotiations under GATT. While these negotiations were among the developed countries, developing countries benefited from the reduced trade barriers that resulted.

6. See chapters 3 and 6 for elaboration of this point.

7. The heritage of the United States, especially the history of the American revolution, also contributed to strong U.S. sympathies with the newly independent nations.

8. Moreover, even in those developing countries politically independent before World War II, many citizens regarded the world economy as a system of "economic colonialism," because poverty, specialization in primary commodity production, and vulnerability to international economic fluctuations had long characterized their economies.

9. See chapter 3 for an elaboration of this argument.

10. See chapter 5 for a discussion of U.S. policy toward the multilateral institutions.

11. Simultaneously, most leaders of developing countries perceived their economic interests to be—at least in many regards—in conflict with those of the industrialized countries. Even worse, they embraced economic policies often inimical to development, as discussed in chapter 3.

12. Less developed countries, or LDCs, was the term used to cover the entire group during the 1960s. Originally, they had been referred to as "underdeveloped countries." Subsequently, the term "LDCs" lost favor and was replaced by "developing countries."

13. Article 18 permits developing countries to use quantitative restrictions to support their economic development objectives and also when they encounter balance-of-payments difficulties. See Kenneth W. Dam, *The GATT*,

Law and International Economic Organization (University of Chicago Press, 1970), p. 21.

14. See chapter 3 for an analysis of restrictive trade policies in developing countries and their impact on LDC growth. Until the 1980s it was not fully understood how damaging highly restrictive trade regimes were to developing countries' growth.

15. The estimate is for 1960. As late as 1977, 37 percent of U.S. exports were destined for developing countries. Data are from World Bank, *World Development Report, 1979* (Oxford University Press, 1979), table 11.

16. Dollar prices of internationally traded goods rose very slowly between 1950 and 1970, so that most of the recorded increase in the value of world exports reflects expanding volume. Between 1970 and 1980, however, the increase in the dollar value of exports reflects worldwide inflation and higher oil prices, as well as continuing real growth of world exports of about 5 percent annually.

17. Jeffrey G. Williamson, *Inequality, Poverty, and History* (Cambridge, Mass.: Basil Blackwell, 1991), pp. 1–2.

18. After the severe worldwide recession of 1974–75, some observers credited the willingness of developing countries to maintain their expenditure programs and to finance their increased current account deficits (for oil imports) as a major stimulus to world economic activity. At the time, their policies were regarded as healthy. See, for example, William Branson, "Trends in United States International Trade and Investment since World War II," in Martin Feldstein, ed., *The American Economy in Transition* (University of Chicago Press, 1980), pp. 184–257.

19. As real wages rise in industrialized countries, pressure on labor-intensive industries inevitably increases. In the United States, for example, employment in the clothing and footwear industries had fallen from 12.2 percent of total employment in 1929 to 10.2 percent in 1950 and 8.2 percent in 1960 *before* imports of those commodities from developing countries began increasing rapidly. See Anne O. Krueger, "LDC Manufacturing Production and Implications for OECD Comparative Advantage," in Irving Leveson and Jimmy W. Wheeler, eds., *Western Economies in Transition: Structural Change and Adjustment Policies in Industrial Countries* (Boulder, Colo.: Westview Press, 1980), pp. 219–50. Thus industrialized countries would encounter difficulties in labor-intensive industries even in the absence of increased import competition. But when import shares are increasing, the natural tendency is to blame all the domestic industry's difficulties on foreign competition.

20. See Joseph Kraft, *The Mexican Rescue* (New York: Group of Thirty, 1984), for an account of the emergence of the Mexican debt issue and the roles of the U.S. Treasury, the chairman of the Board of Governors of the Federal Reserve System, the IMF, the World Bank, and the private commercial banks in the Mexican debt crisis.

21. Brazil is the case with perhaps the most visible contradictions. The United States has given Brazil much policy advice to increase exports to earn foreign exchange for debt servicing. Simultaneously, the United States has penalized Brazil under its countervailing duty trade laws, negotiated a voluntary export restraint governing Brazilian steel exports to the United States, and repeatedly objected, through the U.S. Trade Representative, to Brazilian export subsidies. Brazil was also named an "unfair trader" under the "Super 301" provisions of the 1988 Trade Expansion Act because of some of its import restrictions. See U.S. International Trade Commission, *Operation of the Trade Agreements Program, 41st Report, 1989*, Publication 2317 (September 1990).

Chapter Three

1. Usually, development performance is evaluated by considering a country's overall rate of economic growth, as measured by the rate of growth of real GDP per capita. While the correlation between changes in welfare and the growth of real GDP per capita is not perfect, there is a strong presumption that over reasonable periods of time (say, a decade or more), significant increases in welfare cannot be attained without increases in real output and income. In most developing countries, income distribution has changed little over time, implying that the benefits of growth are rather evenly spread over the population. While this statement deserves qualifications, for purposes of analysis I take higher growth rates to be synonymous with greater increases in welfare. For more careful discussions, see Amartya K. Sen, *The Standard of Living* (Cambridge University Press, 1987), on welfare and per capita income; and Hollis B. Chenery and others, *Redistribution with Growth: Policies to Improve Income Distribution in Developing Countries in the Context of Economic Growth* (Oxford University Press, 1974), on income distribution. For a recent analysis of the relationship between income inequality and growth, see Torsten Persson and Guido Tabellini, "Is Inequality Harmful for Growth? Theory and Evidence," National Bureau of Economic Research Working Paper 3599 (Cambridge, January 1991).

2. In some cases the support of a particular regime or other objectives were undoubtedly paramount, but even then foreign aid was expected to improve economic performance.

3. For in-depth discussions of early development thought, see Heinz W. Arndt, *Economic Development: The History of an Idea* (University of Chicago Press, 1987); and Francis X. Sutton, "Development Ideology: Its Emergence and Decline," *Daedalus*, vol. 118 (Winter 1989), pp. 35–58.

4. Robert H. Bates, *Markets and States in Tropical Africa* (University of California Press, 1981), p. 11.

5. Gottfried Haberler, in his Cairo Lectures, articulated this viewpoint in 1959. The lectures are reprinted in Gottfried Haberler, *International Trade and Economic Development* (San Francisco: International Center for Eco-

nomic Growth, 1988). See also Harry G. Johnson, *Economic Policies toward Less Developed Countries* (Brookings, 1967).

6. Raul Prebisch, for example, stated that "when I started my life as a young economist and professor during the 1920s, I was a firm believer in neoclassical theories. However, the first great crisis of capitalism—the world Depression—prompted in me serious doubts regarding these beliefs. It was the beginning of a long period of heresies." See Prebisch, "Five Stages in My Thinking on Development," in Gerald M. Meier and Dudley Seers, eds., *Pioneers in Development* (Oxford University Press, 1984), p. 175. For a clear statement of these influences, see Economic Commission for Latin America and the Caribbean, *Economic Survey of Latin America, 1949: Growth, Disequilibrium, and Disparities. Interpretation of the Process of Economic Development* (Santiago: United Nations, 1951).

7. Theodore W. Schultz was the first to challenge this view in his *Transforming Traditional Agriculture* (Yale University Press, 1964). He successfully argued that poor peasants were exceptionally responsive to any opportunities offered to them, and that incentives in agriculture mattered greatly. The extent to which the older, "supply inelastic" view was entrenched is implicit in reviews of Schultz's book at the time. See, for example, T. Balogh's review in *Economic Journal*, vol. 74 (March 1964), pp. 996–99.

8. For a discussion of the infant industry argument in theory and in application and the reasons that there were so few successful infant industries, see Anne O. Krueger, "Economists' Changing Perceptions of Government," *Weltwirtschaftliches Archiv*, Band 126, Heft 3 (1990), pp. 417–31.

9. P. N. Rosenstein-Rodan, "Problems of Industrialisation of Eastern and South-Eastern Europe," *Economic Journal*, vol. 53 (June–September, 1943), pp. 202–11, as quoted in Deepak Lal, *The Limits of International Cooperation*, Occasional Paper 83 (London: Institute of Economic Affairs, 1990), p. 17.

10. Jan Tinbergen, "Development Cooperation as a Learning Process," in Meier and Seers, *Pioneers*, p. 326.

11. For an early and explicit statement of this view, see Government of India Planning Commission, *Second Five Year Plan* (New Delhi, 1956).

12. Economists use the term "immiserizing" for a situation in which output growth might result in falling consumption. This could happen only if a country's terms of trade deteriorated so much that import levels had to decline. It is a remote theoretical possibility but in the 1950s the possibility received a great deal of attention.

13. Reluctance to alter nominal exchange rates was almost universal in the 1950s and 1960s. The British effort to avoid devaluation of the pound is perhaps the most dramatic case in point.

14. In most developing countries, the suppression of producer prices was accompanied by other measures designed to increase agricultural output. Many were productive, such as the provision of irrigation, roads, and inputs. However, the value of these measures in general was far less than the cost of the

price suppression, creating a strong disincentive for production of traditional agricultural commodities. In many countries, the result was a decline in the production and export earnings of traditional commodities. Perhaps the most famous case is Ghana, whose production and exports of cocoa fell by half over the two and a half decades following independence in 1957. See J. Dirck Stryker, "Ghana," in Anne O. Krueger, Maurice Schiff, and Alberto Valdés, eds., *The Political Economy of Agricultural Pricing Policy*, vol. 3: *Africa and the Mediterranean* (Johns Hopkins University Press, 1991), pp. 79–121. On the more general point that resources expended on efforts to provide inputs to agriculture were far smaller than the resources extracted from agriculture through the suppression of producer prices, see Maurice Schiff and Alberto Valdés, eds., *The Political Economy of Agricultural Pricing Policy*, vol. 4: *Synthesis of Economic Consequences* (Johns Hopkins University Press, 1992).

15. For a full discussion, see World Bank, *World Development Report, 1986* (Oxford University Press, 1986).

16. David Morawetz, *Twenty-Five Years of Economic Development, 1950 to 1975* (International Bank for Reconstruction and Development, 1977).

17. These numbers are simple averages of individual country data. If they were weighted by population, for example, India and China would figure much more prominently in the Asian per capita income (and growth) estimates, reducing them significantly.

18. Crude death rates fell in all regions of the world, and life expectancies increased. Even in sub-Saharan Africa, the region with the least satisfactory economic performance, crude death rates fell from 29.3 per thousand in 1950 to 22.8 per thousand in 1965, 17.7 per thousand in 1980, and an estimated 15.3 per thousand in 1985–90. See Nancy Birdsall, "Thoughts on Good Health and Good Government," *Daedalus*, vol. 118 (Winter 1989), pp. 89–117. Data are from table 2, p. 92.

19. See World Bank, *World Development Report, 1983* (Oxford University Press, 1983).

20. Eventually, "foreign exchange shortage" was recognized as a major bottleneck to growth, and the now-famous "two-gap" model explained how foreign aid could promote growth by alleviating shortages of both savings and foreign exchange. The model was developed by economists then working at the U.S. Agency for International Development. See Hollis B. Chenery and Alan M. Strout, "Foreign Assistance and Economic Development," *American Economic Review*, vol. 56 (September 1966), pp. 679–733.

21. Import-substituting goods were sold on the domestic market at prices much higher than those obtainable through exporting. Consequently, firms producing import substitutes rarely invested in export capacity (although they occasionally exported out of excess capacity). Instead, it was more profitable to undertake additional new product lines that would also receive high levels of protection.

22. See, for example, Jagdish N. Bhagwati and T. N. Srinivasan, *Foreign*

Trade Regimes and Economic Development, vol. 6: *India* (Columbia University Press, 1975).

23. By contrast, in Korea, Taiwan, Hong Kong, and Singapore—all oil importers—the domestic price of petroleum and petroleum-derivative products changed quickly to reflect the price increase. The 1973–75 period was a period of difficult adjustment, but growth resumed and rates reached even higher than those of the late 1960s.

24. The nominal value of the developing countries' long-term debt increased from U.S. $195 billion in 1976 to U.S. $437 billion in 1980. World Bank, *World Debt Tables, 1989–90* (Washington, 1989). Export unit values of developing countries rose over the same period from 49.6 to 100.0. Using this deflator, the real value of developing countries' debt at 1976 prices was U.S. $216 billion in 1980, or only 11 percent more than in 1976. Average annual borrowing, however, had been $55 billion, which represented more than 20 percent of nominal debt each year.

25. For a recent discussion and bibliography, see the articles in George Psacharopoulos, ed., *Economics of Education: Research and Studies* (Oxford University Press, 1987).

26. See Government of India, Ministry of Food and Agriculture and Ministry of Community Development and Cooperation, *Report on India's Food Crisis and Steps to Meet It* (New York: Ford Foundation, 1959), a key report that documented the difficulties of that country.

27. See Anne O. Krueger, Constantine Michalopoulos, and Vernon Ruttan, *Aid and Development* (Johns Hopkins University Press, 1989).

28. See chapter 4 for a discussion of U.S. program aid.

29. Carlos Diaz-Alejandro noted the frequent success of IMF programs in improving the balance of payments and attributed it largely to short-term flows. Before devaluation, individuals shifted funds abroad as much as possible, and after devaluation, they repatriated them. See Carlos F. Diaz-Alejandro, "Southern Cone Stabilization Plans," in William R. Cline and Sidney Weintraub, eds., *Economic Stabilization in Developing Countries* (Brookings, 1981), pp. 119–41.

30. IMF, *International Financial Statistics Yearbook*, vol. 41 (Washington, 1988), p. 167.

31. World Bank, *World Development Report, 1985* (Oxford University Press, 1985), p. 138.

32. See the studies in Robert H. Bates and Anne O. Krueger, *Political and Economic Interactions in Economic Policy Reform: Evidence from Eight Countries* (Oxford: Basil Blackwell, 1993), for analysis of the political economy of policy reform in several countries.

33. Difficulties similar to those in Turkey occurred in Ghana in 1984. Care must be taken, of course, to see that the exchange rate is realistic, and that assistance is not simply used to avoid necessary adjustment of the exchange rate.

34. It is important, however, that additional assistance be associated with increases in the rate of investment, not with appreciation of the real exchange rate. For an elaboration of this danger, see Ronald I. McKinnon, *The Order of Economic Liberalization: Financial Control in the Transition to a Market Economy* (Johns Hopkins University Press, 1991).

35. Johnson, *Economic Policies*, pp. 55–56.

Chapter Four

1. Even for India, foreign aid was equal to 2–3 percent of GNP in the 1950s, when the domestic savings rate was less than 10 percent. Vasant Sukhatme, "Assistance to India," in Anne O. Krueger, Constantine Michalopoulos, and Vernon W. Ruttan, eds., *Aid and Development* (Johns Hopkins University Press, 1989), p. 205.

2. Foreign aid programs have provided a great deal of technical assistance. In some instances, that assistance has been a component of aid projects. In others, it has consisted of financing the training of technical workers, compensating U.S. experts for work in the recipient country, supporting research efforts (as with the high-yielding varieties of grain developed in the "Green Revolution"), and funding other technical support programs directly. Foreign aid is necessarily measured by the amount spent on it; many observers believe that the technical assistance component of aid has contributed disproportionately to economic development.

3. Historically there have been two broad groups of aid supporters. As Harry Johnson has written: "In the case of the United States, broad humanitarianism and the moral obligation of the rich to assist the poor have been inextricably intermingled with the belief in rapid economic development as a potent strengthener of resistance to domestic communist influences and generosity in development assistance as an effective means of commanding the political and military support—or at least neutrality—of the less developed nations." Harry C. Johnson, *Economic Policies toward Less Developed Countries* (Brookings, 1967), p. 2.

4. For a discussion, see Vernon W. Ruttan, "Solving the Foreign Aid Vision Thing," *Challenge*, vol. 34 (May–June 1991), pp. 41–46.

5. See chapter 5 for analysis of the U.S. role in the multilateral institutions, which also include the regional development banks.

6. The members of the Development Assistance Committee are the seventeen member countries that are aid donors. The nondonors are Greece, Iceland, Luxembourg, Portugal, Spain, and Turkey. See Development Assistance Committee, *Development Cooperation in the 1990s* (Paris: OECD, 1989).

7. Data are estimates taken from *Presentation of the Task Force on Foreign Assistance to the House Foreign Affairs Committee*, 101 Cong. 1 sess. (February 1989). Known as the Hamilton Report, it derived its name from the task force's chairman, Congressman Lee Hamilton.

8. In 1988, the latest year for which data are available, the OECD donor

countries as a group provided official development assistance (ODA) equal to 0.36 percent of their GNP. Norway's percentage contribution was largest, at 1.10 percent of GNP, while the programs of the other Scandinavian countries and the Netherlands were about 0.9 percent of GNP. At the other end of the spectrum, Ireland's aid program constituted a smaller share of GNP (0.2 percent) than that of any other OECD donor, but the United States was second lowest with 0.21 percent of GNP. Data are from Development Assistance Committee, *Development Cooperation in the 1990s*, pp. 266–67. At one point in the 1960s, the donor group, through the Development Assistance Committee of the OECD, made a formal statement of intent to commit 1 percent of GNP to development assistance. The goal has never been realized, as only the Scandinavian countries and the Netherlands came close to this objective.

9. In the late 1970s yet another reorganization was attempted. A body called the International Development Cooperation Administration (IDCA) was established within the State Department, charged with the mission of overseeing foreign aid and ensuring its coordination with other U.S. international economic programs toward recipient countries. IDCA never filled the functions that its proponents had hoped it would.

10. The World Bank and IMF have, in recent years, established resident representative offices in many member countries. Those offices, however, have small staffs and serve primarily as a base for headquarters staff when they are working temporarily in the country. USAID's missions have been larger than those of most donor countries because of both the size and the style of the U.S. program.

11. In several countries it is widely believed that many currently successful entrepreneurs learned the business when employed on USAID-financed projects and working with or being supervised by U.S. technicians. For a discussion of many particulars of development assistance, see Vasant Sukhatme, "Assistance to India," pp. 203–25, Anne O. Krueger and Vernon W. Ruttan, "Assistance to Korea," pp. 226–49, Krueger and Ruttan, "Assistance to Turkey," pp. 250–68, and J. Dirck Stryker and Hasan A. Tuluy, "Assistance to Ghana and the Ivory Coast," pp. 269–302, all in Krueger, Michalopoulos, and Ruttan, *Aid and Development*.

12. See David C. Cole and Princeton N. Lyman, *Korean Development: The Interplay of Politics and Economics* (Harvard University Press, 1971).

13. For a discussion of these interactions, see Keith Jay and Constantine Michalopoulos, "Interaction between Donors and Recipients," in Krueger, Michalopoulos, and Ruttan, *Aid and Development*, pp. 89–108.

14. Project financing has almost always been limited to the foreign exchange component, in both U.S. aid policy and that of other donor countries and the multilateral institutions. That arrangement has had some unfortunate implications, as (a) it has provided an incentive for governments to plan projects with a high import content; (b) it has therefore provided an incentive for the use of capital-intensive techniques; and (c) it has precluded the financing

of the maintenance of existing projects with aid, even when maintenance would have generated a very high return.

15. See, for example, Anne O. Krueger, *Foreign Trade Regimes and Economic Development*, vol. 1: *Turkey* (Columbia University Press, 1974), for an account of Turkish policies in the mid-1950s, which were ill-advised and clearly unsustainable. Yet top Turkish officials persisted in those policies until they ran out of foreign exchange in 1958, having disregarded the evidence of economic dislocation and the warnings of USAID officials until a crisis forced action.

16. L. Ronald Scheman, ed., *Alliance for Progress: A Retrospective* (Praeger, 1988).

17. There is a genuine issue here, long recognized by the development community. When a donor provides assistance for a particular project, that aid frees resources and allows the recipient to undertake another project. So long as the donor finances a project that the recipient would have undertaken in any event, the resources thereby freed for other purposes are, in an important sense, the "true" effect of aid.

A recent study of aid to Indonesia suggests, however, that more aid may be allocated to its intended purposes than economists have sometimes believed. See Howard Pack and Janet Rothenberg Pack, "Is Foreign Aid Fungible? The Case of Indonesia," *Economic Journal*, vol. 100 (March 1990), pp. 188–94.

18. The IDA was formed under World Bank auspices. By the late 1950s it was evident that very poor countries could not borrow from the World Bank on commercial terms and that they needed concessional assistance, which the IDA was to provide. It is financed by contributions from the major donor countries, with a replenishment every third year. Those contributions are then extended to countries with sufficiently low per capita incomes in support of their development efforts. See chapter 5 for further discussion.

19. There have been many consortia, and that mechanism for coordinating assistance is still in wide use. Each consortium is chaired by a representative of a major donor, be it the World Bank, the United States, or another country with strong interests in the recipient country.

20. See John White, *Pledged to Development: A Study of International Consortia and the Strategy of Aid* (London: Overseas Development Institute, 1967), for a description and analysis of the functioning of consortia in the 1960s.

21. See Cole and Lyman, *Korean Development*, for a detailed account of U.S. policy discussions with Korean authorities.

22. See table 4-3 for estimates of U.S. aid in constant dollars. Interpreting constant dollar estimates is difficult for a number of reasons. First, the year aid is allocated is not often the year it is spent, so there are ambiguities as to which year price deflators should be applied. Second, many estimates of aid (including those in tables 4-1 and 4-2) are for multiyear periods, which again creates difficulties for the use of constant dollar deflators. Finally, there are

important unresolved problems regarding exchange rate fluctuations: the real value of one dollar of aid to the recipient country varies with the purchasing power and with the real exchange rate of the U.S. dollar.

23. Whereas U.S. aid officials exercised great influence in many recipient countries, they had significant difficulty discussing economic policies with Israel and Egypt, because U.S. assistance was a political commitment that officials were virtually obliged to approve regardless of Israeli and Egyptian policies.

24. See chapter 7 for a discussion of the Caribbean Basin Initiative and the role of foreign aid in it.

25. Food aid increased somewhat in the mid-1980s in response to famine in Africa. Measured in volume of shipments, food aid has diminished even more than these data suggest, as the price of the transferred commodities has increased relative to the price level. Hamilton Report, p. 9.

26. There are countries, such as France and Australia, whose foreign aid consists entirely of grants.

27. As chapter 5 details, the World Bank lends to middle-income countries at interest rates close to those prevailing in private international financial markets, but with longer maturities. For low-income countries, the World Bank provides credits, which are highly concessional and have even longer maturities.

28. The countries declared eligible for write-off included Ghana, Kenya, Madagascar, Malawi, Mozambique, Senegal, Tanzania, and Uganda. In total, those countries owed more than $400 million in official debt to the United States. "Debt Forgiveness Tops $400 Million," *Africa News*, vol. 35 (September 23, 1991), pp. 6–7.

29. The U.S. Export-Import (Ex-Im) Bank has also written off some of its loans to very poor countries, in concert with other OECD members. When Ex-Im loans are written off, the loan becomes equivalent to unrestricted program aid. Since Ex-Im financing to date has largely operated without regard to the use of funds, grants may finance projects far removed from those intended by supporters of economic development. In Africa, for example, a loan that financed the personal transportation of one ruler was eventually written off.

30. Data for U.S. share of bilateral aid are from USAID, *Development and the National Interest: U.S. Economic Assistance into the 21st Century* (Washington, 1989), p. 24.

31. Ibid., pp. 148–49.

32. World Bank, *World Development Report, 1991* (Oxford University Press, 1991), table 20.

33. The Asian Development Bank, the African Development Bank, and the Inter-American Development Bank all carry out regional lending programs similar to the global program of the World Bank. See chapter 5 for further discussion.

34. The most visible critic of aid has been P. T. Bauer. See, for example,

"Foreign Aid: Issues and Implications," in P. T. Bauer, *Reality and Rhetoric: Studies in the Economics of Development* (Harvard University Press, 1984), pp. 38–62. See also Melvyn Krauss, *Development without Aid: Growth, Poverty, and Government* (McGraw-Hill, 1983).

35. The literature is far too vast to provide a complete bibliography. Some recent works with more bibliographic references may prove helpful. In the early 1980s a number of donor governments formed an intergovernmental task force that commissioned a study of aid effectiveness. The findings appeared in Robert Cassen and associates, *Does Aid Work?* (Oxford: Clarendon Press, 1986). See also Krueger, Michalopoulos, and Ruttan, *Aid and Development*. For earlier analyses, see Ian M. D. Little and J. M. Clifford, *International Aid* (London: Allen and Unwin, 1965) and the collection of essays in Jagdish Bhagwati and Richard S. Eckaus, eds., *Foreign Aid: Selected Readings* (Harmondsworth, Middlesex: Penguin Books, 1970). For a recent assessment by the U.S. government, see USAID, *Development and the National Interest*.

36. See the discussion in chapter 8.

37. Shirley W. Y. Kuo, *The Taiwan Economy in Transition* (Boulder, Colo.: Westview Press, 1983), p. 14.

38. For further analysis of project aid in Korea, see Krueger and Ruttan, "Korea."

39. U.S. officials also arranged for consultants to analyze various aspects of economic policy in Korea, Taiwan, and many other recipient countries. For an account of the dialogue during the 1950s in Korea, see Cole and Lyman, *Korean Development*.

40. The Turkish policy reform of the 1980s included major changes in the trade and payments regime and greatly reduced government control of economic activity. The reforms successfully reoriented trade policy and liberalized many aspects of the economy, but failed to achieve macroeconomic equilibrium. Nonetheless, exports grew rapidly during the 1980s, and growth rates surpassed even those of the boom years of the 1960s. See Anne O. Krueger and Okan H. Aktan, *Swimming against the Tide: Turkish Trade Reform in the 1980s* (San Francisco: ICS Press, 1992).

41. See Paul Collier, "Aid and Economic Performance in Tanzania," in Uma Lele and Ijaz Nabi, eds., *Transitions in Development: The Role of Aid and Commercial Flows* (San Francisco: ICS Press, 1991), pp. 151–71.

42. However, a few questions do arise with regard to individual project evaluation. For example, if aid projects provide higher wages to local workers, thereby attracting some of the most skilled, part of the project's success may be at the cost of other activities. Those employed on individual projects, however, may gain experience and skills they then apply in ongoing economic activities, so the net impact is very difficult to gauge.

43. Development Assistance Committee (DAC), *Twenty Five Years of Development Co-operation: A Review* (Paris: OECD, 1985), pp. 255–56.

44. This theme is prominent in the 1991 *World Development Report* of

the World Bank. Life expectancies and literacy rates have clearly risen significantly in most developing countries since the 1940s. Certainly rapid and sustained economic development is not possible without significant increases in the educational attainments of the population.

45. For a full discussion, see Vernon W. Ruttan, "Assistance to Expand Agricultural Production," in Krueger, Michalopoulos, and Ruttan, *Aid and Development*, pp. 140–69.

46. In this sense, "social" implies that the bundle of goods and services available to society would be larger were resources allocated to export crops in place of food crops.

47. Even with project aid, issues can arise concerning corrupt local administrations and the manner in which funds are expended, as they did in Korea in the 1950s. See Cole and Lyman, *Korean Development*, for a discussion. In addition, national leaders often have "pet projects" that may not be fully consistent with development objectives; in some cases, aid officials have had to judge the political costs and benefits of supporting such projects.

48. Congress eventually inserted a proviso in foreign assistance appropriations directing aid officials to certify that aid to Egypt was spent for developmental purposes. No more than 13 percent could be in the form of cash grants unless "Egypt will undertake significant economic reforms which are additional to those which were undertaken in previous fiscal years." See *1989 Congressional Quarterly Almanac*, p. 782.

49. For a fuller discussion, see Jay and Michalopoulos, "Interactions."

50. For further discussion, see the papers in Williamson, *IMF Conditionality*, and Manuel Guitian, "Fund Conditionality: Evolution of Principles and Practices," Pamphlet Series 38 (Washington: IMF, 1981).

51. For an interesting discussion of why OECD governments failed to persuade the Sri Lankan government to reduce its ambitious program for Mahaweli development to realistic dimensions, see Brian Levy, "Foreign Aid in the Making of Economic Policy in Sri Lanka, 1977–1983," Williams College Research Memorandum Series RM-106 (March 1987).

52. Developing countries as a group have spent an estimated 5 to 6 percent of GNP on their militaries in the past two decades. IMF, *IMF Survey* (Washington, June 24, 1991), p. 203.

53. Data from Development Assistance Committee, *Development Cooperation* (Paris: OECD), various issues. See also Catrinus J. Jepma, *The Tying of Aid* (Paris: OECD Development Centre, 1991). Jepma estimates that for 1985–87, 26 percent of U.S. aid was totally untied cash, compared with an average of 33.4 percent among OECD donors as a whole.

54. On this account, Japan's tied aid would presumably be less costly to recipients than that of Denmark, because the range of goods in which Japan is competitive exceeds that of Denmark. In 1985–86 Japan tied 59 percent of its bilateral aid, while Denmark only tied 38 percent. OECD, *Development Cooperation, Annual Report, 1987* (Paris, 1987).

55. Tied aid can give considerable monopoly power to a domestic pro-

ducer, who is aware that the potential buyer cannot search in foreign markets for alternative sources of supply.

56. Lester Pearson and others, *Partners in Development. Report of the Commission on International Development* (Praeger, 1969). See also the estimates in Jepma, *Tying of Aid*.

57. See Jagdish N. Bhagwati, "The Tying of Aid," in Bhagwati and Eckaus, eds., *Foreign Aid*, pp. 235–93.

58. See OECD, *The Export Credit Financing Systems in OECD Member Countries*, 4th ed. (Paris, 1990). Chapter 25 contains the Arrangement on Guidelines for Officially Supported Export Credits.

59. The United States generally relied less on subsidized export credits than other countries. In 1979 the U.S. Export-Import Bank financed an estimated 5 percent of U.S. exports, compared with 39 percent for the United Kingdom and 38 percent for Japan. See G. Edward Schuh, *The United States and the Developing Countries: An Economic Perspective* (National Planning Association, 1986), pp. 76–77.

60. The question of how to value aid is highlighted by some of the provisions regarding Israel in the 1988 bill. For example, Israel was named a "major non-NATO ally," which permitted procurement from the Pentagon at favorable terms. Also, Congress decided that in pricing weapons sales to Israel, the government would apply marginal cost pricing, thus excluding the costs of research, development, and overhead. Israel also requested but failed to obtain authorization to lease some big-ticket weapons previously available by purchase only. See *1988 Congressional Quarterly Almanac*, p. 689.

61. OPIC is an institution established to provide insurance against political risk for U.S. citizens investing directly in foreign countries.

62. *1988 Congressional Quarterly Almanac*, pp. 682–85.

63. Ibid., p. 694.

64. USAID, *Development and the National Interest*, p. 114.

65. The first was known as the Pearson Commission. Its report is Lester Pearson and others, *Partners in Development*. The second was the Brandt Commission. Its report is *North-South, A Program For Survival: Report of the Independent Commission on International Development Issues* (MIT Press, 1980).

66. *Presentation of the Task Force* (Hamilton Report), p. 28.

67. See Larry Q. Nowels and Ellen C. Collier, "Foreign Policy Budget: Priorities for the 102nd Congress," IB91014 (Congressional Research Service, May 22, 1992), p. 13.

68. U.S. International Trade Commission (USITC), *Operation of the Trade Agreements Program, 39th Report, 1987*, Publication 2095 (July 1988), p. 5-12 and table 5-2.

69. Victoria Griffith, "Brazilian Oranges Caught in Squeeze," *Financial Times*, March 12, 1991, p. 32.

70. USITC, *Operation of the Trade Agreements Program, 41st Report, 1989*, Publication 2317 (September 1990), pp. 81, 122–26, 139.

71. See chapter 6 for a further discussion of administered protection and its effect on potential exporters.

72. James Bovard, *The Fair Trade Fraud* (St. Martin's Press, 1991), p. 3.

73. Economists have long recognized that resources are fungible and that money provided for development assistance may be diverted to other uses if the recipient responds to aid by reducing its own development expenditures. However, the same argument applies in reverse: providing military assistance to a country may permit its government to spend more resources for development.

Since there is no way in practice to establish what would otherwise have been done, development assistance is usually defined by the donor's stated purpose, not by incremental expenditures in the recipient country that are difficult to trace.

74. Alasdair I. MacBean and P. N. Snowden, *International Institutions in Trade and Finance* (London: Allen and Unwin, 1981), p. 220.

75. These "mixed credits" usually finance the machinery and equipment imports of a development project with a combination of foreign aid and export credits. Many governments use their export and mixed credits to secure additional orders for domestic exporters. See the discussion of tied aid in chapter 4.

76. The practice of requiring recipients to spend resources in the home country is known as "aid tying." Tied aid is clearly worth less to the recipient than fully fungible aid. See Bhagwati, "Tying of Aid," for further discussion.

Chapter Five

1. All the multilateral lending institutions are owned by their members, which hold shares in them. When the World Bank was founded, the U.S. shares of its capital subscription and voting were 41.40 and 37.12 percent respectively; those of the United Kingdom were 16.95 and 15.37 percent respectively. The initial U.S. capital subscription and voting shares in the IMF were 36.80 and 32.85 percent, while those of the United Kingdom were 17.40 and 15.61 percent. See International Bank for Reconstruction and Development, *First Annual Meeting of Governors, Washington, D.C., September 27– October 3, 1946, Proceedings and Related Documents* (Washington, 1946), p. 147, and IMF, *First Annual Meeting of the Board of Governors, Report of the Executive Directors and Summary Proceedings, September 27 to October 3, 1946* (Washington, 1946), p. 117. These percentages insured that the two countries together would command a majority of the votes in each institution's board. See Richard N. Gardner, *Sterling-Dollar Diplomacy: The Origins and the Prospects of Our International Economic Order* (McGraw-Hill, 1969) for an account of the founding of the two institutions.

2. The reader interested in more detailed analyses of the multilateral institutions can consult Anne O. Krueger, "The Role of the World Bank as an International Institution," *Carnegie-Rochester Conference Series on Public Policy*, vol. 18 (Spring 1983), pp. 281–311; John Williamson, ed., *IMF Conditionality* (Washington: Institute for International Economics, 1983); Jacques J. Polak, *The Changing Nature of IMF Conditionality*, Essays in International Finance 184 (Princeton University Department of Economics, September 1991); Manuel Guitian, "The Unique Nature of the Responsibilities of the International Monetary Fund," Brookings, May 1991; and Alasdair I. MacBean and P. N. Snowden, *International Institutions in Trade and Finance* (London: Allen and Unwin, 1981).

3. A large number of United Nations agencies support economic development in developing countries. Some of the more prominent are the United Nations Development Program (UNDP), the United Nations Industrial Development Organization (UNIDO), the Food and Agriculture Organization (FAO), the World Health Organization (WHO), the United Nations Conference on Trade and Development (UNCTAD), and the regional economic commissions—the United Nations Economic Commission for Latin America and the Caribbean (ECLAC), the United Nations Economic and Social Commission for Asia and the Pacific (ESCAP), and the United Nations Economic Commission for Africa. These agencies have provided economic analysis of the challenges and performance of various aspects of development and technical assistance on a variety of issues.

4. In the late 1980s the European Bank for Reconstruction and Development (EBRD, or BERD) was established to finance development projects in Eastern Europe and the Soviet Union during their transitions from communism. The United States supported the establishment of the EBRD, although it insisted on restricting loans to the Soviet Union until market mechanisms and democratic institutions were more firmly entrenched. See Peter Riddell, "US Likely to Join Bank to Aid Reform in E. Europe," *Financial Times*, March 26, 1990, p. 5, and Peter Norman, "BERD Gets Ready to Fly," *Financial Times*, May 29, 1990, p. 19. It may arguably have been preferable, from the U.S. and a global viewpoint, to strengthen the existing multilateral lending institutions, rather than create a new one. But since the East European and former Soviet economies are not regarded as developing, analysis of U.S. policies toward them is beyond the scope of this work.

5. Greater U.S. influence in the multilateral lending institutions derives in part from their weighted voting procedures, contrasted with the one-country, one-vote U.N. procedures. In addition, as a matter of policy, the United States has chosen to rely more on the World Bank and the IMF than on other U.N. agencies.

6. The initial Bretton Woods institution was the International Bank for Reconstruction and Development (IBRD), which was designed to lend on hard terms. When it became evident that a soft-loan facility would be essential if the poorer developing countries were to obtain resources, the Interna-

tional Development Association (IDA) was formed. The International Finance Corporation (IFC) was also founded to promote private sector development. At that stage, the name World Bank was officially given to the entire group.

7. See Kenneth W. Dam, *The Rules of the Game: Reform and Evolution in the International Monetary System* (University of Chicago Press, 1982).

8. The charter for the International Trade Organization was never ratified. The General Agreement on Tariffs and Trade (GATT) eventually articulated the principles on which world trade would be conducted. See Kenneth W. Dam, *The GATT, Law and International Economic Organization* (University of Chicago Press, 1970). See also chapter 6.

9. The IBRD was intended to lend in support of activities yielding a market rate of return. It was assumed that the private international capital market would not function effectively for this purpose, given the legacy of the Great Depression. IBRD lending was to be directed both to postwar reconstruction when returns were high and to developing countries that promised high returns as they caught up with developed countries.

10. Each institution has some paid-in capital from member countries, but it represents a small share of each country's subscription. Member governments effectively provide financing guarantees with their subscriptions, which help ensure the institutions' credit ratings. With these guarantees, the World Bank can borrow on the private international capital market at more favorable terms than most individual countries.

11. IMF staff also work closely with the Group of Seven (G-7), which includes the finance ministers of Canada, France, Germany, Italy, Japan, the United Kingdom, and the United States. IMF staff provide important input for G-7 deliberations, and much of the IMF's role in international monetary relations grows out of its G-7 work.

12. The IMF's ability to influence a member's policies depends in part on its technical competence and authority and in part on its resources. Any member with balance-of-payments difficulties can draw a "reserve tranche" (equal to 25 percent of its IMF subscription) on request. Another 25 percent is available as a "first credit tranche," once the country has demonstrated that it will make "reasonable efforts" to overcome its balance-of-payments difficulties. Three additional tranches, each equal to 25 percent of the member's subscription, may be made available as a stand-by facility only after formal agreement with the IMF.

Until the mid-1970s almost all IMF lending was much shorter-term than that of the World Bank, with repayment terms of three to five years. All IMF facilities operated at market interest rates. In the mid-1970s it became evident that short-term maturities were inappropriate given the magnitude of the adjustments required in many developing countries, and the IMF created several additional lending facilities, some longer-term and some concessional. These included an extended fund facility (EFF), a structural adjustment facility (SAF), an extended SAF (ESAF), and a supplementary financing facility to provide larger loans. For a description, see Polak, *Changing Nature*; and

Richard B. Goode, *Economic Assistance to Developing Countries through the IMF* (Brookings, 1987).

13. For an excellent account of IMF programs and treatment of IMF conditionality, see Polak, *Changing Nature*.

14. See Polak, *Changing Nature*, pp. 12–13, for a description.

15. These IMF resources are often only part of the package made available to a country in the process of policy reform. Support from the World Bank, a regional bank, and from bilateral donors, including the United States, is often also forthcoming.

16. Because they pertain to such sensitive matters as the exchange rate regime, import regulations, and government finance, the letters of intent are rarely made public. The government of the country in question retains discretion over whether the agreement is publicized. Often the government reveals the broad outline of an agreement but not its details. For a good account of one set of negotiations, see Osman Okyar, "Turkey and the IMF: A Review of Relations 1978–82," in Williamson, ed., *IMF Conditionality*, pp. 533–61.

17. See chapter 7 for a discussion of some IMF programs in the Caribbean.

18. For a recent review of the effects of IMF programs, see Mohsin S. Khan, "The Macroeconomic Effects of Fund-Supported Adjustment Programs," *IMF Staff Papers*, vol. 37 (June 1990), pp. 195–231.

19. Until the 1970s the Fund strongly supported the maintenance of fixed nominal exchange rates. Since that time, however, it has countenanced crawling peg and floating exchange rate regimes as well. In all circumstances, however, it has focused on measures that will reduce inflationary pressures.

20. The IBRD was active in lending to Europe and Japan, but its resources were small compared with those provided by the United States under the Marshall Plan.

21. Replenishments are contributions by the donor members of IDA. Because IDA credits are highly concessional, the organization does not generate sufficient repayments to sustain borrowing without replenishment—hence the name.

22. All international institutions need criteria that establish eligibility for their activities. In 1991 countries with per capita incomes below $1,195 in 1990 U.S. dollars were eligible for IDA assistance, while those with per capita incomes up to $4,300 were eligible for IBRD loans. When per capita incomes exceed the upper limit, technical assistance may still be available for a limited period of time, but World Bank lending is phased out.

In a few instances, countries receive a combination of IDA and IBRD loans, because IDA funds are scarce and must be shared by a large number of recipients. India and China have both received such mixed packages. See World Bank, *IDA in Retrospect: The First Two Decades of the International Development Association* (Oxford University Press, 1982), chap. 2.

23. The World Bank is not required by its charter to lend only to govern-

ments, though every loan does need a government guarantee. To date, all lending has been to governments, although some government agencies (such as industrial development banks) have then lent the proceeds to private sector enterprises. The guarantee in effect doubly insures the loan, with one pledge from the borrowing country and another from the shareholders of the World Bank. Thanks in part to these guarantees, the World Bank has had little difficulty borrowing on private international capital markets to finance its lending operations.

24. To be sure, World Bank officials met with policymakers in developing countries and discussed growth prospects. Such exchanges may have led to substantial learning that contributed significantly to policy formulation and reform. However, those informal influences were not part of the Bank's mission. For a discussion of early Bank policies, see Edward S. Mason and Robert E. Asher, *The World Bank since Bretton Woods* (Brookings, 1973), pp. 447–56.

25. See World Bank News, *The World Bank and the Heavily Indebted Middle-Income Countries*, Special Report (Washington, May 1988).

26. Although by definition SAL lending could not continue indefinitely, successful reform processes have lasted several years and have been supported by more than one SAL or SECAL. In Turkey, for example, there were five SALS between 1980 and 1984.

27. World Bank News, *World Bank*, annex A, p. 1.

28. World Bank, *Adjustment Lending Policies for Sustainable Growth*, Policy and Research Series 14 (Washington, September 1991), annex table 5.3.

29. Ibid.

30. Ibid., p. 49. See also Polak, *Changing Nature*, p. 42.

31. See World Bank, *Adjustment Lending Policies*, annex table 5.5, pp. 72–78.

32. Japan is the largest shareholder in the ADB, and U.S. officials have tended to view it as primarily a Japanese concern. In 1992, however, U.S. officials raised a number of issues regarding ADB lending policies and demanded that they be resolved before any consideration of a general capital increase. Alexander Nicoll, "US Stance Rattles Asian Development Bank Consensus," *Financial Times*, May 6, 1992, p. 8.

33. Data are from World Bank, *World Debt Tables, 1990–91* (Washington, 1990), table 3.

34. World Bank, *Annual Report, 1991*, p. 200. Paid-in or callable capital is the amount subscribed that the World Bank could rely on if borrowers failed to service their loans. The World Bank raises resources on world capital markets, then lends them to developing countries with government guarantees. To date, the IMF and World Bank have both refused to reschedule loans.

35. Part I members are those who make all subscription payments to IDA in convertible currencies that can be used to provide IDA credits. Part II

members are those who make at least 10 percent of their initial subscription in convertible currencies, with the remaining portion in their own currency or convertible currencies. Funds subscribed by Part II members may not be used outside their own territory without their permission. World Bank, *Annual Report, 1991*, p. 212.

36. In the late 1970s under President Jimmy Carter, the United States did object to some World Bank loans because of concerns about human rights in recipient countries.

37. Department of the Treasury, *United States Participation in the Multilateral Development Banks in the 1980s* (February 1982). See appendix C for the list of criticisms and discussion of them.

38. The U.S. executive director is instructed by law to vote against lending to countries under certain circumstances; the most prominent example is U.S. opposition to lending to countries that have expropriated U.S. property.

39. See the interview of James Burnham, then U.S. executive director of the World Bank, in Clyde Farnsworth, "U.S. Votes No at World Bank More Often under Reagan," *New York Times*, November 26, 1984, pp. A1, D14. Burnham was quoted as saying, "The Bank's resources should be used only where they do not run the risk of displacing alternative sources of finance." The real dispute, of course, was ascertaining when Bank lending actually displaced private sources. The U.S. administration appeared to believe that private lending was a viable alternative in many instances in which Bank staff and officials in the borrower country stated otherwise.

40. In addition to these issues, on many occasions private U.S. producers have persuaded their congressmen that individual activities of the World Bank or other multilateral institutions (including regional development banks) compromised their interests. These congressmen in turn have criticized the activities of the Bank and Fund and been a leading source of opposition to them. In some instances, they opposed lending that would allegedly promote a particular economic activity in competition with U.S. producers. One widely publicized example occurred in 1988, when the Senate passed a resolution opposing a $400 million World Bank loan to Mexico to help upgrade the Mexican steel industry. See "Senate Decries World Bank's Mexico Loan," *Chicago Tribune*, March 3, 1988, sect. 1, p. 5. The World Bank nonetheless proceeded with the loan, despite the vote of the U.S. executive director against it. See "World Bank Clears Loan for Mexico Steel Industry," *Wall Street Journal*, March 4, 1988, p. 10.

41. See Barend A. De Vries, *Remaking the World Bank* (Washington: Seven Locks Press, 1987), chap. 8.

42. For an account of congressional opposition to an increase in IMF capital, see, for example, Keith Bradsher, "Lawmakers Balk on IMF Funds," *New York Times*, July 22, 1991, p. D2. Democrats were quoted as opposing it because they believed the IMF was not paying enough attention to environmental issues, nor making sufficient efforts to alleviate poverty.

43. See, for example, the papers in Jeffrey D. Sachs, ed., *Developing Country Debt and the World Economy* (University of Chicago Press, 1989), and in Rudiger Dornbusch and Steven Marcus, eds., *International Money and Debt: Challenges for the World Economy* (San Francisco: ICS Press, 1991). The World Bank's *World Development Report, 1985* (Oxford University Press, 1985), provided a systematic analysis of understanding of the debt problem at that time.

44. For a fuller analysis of this argument, see Anne O. Krueger, "Aid in the Development Process," in Hans Singer, Neelamber Hatti, and Rameshwar Tandon, eds., *Aid and External Financing in the 1990s*, New World Order Series, vol. 9 (New Delhi: Indus Publishing Company), pp. 64–65; and Anne O. Krueger, "Aid in the Development Process," *World Bank Research Observer*, vol. 1 (January 1986), pp. 57–78.

45. As late as 1970, private foreign direct investment in all developing countries totaled $3.69 billion, contrasted with $8 billion in ODA and a total of $19 billion in net external financial receipts. See Development Assistance Committee, *Development Cooperation 1980* (Paris: OECD, 1980), p. 85.

46. The same had been true in the 1960s and 1970s. The rate at which countries approached the IMF and World Bank in the 1970s was not noticeably different from that of the preceding decade, in part because of the worldwide expansion and inflation.

47. Joseph Kraft, *The Mexican Rescue* (New York: Group of Thirty, 1984).

48. For a more detailed description, see Anne O. Krueger, "Decision Making at the Outset of the Debt Crisis: Analytical and Conceptual Issues," in Dornbusch and Marcus, *International Money and Debt*, pp. 27–49.

49. See, for example, Barry Eichengreen and Peter H. Lindert, eds., *The International Debt Crisis in Historical Perspective* (MIT Press, 1989).

50. Turkey had experienced serious economic difficulties in the late 1970s and initiated a major economic policy reform program in 1980. The program continued throughout the 1980s, significantly restructuring the Turkish economy. Turkey managed to service its debt voluntarily after the reschedulings associated with the 1980 policy reforms. See Anne O. Krueger and Okan H. Aktan, *Swimming against the Tide: Turkish Trade Reform in the 1980s* (San Francisco: ICS Press, 1992).

51. Countries that managed to maintain voluntary debt-servicing did so through restrictive economic policies in the short run. The measures they undertook were necessarily somewhat painful. See, for example, the discussion of Korea and debt in chapter 8. Many other countries had not borrowed heavily on the international capital markets, accepting low economic growth rates in place of increasing indebtedness. Among them were the very low-income South Asian countries and, at that time, China.

52. Some countries made threats of repudiation. Peru made the most publicized action suggesting an unwillingness to pay. Its government announced that it would pay no more than 10 percent of export earnings to service the debt. Evidently, Mexican officials also considered a unilateral moratorium

during July and August of 1982. Finance Minister Jesús Silva-Herzog several times left negotiations with U.S. Treasury officials and received instructions to reject their conditions for assistance. The most serious rift apparently occurred when the United States requested a $100 million fee for opening an oil facility, which would provide the United States favored guaranteed access to Mexican oil. When Silva-Herzog left the Treasury Department, U.S. officials contacted him by phone to notify him that the fee would be halved. Kraft, *Mexican Rescue*, pp. 15–16.

53. Moreover, drastic import cuts would have caused economic stagnation that would not have been politically acceptable in developing countries themselves.

54. See, for example, the lucid analysis by Martin Feldstein, "Muddling Through Can Be Just Fine," *Economist*, June 27, 1987, pp. 21–25.

55. Simple arithmetic showed that the developing countries as a group would have to increase their nominal export earnings at an average annual rate in excess of the world nominal interest rate if their debt-service ratios were to decline. If trade barriers in developed countries held the growth rate of developing countries' exports at a constant share of their nominal income, which was growing at 4 to 5 percent annually, their debt problem could not be resolved.

56. The crisis was also fundamentally different because the global economic environment had changed. Reduced inflation rates in the major OECD countries and the accompanying move to positive real interest rates implied much less room for policy mistakes—a forgiving environment had become much harsher.

57. See William R. Cline, *International Debt: Systemic Risk and Policy Response* (Washington: Institute for International Economics, 1984). Cline's analysis was widely circulated in the Washington community, and his conclusions were broadly similar to those of most other analysts at the time. For an official statement, see *Economic Report of the President, February 1984*, p. 72. These assumptions were criticized in academia. See, for example, Jeffrey Sachs and Richard N. Cooper, "Borrowing Abroad: The Debtor's Perspective," in Gordon Smith and John Cuddington, eds., *International Debt and the Developing Countries* (Washington: World Bank, 1985), pp. 21–60.

58. Some observers believe there was an additional objective—buying the commercial banks time to strengthen their capital positions before they took inevitable losses in writing down their loans to developing countries.

59. Sub-Saharan African countries constituted an exception. They did not carry large amounts of debt, but given their economic situations, they were clearly incapable of voluntary debt-servicing and in need of radical policy reforms. In regard to the sub-Saharan African countries, the United States was passively supportive of the multilateral institutions. The contradictions and dilemmas inherent in U.S. debt policy were much greater in regard to the major countries, which are therefore the focus of this discussion.

60. Poorer countries remained eligible for concessional assistance, while

there was no proposal to support heavily indebted middle-income countries with concessional funds. Nonetheless, some proposals for partial debt forgiveness appeared to rely on resources that could otherwise have gone to low-income countries.

61. The author happened to be in Colombia when the Brady Plan for debt forgiveness was announced. Colombia had maintained voluntary debt-servicing throughout the 1980s, and its representatives were in New York seeking a loan when the Brady Plan was announced. The New York bankers immediately informed the Colombians that they did not wish to negotiate further until particulars of the Brady Plan became known. The Colombian economics team came under political attack—irate Colombians wanted to know why they had so faithfully serviced the debt when it had not been necessary. At the same time, Colombia's cut flower exports—a major new industry—were under investigation in the United States for dumping, and Washington eventually imposed an antidumping duty. As if these economic pressures were not enough, U.S. authorities were also attempting to persuade the Colombians to intensify their antidrug efforts.

62. Chapter 8 discusses U.S. negotiations with Korea on the "unacceptably large" Korean current account surpluses that emerged between 1986 and 1989. These surpluses enabled Korea to pay back some debt, a measure that enjoyed widespread domestic support. U.S. officials objected to the size of Korea's bilateral current account surplus with the United States and insisted that the Koreans reduce it at the same time as other U.S. officials urged heavily indebted countries to take measures to reduce their indebtedness. One of the puzzles of the late 1980s is why U.S. pressure on Korea to reduce the current account surplus was not challenged publicly by other heavily indebted countries.

63. See, for example, *Economic Report of the President, February 1984*, pp. 78–79. Similar statements may be found in Treasury Secretary James Baker's address to the IMF–World Bank meetings in Seoul, in Treasury Secretary Nicholas Brady's announcement of his plan, and in numerous other official policy pronouncements. For Baker's address, see James A. Baker III, "Statement by the Governor of the Fund and the Bank for the United States," in IMF, *Summary Proceedings, Annual Meeting, 1985* (Washington, 1985).

64. Joseph Kraft, *Mexican Rescue*; and Jesús Silva-Herzog, "Problems of Policy Making at the Outset of the Debt Crisis," in Dornbusch and Marcus, *International Money and Debt*, pp. 51–60.

65. The Bank of Mexico did not have and could not obtain enough assets to continue servicing the debt. The debt-service payments due during 1983 exceeded Mexico's anticipated foreign exchange earnings that year.

66. Kraft, *Mexican Rescue*, p. 11. See also Silva-Herzog's description of the Treasury Department's position as "abusive" in "Problems of Policy Making," p. 57. The Mexican team was apparently prepared to return to Mexico City and declare a moratorium after hearing the terms initially outlined by Treasury.

67. Only $13.8 billion of official and commercial debt was rescheduled between 1975 and 1980, whereas $50.6 billion was rescheduled in 1980 alone (including $25 billion by Mexico), and $116.2 billion in 1984. See World Bank, *World Debt Tables*, 1984–85 (Washington, 1984), p. xvi.

68. Federal Reserve Chairman Paul Volcker appears to have played a central role in instituting these arrangements. Kraft describes Treasury Secretary Donald Regan as being "at odds with the Fed, the IMF, and the Treasury staff." Kraft, *Mexican Rescue*, p. 11.

69. Typically, the indebted country had borrowed from a large number—often more than a hundred—commercial banks. The major lenders usually held more than three-quarters of all outstanding debt, with the remainder spread across many institutions. Since all loan agreements had cross-default clauses, rescheduling was thought to require the agreement of all lenders. Initially, all creditors were expected to contribute their share of the negotiated new money package. A major challenge for officials in developing countries and also for the chairmen of the various advisory committees was to secure the consent of all commercial banks, not just the large lenders with seats on the committee. In retrospect, the small banks should perhaps have been given exit options much earlier than they in fact were.

70. The IMF could increase its lending only by increasing its capital subscription or by borrowing directly from private capital markets, which it had never done. The World Bank was constrained by the understanding that it would not lend any amount unsustainable in the absence of a future general capital increase. While this constraint was not binding in the early 1980s, it would have precluded any large increase in IBRD lending, had one been contemplated.

71. In the *Economic Report of the President, February 1983*, only five pages of the chapter on the international economy were devoted to developing countries and the debt problem. In these few pages, the first section focused on the events of the 1970s, the second was entitled "Causes of the Liquidity Problem," and the third discussed the risks to financial markets and the likely effects on world trade and the U.S. trade balance. At the end, two paragraphs on developing countries noted that these problems "were not insoluble" and pointed to the export growth of developing countries as the solution.

72. Between 1982 and 1988, U.S. officials contributed to the multilaterals' policies toward individual developing countries in a variety of ways. First, as exemplified by the Mexican case, they supported IMF coordination of the commercial banks during the debt crisis. Second, U.S. officials took positions on individual World Bank and IMF programs, depending on their interests in the country concerned, sometimes exercising their influence in support of Bank or Fund lending even when policy reforms were not judged to be adequate. Third, the United States provided bridge loans in some instances, either to permit Fund lending or to promote its political interests in the country. Fourth, through its foreign aid program, the United States sometimes pro-

vided additional support for low-income countries, though there was no in-cremental aid financing. After the announcement of the Brady Plan, discussed later, U.S. officials also became more active on debt reduction and debt re-scheduling. For an example, see the discussions of Costa Rican and Jamaican debt in chapter 7.

73. IMF, *World Economic Outlook* (Washington, November 1990), table A44, p. 171.

74. The Council of Economic Advisers concluded, "The recent gains made by Mexico, Brazil, and several other debtors confirm that their strategies for economic adjustment and repayment are basically sound." The council noted the multi-year rescheduling of Mexico's debt, the declining debt-export ratio, and other "positive steps." It also noted that continued progress depended on the international economy and the ability of developing countries to con-tinue increasing their exports. See *Economic Report of the President, February 1985*, p. 108.

75. World Bank, *World Debt Tables*, 1985–86 (Washington, 1985), p. vii.

76. See, for example, the discussion in *Economic Report of the President, February 1984*, pp. 71–72. That report stated, "If all concerned parties con-tinue their efforts, and there are no unforeseen calamities, the system can be expected gradually to work its way back to normalcy" (p. 72).

77. Jeffrey D. Sachs was a prominent advocate of that position. See his "External Debt and Macroeconomic Performance in Latin America and East Asia," *Brookings Papers on Economic Activity*, 2:1985, pp. 523–73; and "Managing the LDC Debt Crisis," *Brookings Papers on Economic Activity*, 2:1986, pp. 397–432.

78. Net capital flows to developing countries were clearly going to be very small, if not negative, if changes were not made. See table 6-1 for actual capital flows during the 1980s.

79. See Richard N. Cooper, *Economic Stabilization and Debt in Devel-oping Countries* (MIT Press, 1992), pp. 152–53.

80. Baker, "Statement by the Governor of the Fund," p. 52.

81. Ibid., p. 56.

82. Ibid., pp. 50–58.

83. The Baker speech also expressed concern about sub-Saharan Africa and urged additional assistance for countries in that region.

84. The United States, however, along with other OECD donors, did reduce the official debt of some sub-Saharan African countries. See chapter 4.

85. The "Baker fifteen" were Argentina, Bolivia, Brazil, Chile, Colom-bia, Ecuador, Ivory Coast, Mexico, Morocco, Nigeria, Peru, Philippines, Uruguay, Venezuela, and Yugoslavia. Of these, only Chile was close to re-gaining creditworthiness by early 1989.

86. The price of the debt of the heavily indebted developing countries in the secondary market plummeted between the end of 1985 and early 1989. Mexican debt, for example, had been selling at between 50 and 60 percent of face value at the beginning of 1986; by the beginning of 1989 it sold for about

45 percent of face value. Costa Rican debt had fallen from 50 percent to 20 percent, Venezuelan from more than 70 percent to 40 percent, and Argentine from more than 50 percent to 15 percent during the same period. "Brady's Bazaar," *Economist*, May 12, 1990, p. 77. For one negative assessment of the Baker Plan that may have been influential in the U.S. policy shift and the formulation of the Brady Plan, see J. P. Morgan, "LDC Debt Reduction: A Critical Appraisal," *World Financial Markets*, December 30, 1988, pp. 1–12. The Morgan analysis, executed by a large and respected bank, concluded that the Baker Plan had not achieved its goals and that debt reduction had to be given serious consideration.

87. See also Edwin M. Truman, "U.S. Policy on the Problems of International Debt," *Federal Reserve Bulletin*, vol. 75 (November 1989), pp. 727–35.

88. See Polak, *Changing Nature*, pp. 15–16, for a discussion.

89. See, for example, Jonathan Fuerbringer, "Future of Debt Plan," *New York Times*, April 10, 1989, p. D2. Many observers questioned why the multilateral institutions should use their resources to fund the commercial banks. Leonard Silk, "Debt Reduction: Now, the Details," *New York Times*, April 7, 1989, p. D2.

90. Cooper, *Economic Stabilization*, p. 154.

91. The Treasury Department had gained the active support of all G-7 governments for the Brady Plan.

92. World Bank, *Annual Report, 1990*, p. 50.

93. See Cooper, *Economic Stabilization*, p. 155, for a statement of this viewpoint.

94. The IMF has not relied on private capital markets for its resources, so there is less concern about the quality of its portfolio.

95. Peter Truell, "IMF Board Approves Guidelines for Role in U.S.-Backed Efforts at Debt Reduction," *Wall Street Journal*, May 25, 1989, p. A4.

96. If approved, the North American Free Trade Agreement may prove valuable in mitigating Mexico's debt problems. That initiative, however, appears to have emanated from motivations that had little to do with the debt problem.

97. "U.S. Uses Vote on Loan to Protest Chile Policies," *Wall Street Journal*, March 13, 1985, p. 39; and Gerald F. Seib, "Bush Expanding China Sanctions, Suspends High-Level Exchanges," *Wall Street Journal*, June 21, 1989, p. A3.

98. C. David Finch, "Let the IMF Be the IMF," *International Economy*, vol. 1 (January–February 1988), p. 127. The United States was certainly not alone in urging debt rescheduling for Egypt without policy reform. But had the United States not supported it, other countries would have been unlikely to be able to exert very much pressure on the IMF.

99. Clyde Farnsworth, "World Bank and I.M.F. in Conflict over Roles," *New York Times*, September 26, 1988, p. D3; and Steve Greenhouse, "Distress on World Debt," *New York Times*, February 28, 1989, p. D1.

100. John Barham, "IMF Likely to Approve Standby for Argentina," *Financial Times*, July 2, 1991, p. 5.

101. See also Peter Norman, "Bank President Opposes US on Private Lending," *Financial Times*, October 18, 1991, p. 6, where the new World Bank President, Lewis Preston, indicated his opposition to the U.S. proposal.

102. Irving S. Friedman, "The Development Role of the IMF and the World Bank: The U.S. Stance," in John Yochelson, ed., *Keeping Pace: U.S. Policies and Global Economic Change* (Cambridge, Mass.: Ballinger, 1987), pp. 119-32, esp. p. 130.

Chapter Six

1. See chapter 8, which reviews the experience of Korea, an outward-oriented, rapidly growing country that was also a large aid recipient.

2. Official U.S. support, however, was entirely consistent with the then-prevailing domestic consensus in support of free trade. See Robert E. Baldwin, *The Political Economy of U.S. Import Policy* (MIT Press, 1985), for an analysis.

3. Data are from World Bank, *World Development Report, 1987* (Oxford University Press, 1987), p. 40. This observation includes all the industrialized countries and those developing countries for which data are available.

4. The objective of growth, of course, is to improve the well-being of a country's citizens. In countries that relied on outward-oriented growth, real wages rose rapidly and income distribution did not worsen, holding virtually constant during the period of rapid growth. See chapter 8 for a more detailed discussion of the Korean case.

5. Some observers argue that "administered protection," discussed further later, is part of U.S. law and is not protectionist. Others, however, have convincingly revealed strong protectionist biases in the ways in which the relevant portions of trade law are interpreted. For a discussion, see Richard Boltuck and Robert E. Litan, eds., *Down in the Dumps: Administration of the Unfair Trade Laws* (Brookings, 1991). In addition, political scientists have shown the circumstances under which those seeking protection pursue administered remedies rather than legislated action. See H. Keith Hall and Douglas Nelson, "Institutional Structure in the Political Economy of Protection: Legislated v. Administered Protection," *Economics and Politics*, vol. 4 (March 1992), pp. 61-77.

6. I am indebted to Robert Slonim for able research assistance in preparing the material covered in this section.

7. The trade policies of the developing countries were so biased against exports that even their share of world agricultural exports fell, from 44.4 percent in 1955 to 25 percent in 1986. See U.N. Conference on Trade and Development (UNCTAD), *Handbook of International Trade Statistics*, various issues, Geneva.

8. For the 1980s, data are from GATT, *International Trade 1988/89* (Geneva, 1990). Other data are from UNCTAD, *Handbook of International Trade Statistics*, various issues. For further details, see Anne O. Krueger, "Global Trade Prospects for the Developing Countries," *World Economy*, vol. 15 (July 1992), pp. 457–74.

9. See chapter 8 for details of the spectacular growth of Korea, one of the four.

10. A fact seldom noted is that the share of employment in textiles and clothing, a major commodity group subject to intense import competition in recent years, had already fallen in the United States from 12 percent in 1929 to 6 percent in 1950. That decrease occurred long before imports became a factor, the consequence both of the shift of consumers away from commodities whose relative price was increasing and of a relatively low income elasticity of demand. See Anne O. Krueger, "LDC Manufacturing Production and Implications for OECD Comparative Advantage," in Irving Leveson and Jimmy W. Wheeler, eds., *Western Economies in Transition: Structural Change and Adjustment Policies in Industrial Countries* (Boulder, Colo.: Westview Press, 1980), pp. 219–50.

11. In some industries, such as textiles and apparel, protection against imports from Japan already existed and was extended to cover other countries.

12. The cornerstone of this system was the proviso, contained in treaties governing bilateral commercial relations, that neither party to an agreement would be treated less well than the other's "most favored nation." The move toward regional trading blocs, discussed below, represents a distinct departure from this principle.

13. GATT rules do provide for the formation of free trade agreements and customs unions. Essentially, these arrangements are compatible with GATT as long as they are across the board, and not sectoral in nature.

14. For a detailed exposition of the legal, institutional, and economic aspects of the GATT, see Kenneth W. Dam, *The GATT, Law and International Economic Organizations* (University of Chicago Press, 1982).

15. The IMF was also active in counseling exchange rate regimes consistent with liberal trade regimes.

16. For a statement of that view, see Robert E. Baldwin, *Nontariff Distortions of International Trade* (Brookings, 1970), p. vii. In the successive GATT rounds of tariff negotiations, countries have bargained, offering to reduce tariffs on commodities of interest to their major trading partners if those partners in turn reduced tariff barriers on items of interest to them. Once bargains were struck, these tariff rates were "bound"—that is, under GATT arrangements, once tariffs were reduced they could not be increased above the negotiated levels. Many developing countries in recent years have unilaterally reduced their tariff rates. Those rates are not bound and could, therefore, be increased without violating GATT obligations.

17. At the inception of GATT, the United States had insisted that U.S. price supports for agricultural commodities and other practices then in effect could not be altered and thus had to be exempted from GATT rules. See Dam, *The GATT*, for an account.

18. Throughout the period, however, the structure of protection in the United States and other industrialized countries has been somewhat biased against developing countries. Edward J. Ray and Howard P. Marvel estimated the extent of protection by individual import categories according to their source. They demonstrated statistically that imports from developing countries were systematically subject to higher protection than those from developed countries. Their conclusion does not imply that discrimination against products from developing countries is deliberate. Rather, it points to the fact that protectionist pressures are greatest toward imports of commodities of special importance to the developing countries. See Edward J. Ray and Howard P. Marvel, "The Pattern of Protection in the Industrialized World," *Review of Economics and Statistics*, vol. 66 (August 1984), pp. 452–58.

19. Economists almost unanimously agree that over the long run the current account deficit of any country is a consequence of macroeconomic policies, including the fiscal deficit and factors affecting savings rates, rather than of foreign or domestic trade practices. The latter affect the levels of both exports and imports, while macroeconomic variables determine the difference between current payments to and from foreigners.

20. For a careful analysis of the old and new Section 301 articles, see Robert Hudec, "Thinking about the New Section 301: Beyond Good and Evil," in Jagdish Bhagwati and Hugh Patrick, eds., *Aggressive Unilateralism: America's 301 Trade Policy and the World Trading System* (University of Michigan Press, 1990), p. 121 and appendix. See also the introductory essay by Bhagwati in the same volume for an analysis of the issues in far greater depth than is possible here.

21. Brazil is one of the heavily indebted countries affected by U.S. policy toward debt. While citing Brazil as an unfair trader, the United States also urged that it (and other indebted countries) undertake export promotion policies to service its debt obligations.

22. See U.S. International Trade Commission (USITC), *Operation of the Trade Agreements Program, 41st Report, 1989*, Publication 2317 (September 1990), pp. 1–7.

23. Ibid., p. 5.

24. Ibid., p. 6.

25. Ibid. Most observers believe that the pressures in the United States for intellectual property rights protection originate largely in the U.S. pharmaceutical industry. See Julio Nogués, "Patents and Pharmaceutical Drugs: Understanding the Pressures on Developing Countries," World Bank International Economics Department, Working Paper 502 (September 1990). In

Nogués's analysis, these pressures have arisen in response to losses in the market shares of major pharmaceutical firms associated with increasingly stringent drug safety regulations and increased competition from generic drugs.

26. See Judith Hippler Bello and Alan F. Holmer, "The Heart of the 1988 Trade Act: A Legislative History of the Amendments to Section 301," in Bhagwati and Patrick, eds., *Aggressive Unilateralism*, pp. 65–68.

27. For a discussion, see the papers in U.S. Department of Labor, Bureau of International Labor Affairs, *Labor Standards and Development in the Global Economy* (Washington, 1990).

28. For a report of growing Thai resentment, see Stephen Coats, "Seeding Hostility among the Thais," *New York Times*, November 25, 1988, p. A31. In December 1990 Thailand and the United States were on the same side of the farm subsidies issue at GATT. At that time, however, the following subjects were listed as being in dispute between the two countries: intellectual property rights, textile quotas, tuna fish, and bilateral air traffic. Under pressure from the United States, Thailand in November 1990 opened up its market for U.S. cigarette imports. See Paul Taylor, "US and Thailand in Brief Harmony and Discord," *Financial Times*, December 6, 1990, p. 3.

29. For an analysis of aggressive unilateralism, see Thomas O. Bayard, *Reciprocity and Retaliation: An Evaluation of Aggressive Trade Policies* (Washington: Institute for International Economics, 1991); and Jagdish Bhagwati, *The World Trading System at Risk* (Princeton University Press, 1991).

30. "Secretariat: Uncertainties and Tensions despite High Trade Growth," *GATT Focus* (newsletter), vol. 63 (July 1989), p. 6.

31. *International Trade Reporter* (Washington: Bureau of National Affairs), May 30, 1990, p. 766.

32. Bovard, *Fair Trade Fraud*, p. 78. In the 1970s, the United States had imposed a steel trigger pricing mechanism after steel producers alleged dumping.

33. For an excellent discussion of the protectionist impact of these provisions from the Canadian perspective, see Alan M. Rugman and Andrew D. M. Anderson, *Administered Protection in America* (London: Croom Helm, 1987).

34. In addition to the measures discussed here, rules of origin, product definitions, and other administrative matters are also being enforced and interpreted in ways that provide protection to U.S. firms. See Bovard, *Fair Trade Fraud*, especially chapter 2.

35. GATT, *Trade Policy Review, United States* (Geneva, 1990), tables IV.1, IV.4.

36. Ibid., tables IV.2, IV.3.

37. See Brian Hindley, "Protectionism in the GATT," *Financial Times*, June 7, 1991, p. 12.

38. Nancy Dunne, "Knitwear Quotas in U.S. 'Fail to Stop Dumping,'" *Financial Times*, November 3, 1989, p. 4.

39. Hong Kong exporters were reportedly angered because (a) the im-

ports allegedly dumped were already restricted by quota; (b) the USITC omitted the high margin item among Hong Kong's imports in calculating the reference price; and (c) the USITC expects a minimum of 8 percent profit margin and 10 percent selling expense in determining whether dumping has occurred, and the Hong Kong exporters claimed that their costs were below these levels. Angus Foster, "Ruling Angers Hong Kong Textile Manufacturers," *Financial Times*, July 7, 1990, p. 7.

40. Richard Boltuck and Robert E. Litan, "America's 'Unfair' Trade Laws," in Boltuck and Litan, eds., *Down in the Dumps*, p. 17.

41. Even Norway, not a poor country, has protested the antidumping provisions of U.S. law. Terming the administration of antidumping laws "capricious," the Norwegian Secretary for Trade and Shipping stated that "you have to have large resources to risk entering the U.S. market." At the time, the Norwegian government was appealing an antidumping ruling on salmon fishing, under which the United States levied a 23.8 percent antidumping duty and a 2.27 percent countervailing duty. He claimed the duties excluded Norwegian salmon from the U.S. market, placing Norway at a competitive disadvantage of 40 percent compared with other exporters. Nancy Dunne, "Norway Criticizes Anti-Dumping Law," *Financial Times*, September 20, 1991, p. 6.

42. There were forty-eight outstanding antidumping orders in effect against Japan at the end of 1989, fifteen against Canada, eight against France, and ten against Germany. Countervailing duty orders against exports from developed countries were less numerous, with six against Canada, six against New Zealand, two against Sweden, and one each against the European Community, France, Italy, and the Netherlands. See USITC, *Operation of the Trade Agreements Program, 41st Report*, tables A-28, A-29.

43. For an analysis of the welfare impact of patent protection on developing countries, see Alan V. Deardorff, "Should Patent Protection Be Extended to All Developing Countries?" *World Economy*, vol. 13 (December 1990), pp. 497–507.

44. As noted, the 1988 Trade Expansion Act encouraged the USTR to consider labor standards and practices. In debating free trade with Mexico, representatives of U.S. labor have insisted that "fair labor standards" be included in any agreement. To date, labor practices have been a subject of discussion, as the United States has suspended Burma, Nicaragua, Romania, and Liberia from GSP eligibility on the basis of worker rights. Although labor standards are not further discussed here, U.S. provisions that exclude imports from countries with wages below a certain level would clearly have very protectionist effects vis-à-vis some developing countries. See, for example, Gary S. Fields, "Labor Standards, Economic Development, and International Trade," in *Labor Standards and Development in the Global Economy* (U.S. Department of Labor, Bureau of International Labor Affairs, 1990), pp. 19–34.

45. See, for example, Robert E. Baldwin and Tracy Murray, "MFN Tariff

Reductions and Developing Country Trade Benefits under the GSP," *Economic Journal*, vol. 87 (March 1977), pp. 30–46.

46. See Martin Wolf, "Differential and More Favorable Treatment of Developing Countries and the International Trading System," *World Bank Economic Review*, vol. 1 (September 1987), pp. 647–68. See also Colleen Hamilton and John Whalley, "Introduction," in John Whalley, ed., *Developing Countries and the Global Trading System*, vol. 1 (University of Michigan Press, 1990), p. 13.

47. For a description of the evolution of this approach, see Hamilton and Whalley, "Introduction," p. 13.

48. For a concise history of the GSP provisions, see Andre Sapir and Lars Lundberg, "The U.S. Generalized System of Preferences and Its Impacts," in Robert E. Baldwin and Anne O. Krueger, eds., *The Structure and Evolution of Recent U.S. Trade Policy* (University of Chicago Press, 1984), pp. 195–229.

49. Ömer Gokcekus provided research and gathered some material used in the analysis of GSP.

50. USITC, *Operation of the Trade Agreements Program, 42nd Report, 1990*, Publication 2403 (July 1991), p. 179.

51. See Edward J. Ray, "The Impact of Special Interests on the Preferential Tariff Concessions by the United States," *Review of Economics and Statistics*, vol. 69 (May 1987), pp. 187–93.

52. USITC, *Operation of the Trade Agreements Program, 41st Report*, pp. 149–50.

53. Canada has exported automobiles to the United States under these provisions. See USITC, *Production Sharing: U.S. Imports under Harmonized Tariff Schedule Subheading 9802.00.60 and 9802.00.80, 1986–1989*, Publication 2365 (March 1991), p. xvii.

54. Ibid., p. xv.

55. Ibid., pp. xv–xix.

56. See GATT, "Textiles and Clothing in the World Economy," Geneva, May 4, 1984, Spec(84)24, pp. 4–5, for further elaboration. See also William R. Cline, *The Future of World Trade in Textiles and Apparel*, rev. ed. (Washington: Institute for International Economics, 1990).

57. The MFA contradicts the GATT charter, both in imposing quantitative restrictions and in being discriminatory and bilateral in application. Nonetheless, the umbrella agreement has been negotiated under GATT auspices and is recognized as a derogation from GATT. See Refik Erzan and Paula Holmes, "Phasing Out the Multi-Fibre Arrangement," *World Economy*, vol. 13 (June 1990), p. 191.

58. See Cline, *Textiles and Apparel*, chap. 1, for a more detailed discussion.

59. Cline, *Textiles and Apparel*, analyzes the 1987 textile and apparel bill before Congress, which would have limited imports globally (not just from developing countries) to growth of 1 percent annually. A 1990 bill would also

have restrained imports of textiles and apparel to that growth rate. See Clyde H. Farnsworth, "Senate Votes Import Curbs on Apparel but Veto Looms," *New York Times*, July 18, 1990, pp. D1, D4.

60. Erzan and Holmes, "Phasing Out the Multi-Fibre Arrangement," p. 196.

61. See Cline, *Textiles and Apparel*, p. 190.

62. GATT, *Trade Policy Review, United States* (Geneva, 1990), table AV.2, p. 303.

63. They estimate that the losses to the United States (to consumers and producers in the form of excess costs) were $15 billion. According to their estimates, Americans could thus have been better off by $15 billion—more than the entire foreign economic assistance program—and improved the welfare of developing countries by removing the MFA. Irene Trela and John Whalley, "Global Effects of Developed Country Trade Restrictions on Textiles and Apparel," *Economic Journal*, vol. 100 (December 1990), table 4, p. 1201.

64. Nancy Dunne, "MFA Edges toward 17-Month Extension," *Financial Times*, July 30, 1991, p. 5.

65. In May 1990 the U.S. textile industry set its conditions for supporting a ten-year phaseout of the MFA. The USTR appeared to agree with the terms, which called for (a) a transition mechanism to slow the growth of textile imports to 1 percent annually; (b) stronger GATT rules against subsidies, dumping, and "import surges"; (c) a commitment from all other nations to open their markets, and (d) tariffs high enough to compensate for the costs of U.S. wage rates, environmental standards, and worker safety programs. Under these conditions, it was questionable whether the phase-out would benefit any foreign textile exporters. Nancy Dunne, "U.S. Names Price for Dropping Textile Quotas," *Financial Times*, May 18, 1990, p. 4.

66. See USITC, *Operation of Trade Agreements Program, 42nd Report*, pp. 11–13.

67. As noted, Trela and Whalley, "Global Effects," estimate that Korea and Taiwan are both net losers under the MFA, as their losses in lower export volume outweigh their gains in higher prices.

68. A vivid example of this effect occurred in Bangladesh, whose garment industry began booming in the mid-1980s. The United States then imposed quotas under the MFA on Bangladeshi imports. See David Housego, "Textiles: Low-Cost Labour Sets Off Helter-Skelter Growth," *Financial Times*, March 26, 1990, p. 31.

69. Jaime de Melo and David Tarr, "Welfare Costs of U.S. Quotas in Textiles, Steel, and Autos," Discussion Paper 401 (London: Centre for Economic Policy Research, April 1990), p. 13.

70. *Federal Register*, April 9, 1986, p. 12356, as cited in Bovard, *Fair Trade Fraud*.

71. Bovard, *Fair Trade Fraud*, p. 3.

72. World Bank, *World Development Report, 1986* (Oxford University Press, 1986), pp. 128, 131.

73. There are exceptions. Australia, for example, is a large exporter and low-cost producer of sugar.

74. In addition to the topics discussed in the section, price stabilization schemes have been advocated. Developing countries have consistently urged the United States and other consuming countries to negotiate commodity agreements to "stabilize" the price of primary commodities. The economic benefits of such agreements to developing countries would be highly uneven, and commodity price schemes could seek price increases in the name of stabilization. The United States has been uniformly reluctant to enter into these schemes. See, for example, the recent description of the U.S. position on a possible coffee agreement in "U.S. Support Is Sought for Coffee Limits," *New York Times*, March 16, 1992, p. D1.

75. The mere fact that there are threats to the system strengthens those who oppose policy reforms in developing countries. Opponents of reform argue frequently that outward-oriented policies, which were so successful for developing countries that adopted them in earlier decades, are no longer appropriate because export markets in the developed countries are prospectively less open. For a discussion of Indian export prospects, see, for example, Sukhamoy Chakravarty, *Development Planning: The Indian Experience* (Oxford University Press, 1987), p. 70.

76. See Roy Denman, "Why the Trade Talks Fizzled," *New York Times*, December 20, 1990, p. A31. Denman pointed out not only that Europeans felt they could not entirely abolish the CAP on the U.S. timetable, but that they viewed Washington's promise to reciprocate by removing sugar, dairy, and other agricultural protection in the United States as incredible. See also Keith Bradsher, "Talking Deals," *New York Times*, August 8, 1991, p. C2. Bradsher quoted U.S. officials as believing that American objectives on agriculture had been unrealistic.

77. The U.S. position to date has been to reject most-favored-nation (MFN) rules in shipping. The United States has also resisted any effort to liberalize coastal shipping (cabotage), reserving that for U.S. vessels. William Duitforce, "Nordic Shipping Plan May Help Uruguay Round," *Financial Times*, September 30, 1991, p. 6.

78. Clyde H. Farnsworth, "U.S. Is Changing Its Tune on Liberalization of Trade," *New York Times*, October 29, 1990, p. C1.

79. William Duitforce, "US Blocks GATT Telecoms Deal at Last Minute," *Financial Times*, October 19, 1990, p. 4.

80. William Duitforce, "US and EC in Tariff Deadlock," *Financial Times*, December 21, 1989, p. 3.

81. Jeffrey J. Schott, "More Free Trade Areas?" in Jeffrey J. Schott, ed., *Free Trade Areas and U.S. Trade Policy* (Washington: Institute for International Economics, 1989), pp. 1–2.

82. See the papers in Schott, *Free Trade Areas*, for a reflection of these views.

83. Lane Kirkland, "U.S.-Mexico Trade Pact: A Disaster Worthy of Stalin's Worst," *Wall Street Journal*, April 18, 1991, p. A17.

84. Nancy Dunne, "Fears over US-Mexico Free Trade Pact," *Financial Times*, January 30, 1991, p. 4.

85. See Richard Johns, "US and Mexico See Logic of Commercial Integration," *Financial Times*, November 26, 1990, p. 2.

86. On this point, see the excellent discussion by Richard Snape, "A Free Trade Agreement with Australia?" in Schott, *Free Trade Areas*, pp. 167–96, esp. pp. 193–94.

87. See the comments by Robert E. Baldwin on Anne O. Krueger, "American Bilateral Trading Arrangements and East Asian Interests," in Takatoshi Ito and Anne O. Krueger, eds., *NBER–East Asia Seminar on Economies*, vol. 2: *Trade and Protectionism* (University of Chicago Press for the National Bureau of Economic Research, forthcoming).

88. Lim Siong Hoon, "Malaysia Prepares to Pay the Price of Prosperity," *Financial Times*, February 6, 1991, p. 8.

Chapter Seven

1. Although similar tensions are present in U.S. policy toward other industrialized countries, those policies tend to focus on defense and security issues, and when conflict arises it is resolved at high levels within the administration. Moreover, in the absence of foreign aid, lending by multilaterals, and debt problems, the United States has less opportunity for inconsistency in its policies and policy pronouncements. In many cases, the United States reiterates its support of free trade and then adopts some protectionist measures. And the United States recently presumed to identify those Japanese policies and practices prejudicial to U.S. competitiveness in the Structural Impediments Initiative. However, the Japanese had sufficient economic and political power to respond with their own list of U.S. policies and practices whose alteration would improve U.S. competitiveness.

2. Other administration trade actions against Mexico have included steel wire rope, fresh cut flowers, bars, rebars, shapes, iron-metal castings, toy balloons, playballs, and cookware. See U.S. International Trade Commission (USITC), *Operation of the Trade Agreements Program, 42nd Report, 1990*, Publication 2403 (July 1991), p. 211.

3. I am greatly indebted to Ozkan Zengin for preparing an excellent background paper on which much of the analysis in this chapter is based. David Orsmond was invaluable in assembling material on the multilateral institutions' roles in CBI countries.

4. The investment proposal, which Congress never approved, was that

the United States should offer U.S. investors a tax credit worth 10 percent of the amount invested in eligible countries.

5. See "Remarks on the Caribbean Basin Initiative to the Permanent Council of the Organization of American States," February 24, 1982, in *Public Papers of the Presidents of the United States, Ronald Reagan, 1982* (Government Printing Office, 1983), book 1, pp. 210–15; and Daniel Seyler, "The CBI and Caribbean Industrialization: An Assessment of the First Five Years and the Outlook under CBI II," paper presented at the Latin American Studies Association Congress xv, San Juan, Puerto Rico, September, 1989, p. 4.

6. Some congressmen remained very nervous about the impact of the act's trade provisions on the United States. In Section 216 they required the secretary of labor to issue a report each year analyzing the impact of the act on U.S. labor. See, for example, Robert C. Shelburne and Clinton R. Shiells, *Trade and Employment Effects of the Caribbean Basin Economic Recovery Act*, Economic Discussion Paper 35 (Bureau of International Labor Affairs, December 1990). Section 215 (a) of the act required a similar report from the USITC on the impact on U.S. industries and consumers. See USITC, *Annual Report on the Impact of the Caribbean Basin Economic Recovery Act on U.S. Industries and Consumers, Fifth Report, 1989*, Publication 2321 (September 1990).

7. In some instance, the act provided preferences within the limits permitted by other U.S. policies; in others (as with beef imports), the Agriculture Department had to approve an overall agricultural plan for the country in question, the stated purpose of which was to "insure the self-sufficiency of the economy" in the agricultural commodities in question. U.S. Department of Commerce, *1987 Guidebook, Caribbean Basin Initiative* (Washington, 1987).

8. Department of State, *Report by the Department of State on the Caribbean Basin Initiative (CBI)* (November 1990), p. 1. Subsequently, the duty-free tourism allowance for U.S. tourists was increased from $400 to $600, giving a 50 percent preference to goods brought back by tourists from CBI countries relative to those of other countries. GSP, however, also applied to items imported by tourists.

9. See USITC, *Operation of the Trade Agreements Program, 40th Report, 1988*, Publication 2208 (July 1989), p. 156. One of the conflicts the bill caused concerned U.S. policy toward its overseas territories, especially Puerto Rico. Puerto Rico and the Virgin Islands immediately complained that the proposed CBI would adversely affect them by extending privileges only they enjoyed to other countries in the Caribbean. In response, several provisions granted more favorable treatment to U.S. territories, including one that mandated the transfer of all rum tax revenues to their treasuries and another (section 936 of the internal revenue code) that allowed the tax-free repatriation of profits from other countries to Puerto Rican banks.

10. It is significant that, despite the importance attached by the U.S. administration to the CBI, recent analyses of the economic performance of Ca-

ribbean and Central American countries do not even mention it. See DeLisle Worrell, "The Caribbean," and Sylvia Saborio, "Central America," in John Williamson, ed., *Latin American Adjustment: How Much has Happened?* (Washington: Institute for International Economics, April 1990), pp. 257–78, 279–302.

11. Complicating the CBI arrangement was the fact that some eligible countries were beneficiaries of the Lome Convention and received ACP (Asia, Caribbean, and Pacific) preferences from the European Community. Former colonies of EC members receive access to EC markets on preferential, often duty-free terms, but they cannot be members of another trading bloc. See Commission of the European Economic Community, *Annual Report of the ACP-EEC, 1988* (Brussels, 1989).

12. The impetus to amend the bill grew out of recommendations of the House Ways and Means Subcommittee on Oversight after a fact-finding mission went to the Caribbean in 1987. Committee members sought to remedy shortcomings of the original legislation, especially the concern that trade was not sufficiently liberalized. Since the initial CBERA, import restrictions on citrus and ethanol, decreased sugar quotas, and an antidumping order against Costa Rican cut flowers had been implemented. See *Report on the Committee Delegation Mission to the Caribbean Basin and Recommendations to Improve the Effectiveness of the Caribbean Basin Initiative*, Committee Print, Subcommittee on Oversight of the House Ways and Means Committee, 100 Cong. 1 sess. (GPO, 1987).

13. Section 936 funds are repatriated profits deposited in Puerto Rican banks with tax-exempt status under provisions designed to compensate Puerto Rico for its loss of advantage after CBI passed.

14. However, the prospect of a North American free trade agreement offsets that assurance, as whatever advantage the Caribbean countries enjoy vis-à-vis Mexico will be substantially, if not entirely, eroded if Mexico gains duty-free access to the U.S. market.

15. In 1983, supplemental aid was allocated among countries as follows: $75 million each to El Salvador and Costa Rica; $52 million to Jamaica; $41 million to the Dominican Republic; $38 million to Honduras; $24 million to the eastern Caribbean islands; $15 million for regional projects; and $10 million each for Guatemala, Haiti, and Belize. Seyler, "Caribbean Industrialization," pp. 4–5.

16. Those that have qualified for USAID assistance are Antigua and Barbuda, Belize, Costa Rica, Dominica, Dominican Republic, El Salvador, Grenada, Guatemala, Haiti, Honduras, Jamaica, Montserrat, St. Christopher–Nevis, St. Lucia, and St. Vincent. These fifteen countries account for 90 percent of the population of all CBI countries. See James Fox, "Is the Caribbean Basin Initiative Working?" AID/LAC,DP, October 31, 1989. Some critics have alleged that "strategic countries received aid in excess of their absorptive capacities while smaller islands clamored for additional support." Seyler, *Caribbean Industrialization*, p. 12.

17. World Bank, *World Development Report, 1990* (Oxford University Press, 1990), table 20, pp. 216–17.

18. See Joseph Pelzman and Gregory K. Schoepfle, "The Impact of the Caribbean Basin Economic Recovery Act on Caribbean Nations' Exports and Development," *Economic Development and Cultural Change*, vol. 36 (July 1988), pp. 753–96. The United States thus preached open trade for CBI countries but in fact mandated "self-sufficiency in food production," a move that encouraged protection of those agricultural commodities in which Caribbean countries had a comparative disadvantage. Until self-sufficiency was attained, the U.S. policy denied preferential treatment to commodity exports in which the Caribbean had a comparative advantage! The Agriculture Department, which was charged with determining eligibility, could hardly be regarded as an impartial arbiter of the interests of U.S. and Caribbean farmers. As of 1988, five countries had not filed production plans and thus were not eligible.

19. Quotas continued to become increasingly restrictive after 1988, although it is difficult to get data on a consistent basis. Quotas announced in October 1991 for the 1991–92 crop year were one-third smaller than those for 1990–91, despite a plea three months earlier from the Caribbean countries to refrain from additional quota cuts. See Canute James, "Caribbean Sugar Exports Hit by Lower U.S. Quotas," *Financial Times*, October 9, 1991, p. 24.

20. Data are from IMF, *International Financial Statistics, 1990 Yearbook*, country pages for Dominican Republic and Haiti.

21. See USITC, *Operation of the Trade Agreements Program, 40th Report*, p. 156.

22. For particulars of the arrangement, see Shelburne and Shiells, *Trade and Employment*, p. 12.

23. Sylvia Saborio and Constantine Michalopoulos, "Central America at a Crossroads," paper prepared for meeting of the Inter-American Dialogue's Project on Latin America's Integration in the World Economy, Washington, D.C., December 18–20, 1991.

24. U.S. import data from the *Economic Report of the President, February 1991*, p. 404. One qualification is that some CBI exports may have represented reexports; the growth in value added in CBI exports may thus be slightly overstated.

25. Shelbourne and Shiells, *Trade and Employment*, pp. 2–5.

26. Representative Sam Gibbons, chairman of the House Ways and Means Subcommittee on Trade, was quoted as saying that in the CBI "we gave with one hand but took away with a bushel basket in the other." See Arthur G. Wyatt, "The Caribbean Basin Ethanol Industry: Case Study of United States Protectionism Undercutting the Caribbean Basin Initiative," *George Washington Journal of International Law and Economics*, vol. 23, no. 3 (1990), pp. 801–24; quotation from p. 820, fn. 10.

27. Commerce Department, *1987 Guidebook, Caribbean Basin Initia-*

tive. In 1986 the president announced a "special access program" that liberalized textile and apparel import quotas for CBI countries. The liberalization applied to apparel items that consisted entirely of fabric produced and cut in the United States, which enter the United States under HTS 9802.00.8010. See USITC, *Operation of the Trade Agreements Program, 41st Report, 1989,* Publication 2317 (September 1990), p. 148.

28. As of 1983, $1.9 billion of the exports of CBI countries to the United States, or 21.7 percent of their total exports, had entered duty-free under most-favored-nation treatment. No trading partner can gain from the offer of preferential status for commodities that already enter duty-free. However, it is difficult to view the fact that there are no duties on some imports as a limitation to the benefits of preferential status, so this issue is not considered here. See Pelzman and Schoepfle, "Exports and Development," table 4, p. 763.

29. Caribbean exporters cited infrequent air cargo and shipping schedules as a major bottleneck and highlighted transport difficulties more generally. The USITC team reported that producers found it difficult to meet tight deadlines for manufactured exports and that agricultural commodities sometimes rotted before being shipped. See USITC, *Annual Report on the Impact of the Caribbean Basin Economic Recovery Act,* p. 1-3.

30. Ibid.

31. Ibid. Respondents indicated that German regulations, for example, were very strict but very clear. An interesting sidelight on the difficulties of extending preferences is that the eastern Caribbean islands still enjoying preferential market access in the United Kingdom are likely to lose it after 1992.

32. Daniel Seyler, "Caribbean Industrialization," p. 11.

33. Edward John Ray, "The Impact of Special Interests on Preferential Tariff Concessions in the United States," *Review of Economics and Statistics,* vol. 69 (May 1987), pp. 187–93.

34. This discussion is based on Wyatt, "Caribbean Basin Ethanol Industry." The technicalities of the various positions are complex and cannot be exposited within the confines of a few paragraphs. Moreover, they are not essential to the story. The interested reader can glean all the particulars from Wyatt.

35. This tax was designed to protect the U.S. gasohol industry and to encourage domestic production of ethanol. The major groups lobbying for this were U.S. corn producers, as corn is the main feedstock for ethanol in the United States. The congressman who fought hardest to reverse the CBI exemption for ethanol was from Decatur, Illinois, the home of Archer-Daniels-Midland, a major domestic producer of ethanol. See Wyatt, "Caribbean Basin Ethanol Industry," pp. 810, 811, fn. 60.

36. USITC, *Operation of the Trade Agreements Program,* various reports, appendix tables.

37. Members of the European Community have a somewhat similar arrangement under the LOME convention with many of their former colonies.

38. See Saborio and Michalopoulos, "Central America," p. 12; they re-

port that "investment diversion" to Mexico, as well as trade diversion, is already reported to be taking place. They suggest that the relocation of foreign direct investment toward Mexico may be even more serious than trade diversion. The Caribbean countries have formally approached the United States, Canada, and Mexico with requests for free access to NAFTA. Canute James, "Caribbean Textile Makers Seek Open Access to NAFTA," *Financial Times*, October 22, 1991, p. 7.

39. Some Central American countries also received substantial military support because of U.S. concerns about political stability in the region. Saborio notes that aid officials strongly supported an export orientation and other policy reforms, but that military aid was allocated without regard to these criteria: the slowest reformers among the Central American countries received the most aid! Saborio and Michalopoulos, "Central America," pp. 279–302.

40. The interested reader can consult Gladstone Bonnick, "Jamaica: Liberalization to Centralization, and Back?" in Arnold Harberger, ed., *World Economic Growth* (San Francisco: ICS Press, 1984), pp. 265–92. See also Roger J. Robinson and Lelde Schmitz, "Jamaica: Navigating through a Troubled Decade," *Finance and Development*, vol. 26 (December 1989), pp. 30–33.

41. DeLisle Worrell, *Small Island Economies: Structure and Performance in the English-Speaking Caribbean since 1970* (Praeger, 1987), pp. 138–39.

42. The United States, for example, supported a major effort at tax reform with $8 million.

43. World Bank, *World Debt Tables, 1987–88*, vol. 2: *Country Tables* (Washington, 1988), pp. 194–97 (Jamaica country pages).

44. See the plea for debt relief by former Prime Minister Michael Manley in the *Wall Street Journal*, May 3, 1990, p. 18.

45. World Bank, *World Debt Tables, 1989–90*, vol. 2 (Washington, 1990), pp. 91–93 (Costa Rica country pages). Cost Rica's debt was, proportional to GDP, far less than that of Brazil, where debt was equal to one-third of national income.

46. See Peter Passell, "Costa Rica's Debt Message," *New York Times*, February 1, 1989, p. D2.

47. Ibid. Passell noted in passing that the IMF's stand was taken in part in response to European and Japanese "irritation with the way the Reagan Administration allowed the banks to dominate its debt policy."

48. "Costa Rica Breaks the Mold," *New York Times*, November 2, 1989, p. A30.

49. In fact, by the time payment was due on the debt buy-back deal, Costa Rica was out of compliance with the IMF loan and obtained a bridge loan from Mexico and Venezuela to make the payment.

Chapter Eight

1. Much of the analysis of U.S. trade practices in this chapter is based on Chong-Hyun Nam, "Protectionist U.S. Trade Policy and Korean Exports," paper presented at the Second NBER–East Asian Conference on Economics, rev. version, August 1991.

2. At that time the U.S. Congress hotly debated the future of U.S. assistance to Korea. Although development assistance to Korea was finally approved, in the debate many politicians argued that Korea did not have a viable economy nor any hope for economic development. See Anne O. Krueger, *The Developmental Role of the Foreign Sector and Aid*, Studies in the Modernization of the Republic of Korea, 1945–1975 (Harvard University Press, 1979), pp. 9–19, for a description of U.S. policy during the period.

3. Some aid, especially in the period immediately after the Korean War, was given under U.N. auspices. The United States was nonetheless the dominant donor. For expository purposes, therefore, it is useful to discuss aid to Korea in the 1950s as if the United States were the sole donor.

4. For accounts of the aid relationship and the Korean economy during these years, see David C. Cole and Princeton N. Lyman, *Korean Development: The Interplay of Politics and Economics* (Harvard University Press, 1971); Charles R. Frank, Jr., Kwang Suk Kim, and Larry E. Westphal, *Foreign Trade Regimes and Economic Development*, vol. 7: *South Korea* (Columbia University Press, 1975); and Edward S. Mason and others, *The Economic and Social Modernization of the Republic of Korea*, Studies in the Modernization of the Republic of Korea, 1945–1975 (Harvard University Press, 1980).

5. Many observers believe that the land and educational reforms of the 1940s, which were undertaken with U.S. support, were also critical to Korea's successful growth in later years. See Anne O. Krueger and Vernon W. Ruttan, "Assistance to Korea," in Anne O. Krueger, Constantine Michalopoulos, and Vernon W. Ruttan, eds., *Aid and Development* (Johns Hopkins University Press, 1989), pp. 226–49.

6. Mason and others, *Economic and Social Modernization*, p. 98.

7. Ibid., p. 112. These estimates are based on the GNP deflator; if the wholesale price index were used instead, the drop was from an annual average of 37.4 percent from 1954 to 1957 to 2.0 percent from 1957 to 1960.

8. One of the factors that contributed to the downfall of the Rhee government was popular discontent with the corruption and other economic abuses of the control regime that had developed between 1953 and 1959. For an analysis of the political economy of these changes, see Stephan Haggard, Richard N. Cooper, and Chung-in Moon, "Policy Reforms in Korea," in Robert H. Bates and Anne O. Krueger, *Political and Economic Interactions in Economic Policy Reform: Evidence from Eight Countries* (Oxford: Basil Blackwell, 1993).

9. See Frank, Kim, and Westphal, *South Korea*, for a full account.

10. Some analysts believe that Korean government officials intervened in virtually all private sector decisions in the 1960s and 1970s. Others point to the large role of incentives in allocating resources. For this chapter, the important fact is that the degree of direct control over economic activities was considerably less in the 1960s and 1970s than it had been in the 1950s, and at the same time government incentives shifted greatly toward an outward orientation, away from earlier import-substitution policies. For a discussion of these issues from various viewpoints, see the collection of papers in *American Economic Review*, vol. 80 (May 1990, *Papers and Proceedings, 1989*), including Yung Chul Park, "Development Lessons from Asia: The Role of Government in South Korea and Taiwan," pp. 118–21; Susan M. Collins, "Lessons from Korean Economic Growth," pp. 104–07; and Anne O. Krueger, "Asian Trade and Growth Lessons," pp. 108–12.

11. The rate of population growth, which was just under 3 percent annually in the early 1960s, fell to just over 1 percent annually by the mid-1980s.

12. Especially in the 1960s, Korean exporters imported many of the materials they used in production. The growth of net exports was therefore somewhat less than the data in table 8-2 suggest.

13. Data in this paragraph are derived from Frank, Kim, and Westphal, *South Korea*, tables 6-2, 6-4.

14. That Korean exports were destined for countries other than Japan was natural at that time. Korea's initial manufactured exports consisted of labor-intensive products such as woven cotton fabrics, clothing, plywood, and footwear. Japan then had a comparative advantage in these same industries.

15. Numbers are from World Bank, *World Debt Tables, 1986–87* (Washington, 1986), pp. 226–27.

16. Korean authorities were committed to achieving price stability and were therefore unwilling to increase investment. Given the economic growth rate and the level of employment in the economy at the time, additional investment could only have taken place at the expense of an increased rate of inflation.

17. Byung-Nak Song, *The Rise of the Korean Economy* (Oxford University Press, 1990), p. 211.

18. There is no doubt that the Korean economy benefits greatly from the liberalization of her trade restrictions. When confronted with a balance of payments surplus, it is probably preferable to remove those restrictions than to alter the exchange rate, leaving those restrictions in place. While the U.S. government consistently urged the removal of import restrictions, it nonetheless also insisted upon currency revaluation.

19. USITC, *Operation of the Trade Agreements Program, 39th Report, 1987*, Publication 2095 (July 1988). p. 4-49.

20. USITC, *Operation of the Trade Agreements Program, 40th Report, 1988*, Publication 2208 (July 1989), p. 129.

21. Quoted in USITC, *Operation of the Trade Agreements Program, 42nd Report, 1990*, Publication 2403 (July 1991), p. 148.

22. Nam, "Protectionist U.S. Trade Policy."

23. USITC, *Operation of the Trade Agreements Program, 39th Report, 1987*, p. 4-48.

24. Ibid., pp. 4-46, 4-47.

25. Ibid., p. 4-49.

26. USITC, *Operation of the Trade Agreements Program, 40th Report, 1988*, p. 129.

27. USITC, *Operation of the Trade Agreements Program, 41st Report, 1989*, Publication 2317 (September 1990), pp. 118–19.

28. USITC, *Operation of the Trade Agreements Program, 40th Report, 1988*, pp. 128–29.

29. USITC, *Operation of the Trade Agreements Program, 39th Report, 1987*, p. 4-50.

30. Eui Tae Chang, "Barriers to Korea's Manufactured Exports," in John Whalley, ed., *Developing Countries and the Global Trading System*, vol. 2 (University of Michigan Press, 1989), p. 151.

31. USITC, *Operation of the Trade Agreements Program, 41st Report, 1989*, p. 122.

32. See the list of commodities against which Section 337 exclusion orders were filed in table 5-6.

33. USITC, *Operation of the Trade Agreements Program, 42nd Report, 1990*, p. 148.

34. Ibid., p. 144.

35. For comparative purposes, it is estimated that the percentages of Korean exports restricted by other countries were 24 percent for Canada, 22 percent for the European Community, and 24 percent for Japan. The United States was thus slightly below average. Whether this was because U.S. nontariff barriers were more restrictive or for other reasons cannot be determined. See Nam, "Protectionist U.S. Trade Policy," p. 19.

36. Ibid., p. 18.

37. Ibid., p. 21.

38. Even these margins appear to have been high. In the case of color television sets, the preliminary dumping margin was calculated to be 2.9 percent, but the final margin was determined to be 15.8 percent. In the case of photo albums, the preliminary margin was estimated to be 4.0 percent, but the final determination, using constructed cost, was 64.8 percent. See Nam, "Protectionist U.S. Trade Policy," p. 36.

39. Nam, "Protectionist U.S. Trade Policy," pp. 30–32.

40. It should be noted that Nam's estimates also imply that the U.S. imposition of the steel voluntary export restraint worsened the U.S. trade balance, as the price increase outweighed the reduction in quantity.

41. Chungsoo Kim, "The Multi-Fibre Arrangement and Structural Ad-

justment of the Korean Textile Industry," Korea Institute for Economics and Technology, June 1989, table 4.

42. Ibid., p. 20.

43. Ibid., p. 22.

44. Yung Chul Park and Jung Ho Yoo, "More Free Trade Areas: A Korean Perspective," in Schott, *Free Trade Areas*, p. 149.

Chapter Nine

1. There were exceptions, some of which have come back to haunt the United States. For example, at U.S. insistence agriculture was excluded from many of the provisions of GATT: it was felt that the U.S. system of price supports and production controls over agriculture could not be changed. Current arguments over agriculture in the Uruguay Round illustrate the shortsightedness of that position.

2. Jagdish Bhagwati, *Protectionism* (MIT Press, 1988).

3. The International Development Cooperation Administration (IDCA) was established in the late 1970s with the intent of achieving some coordination. IDCA, however, never fulfilled its intended function. In large part, this failure was attributable to an underlying lack of consensus about the objectives of policy instruments.

4. For a statement of this view, see Theodore W. Schultz, "A Critique of the Economics of U.S. Foreign Aid," in Kenneth C. Nobe and Rajan K. Sampath, eds., *Issues in Third World Development* (Boulder, Colo.: Westview Press, 1983), pp. 457–67.

5. Ironically, the U.S. sugar program began in large part as a way to assist the Cuban economy in the 1930s, when U.S. officials thought that economic assistance was essential if complete political instability was to be avoided. The experience with sugar provides an excellent example of why aid, rather than trade preferences, should be the instrument of assistance in such situations. See Anne O. Krueger, "The Political Economy of Controls: American Sugar," in Maurice Scott and Deepak Lal, eds., *Public Policy and Economic Development: Essays in Honor of Ian Little* (Oxford University Press, 1990), pp. 170–216.

6. To argue that assistance should be extended even if its effectiveness is not assured, however, is not to say that the United States should be indifferent about its effectiveness. Insofar as aid furthers foreign policy purposes, its effective use will increase its value.

7. See Nick Eberstadt, *U.S. Foreign Aid Policy—a Critique*, Foreign Policy Association Headline Series 293 (New York, Summer 1990), p. 4. Eberstadt notes the high level of support Americans give to "combating world hunger" contrasted with their low support for aid. He concludes, "The American public, it would seem, is strongly of the opinion that the U.S. foreign aid program is today a highly flawed instrument for the expression of

their considerable goodwill toward the impoverished and the vulnerable overseas."

8. There is arguably little or no case for concessional assistance to middle-income countries undertaking policy reform, although financial support during the reform process can be very valuable, as noted in earlier chapters. "Aid" here implies concessional assistance for low-income countries and financial support for middle-income countries.

9. Chapter 4 mentioned the role of U.S. aid in bringing about significant policy reform in Egyptian agriculture. However, in that study, Robert E. Holt and Terry Roe noted that the ability of U.S. officials to tie the extension of aid to concrete agricultural policy reform permitted the use of leverage. Had aid officials been constrained to spend a given amount on agricultural reform, their ability to influence policy would have been diminished. See Holt and Roe, "The Political Economy of Policy Reform in Egypt," in Robert H. Bates and Anne O. Krueger, *Political and Economic Interactions in Policy Reform: Evidence from Eight Countries* (Oxford: Basil Blackwell, 1993).

10. Some commentators have asked whether this new agency, with its three bureaus, would stand alone or remain housed within the State Department. Those who argued for a separate agency cited the inevitable association of foreign aid with foreign policy concerns and the fact that foreign service officers inevitably staff aid when it is in the State Department. Because the major objective of this chapter's proposal is to clarify the mission of the various bureaus, specific issues of organization are not of central concern. If clarity of purpose was achieved, aid would be more effective independent of organizational details.

11. Public discussions often confuse foreign aid and disaster or humanitarian relief. Humanitarian relief—in the aftermath of floods, earthquakes, and other natural disasters, or in response to famines and health emergencies—is designed to provide relief from an immediate situation. Foreign aid, by contrast, is designed to support efforts to increase future economic performance. While the two clearly overlap, there are also major differences. For example, officials do not establish a rural network of public health clinics and combat a cholera epidemic with the same techniques. In principle, disaster relief could be administered through the basic human needs bureau, a separate agency, or nongovernmental charitable organizations.

12. U.S. aid officials could not avoid the government entirely, but could do most, if not all, of their work with national and local officials in the human services agencies: education, agriculture, health, and so on. The degree of apparent political support for a regime that arises from these programs is greatly different than that perceived from program aid or balance-of-payments support that is more directly subject to the discretion of top government officials.

13. Food aid under P.L. 480 could be in the jurisdiction of more than one bureau in different circumstances. When it is to support development, as opposed to short-term humanitarian concerns, food aid could be adminis-

tered by either the basic human needs or the policy reform bureau. When short-term humanitarian concerns are dominant, the international assistance bureau would handle it.

14. See Anne O. Krueger, "Free Trade Is the Best Policy," in Robert Lawrence and Charles L. Schultze, eds., *An American Trade Strategy* (Brookings, 1990), pp. 68–96.

15. See Anne O. Krueger, "The Political Economy of American Protection in Theory and in Practice," in Horst Herberg and No Van Long, eds., *Trade, Welfare, and Economic Policies: Essays in Honor of Murray C. Kemp* (University of Michigan Press, forthcoming).

16. For example, the 1986 semiconductor agreement with Japan, which guaranteed part of the Japanese market for U.S. producers, resulted in grave difficulties for U.S. firms, which were charged a higher price by Japanese suppliers than were other customers of the Japanese. Similarly, Australia strongly objected to initial pressures on Japan to open its market for imported beef, as the Japanese were giving U.S. imports an unfair advantage. The final arrangement did not discriminate in favor of the United States, because Japan increased beef imports primarily from Australia.

17. Some analysts argue that countries such as Korea, with rising wage costs, benefit from the maintenance of the Multifiber Arrangement (MFA). Existing producers in Korea clearly gain, but the MFA doubtless slows Korea's potential growth rate. At its stage of development, Korea should be moving out of labor-intensive activities, and the MFA retards that process. From a U.S. perspective, however, the MFA stands as a barrier to rapid development in countries considerably poorer than Korea, where lower wages offer comparative advantage in labor-intensive industries.

18. For a discussion of procedural changes that could substantially improve practice with no change in the law, see Richard Boltuck and Robert E. Litan, eds., *Down in the Dumps: Administration of the Unfair Trade Laws* (Brookings, 1991).

19. Economic policy reform was clearly a prerequisite for the resumption of growth. However, the U.S. policy response was open to allegations that the chief concerns of the Treasury Department were the solvency and liquidity of U.S. banks. If securing the goodwill of citizens and officials in developing countries was a policy objective, U.S. pronouncements, even for the same policies, could have been formulated to leave fewer questions about U.S. motives.

Index

124872